Rethinking Cultural Tourism

RETHINKING TOURISM

This series offers a forum for innovative scholarly writing that reflects the new and previously unforeseen challenges, competing interests and changing experiences that tourism faces. It showcases authored books that address key themes from a new angle, expose the weaknesses of existing concepts and arguments, or 're-frame' the topic in an innovative way. This might be through the introduction of radical ideas, through the integration of perspectives from other fields or disciplines, through challenging existing paradigms, or simply through a level of analysis that elevates or sharpens our understanding of the subject.

Rethinking Cultural Tourism

Greg Richards

Professor of Placemaking and Events, Breda University of Applied Sciences and Professor in Leisure Studies, Tilburg University, the Netherlands

RETHINKING TOURISM

Edward Elgar
PUBLISHING

Cheltenham, UK • Northampton, MA, USA

Published by
Edward Elgar Publishing Limited
The Lypiatts
15 Lansdown Road
Cheltenham
Glos GL50 2JA
UK

Edward Elgar Publishing, Inc.
William Pratt House
9 Dewey Court
Northampton
Massachusetts 01060
USA

Paperback edition 2022

A catalogue record for this book
is available from the British Library

Library of Congress Control Number: 2021932283

This book is available electronically in the **Elgar**online
Geography, Planning and Tourism subject collection
http://dx.doi.org/10.4337/9781789905441

ISBN 978 1 78990 543 4 (cased)
ISBN 978 1 78990 544 1 (eBook)
ISBN 978 1 0353 0677 0 (paperback)

Printed and bound by CPI Group (UK) Ltd, Croydon, CR0 4YY

For Chris Devereux (1946–2020)
A great teacher and an even better friend.

Contents

Acknowledgements

This book is the result of decades of collaboration with colleagues around the world – far too many to thank them all individually, and I apologise for the impersonal approach. I would like to acknowledge the crucial role of members of the ATLAS Cultural Tourism Research Group, who since 1991 have helped to gather data on cultural tourism in more than 40 different countries. This work has been fundamental to furthering our knowledge of cultural tourism, the people who perform it and the contexts of this performance. The data they have collected have already formed the basis of many books and articles over the years, illuminating different aspects of the cultural tourism practice. Among the members of the ATLAS project there are a handful of people who should be highlighted for their outstanding contribution to the development of cultural tourism research over the years. I will list them in the order in which they joined the project to avoid any suggestion of a ranking.

Wil Munsters from the Zuyd University in the Netherlands was one of the founder members of the ATLAS project and has been a stalwart participant over the years. I am also grateful to him for pointing out the origin of overtourism, which in its Dutch form *overtoeristisering* dates back several decades. Carlos Fernandes from Viana do Castelo produced a phenomenal overview of cultural tourism in Portugal as well as developing the gastronomic tourism niche. I am also grateful that our joint studies of Portuguese gastronomy have been practical as well as theoretical. Ilie Rotariu from Sibiu in Romania developed the longest-running longitudinal study of urban cultural tourism, helping to capture the effects of the European Capital of Culture in 2007 before, during and after the event. Melanie Smith joined the ATLAS project when she was in London, and we continued collecting data and writing together when she moved to Budapest. She also found time to produce the definitive textbook on cultural tourism.

The practice approach developed here owes much to colleagues at Tilburg University and later at Breda University of Applied Sciences, who also allowed me time to work on the text. Hugo van der Poel linked practices to leisure studies, and introduced us to the work of Randall Collins. Bertine Bargeman has worked with me on leisure practices for many years, and the ideas outlined in this book owe much to our sparring over the relationship between practices and interaction rituals.

Thanks also go to Leontine Onderwater and the team at ATLAS for their untiring support of the Cultural Tourism Research Project over the years. This has included not only the data collection process, but also the hosting and supervision of many project staff, organizing international events and producing many publications.

Work for this book received funding from the SmartCulTour Project within the European Union's Horizon 2020 research and innovation programme under grant agreement No. 870708. The opinions expressed in this book are solely those of the author.

Co-funded by the European Union

Preface

In the preface to his fascinating *Recent Earth History*, my mentor Claudio Vita-Finzi revealed that his book was an intended elephant that became a mouse. In producing *Rethinking Cultural Tourism*, I failed to follow Claudio's good example, managing to conjure an elephant from my intended mouse. I must thank my editor at Edward Elgar, Katy Crossan, for her creativity in dealing with this transformation.

The space afforded by placing this book in the *Rethinking* series allowed me to diverge from my previous work. Although the text is the product of 30 years of research on cultural tourism, this book provides a radical departure from traditional approaches based on production and consumption. It has also been an opportunity to move beyond cultural tourism in a narrow sense, as culture produced for and consumed by tourists. The holistic view adopted here is important because the cultural tourism field is constantly expanding and changing, incorporating new cultural trends as it does so.

I make no apology for drawing extensively on my own research for this text. This is the material I know best, and it reflects my developing thinking on the subject. This book does not attempt to provide an objective view, rather a personal curation of information I consider useful for analysing the cultural tourism field. It reflects the positive sociology approach of an itinerant geographer turned jack of all trades. The approach is European in outlook, urban in content and focussed on contemporary culture rather than the past. This book attempts to develop new perspectives on cultural tourism rather than repeating analyses offered elsewhere.

The book presents a model that I hope will be useful for students and researchers in understanding and analysing cultural tourism as a field of practice. The main innovation lies in developing a 'third generation' practice approach which highlights the mechanisms through which cultural tourism practices are propagated and maintained.

1. Cultural tourism as a dynamic social practice

THE EVOLUTION OF CULTURAL TOURISM

Recent decades have seen a significant increase in the scale and importance of cultural production and consumption. Tourism has also contributed to these trends, with culture becoming an object of travel for growing numbers of people around the globe, and destinations profiling themselves through their cultural assets to distinguish themselves and attract tourist attention. This combination of culture and tourism, which only relatively recently came to be labelled cultural tourism, has become a global social practice.

The traditional view of cultural tourists as cultured people visiting high culture attractions arose during the Grand Tour, which reached its peak in 19th century Europe. This form of 'conspicuous leisure' (Veblen, 1899) was originally reserved for the social elite, those who could afford to spend long periods of time travelling to complete their cultural education. The democratization of tourism, springing from the package tours organized by Thomas Cook in the mid-19th century, gradually broadened the market for cultural tourism, and opened a wider range of cultural destinations. Cultural tourism was further boosted by the growth of mass tourism during the 20th century, as air travel allowed people to travel further afield and discover new and relatively exotic long-haul destinations.

By the 1990s, cultural tourism had become established as a major segment of global tourism, with the United Nations World Tourism Organization (UNWTO) claiming that 40 per cent of international tourists were cultural tourists (Bywater, 1993). Surging cultural tourism demand was met by a flood of places seeking to put themselves, and their cultures, on the global map. Countries used culture to forge new identities and create homogeneous national cultures. Regions and cities employed culture for economic development, fed by the spending of relatively wealthy visitors. Cultural tourism was also seen as a relatively 'good' form of tourism, with high-spending visitors supporting local cultural heritage and economies (Richards, 2001). The role of cultural tourism in supporting heritage also meant it made an important contribution to the 'heritage boom' in the developed world in the 1980s (Hewison, 1987).

The 1990s saw increased attention for cultural tourism as an emerging form of mass consumption, and destinations began to tap into the economic potential of this market by opening new museums and monuments. In the 1990s, the growth rate of cultural attractions in Europe outstripped the growth of cultural tourism demand (Richards, 2001), producing an increasingly competitive cultural tourism marketplace. This period also saw the extension of cultural tourism through globalization, raising concerns about the effects of cultural tourism on the places being visited, and the homogenization of local cultures (Kirshenblatt-Gimblett, 1998; Pickel-Chevalier, Violier and Sari, 2016). The contrast between cultural tourism as a supporter and violator of cultures created 'a heated debate between two schools of thought; one is well placed in the anti-globalization camp, who see the destruction of authentic culture and identity by global forces ...., and the other is those who see culture and identity as a worthwhile commodity in the global market' (Debeş, 2011, p. 236).

The growing scale of cultural tourism, its increasing impacts on the people and places visited and the emerging links with questions of cultural heritage and identity led to a shift from management and marketing approaches in research towards more attention from cultural studies and anthropology. This also marked a wider transition as part of the 'cultural turn' in the social sciences, which also had a profound impact on the study of cultural tourism.

The Cultural Turn

The growth of tourism as a social practice attracted more attention from sociologists and other mainstream social scientists. In the 1980s, studies emerged of the role of culture in supporting different lifestyles or patterns of consumption. The work of French sociologist Pierre Bourdieu (1984) highlighted the role of lifestyle in cultural consumption. He argued that social stratification was not just related to traditional markers such as age, income or social class, but also to lifestyles that distinguished groups in terms of their consumption. Culture played an important role in distinguishing these social groups, for example, between those who consumed high culture and consumers of popular culture. One of Bourdieu's important observations was that the ability to consume culture depended on the skills of the consumer, or the amount of cultural capital they possess. Bourdieu argued that cultural capital was acquired from the habitus, or home environment, and through formal education.

Certain lifestyle groups, and particularly people with a high level of education, were found to consume more high culture than others. These were most likely to visit museums, monuments and cultural performances at home, and they were also frequent cultural tourists (Richards, 1996). In their study of cultural tourists at a Rotterdam museum, Jansen-Verbeke and van Rekom (1996) confirmed that highly educated visitors were very likely to be enticed to travel by art museums. Similarly, in Canada and the USA, Silberberg (1995) found the cultural tourism audience to be older, more highly educated, high spending and more likely to be female. He also found that only 15 per cent of tourists were greatly motivated by culture, compared with 20 per cent partly motivated by culture and 20 per cent who were 'accidental cultural tourists'. As we will see in Chapter 2, in this respect, little seems to have changed in the cultural tourism field in recent decades.

As international travel expanded, it also formed part of the lifestyle of those highly educated, high earning people interested in culture. In his seminal volume *The Tourist*, Dean MacCannell (1976) charted how visitors to Paris and other centres of high culture would celebrate the differentiations of modernity by visiting famous landmarks and sights. John Urry (1990) in *The Tourist Gaze* argued that people wanted to experience things that were different from their everyday life, and that this was creating a 'culture of tourism' (Craik, 2002). Interest in cultural tourism continued to grow among sociologists and anthropologists, who examined emerging styles of tourism in the developing world (Hitchcock and King, 2003), and the growth of heritage production and commodification in the developed world (Halewood and Hannam, 2001; MacLeod, 2013). Concern emerged for the alteration of local and traditional cultures and their resulting commodification by tourism, often spearheaded by the cultural tourists in search of 'authentic' local culture.

The cultural turn was sharpened by the recognition of culture as an economic force. Studies of the cultural economy in the 1990s often cited tourism as an important driver and as a means for spreading wealth to peripheral or depressed regions. Many economic impact studies demonstrated the important role of tourism in economic development, and culture was seen as an important factor attracting tourists (Smith, 2007). Economists began to demonstrate the important job creation role of cultural tourism, not just for static cultural attractions such as museums, but also for events such as the Edinburgh Festival or Salzburg (Gratton and Richards, 1996).

The economic role of cultural tourism fitted the political climate of the time, spurred on by the liberalization of the 1980s and 1990s, and the rise of Thatcherism and Reaganomics. Heritage developments provided opportunities to support entrepreneurship (Corner and Harvey, 1991) and publicly funded museums were encouraged to earn more of their own income (McDonald, 1998). The need for cultural institutions to find new audiences in the face of economic austerity also led them to adopt a more marketing-orientated approach, in which tourism became an attractive and lucrative market.

Cities began to feel the cold winds of austerity as globalization removed the relative protection of the nation state. City centres became hubs for cultural development (Zukin, 1995), and cultural resources were employed in the competitive struggle to attract more consumers, tourists and attention. New postmodern museums and cultural attractions began to emerge, stimulated by increasingly fragmented consumer markets and demand for greater inter-activity and involvement. New areas of cities were highlighted as culturally interesting places to visit, leading to what Maitland (2007) termed 'new tourist areas'. These were often based on ethnic diversity and the novelty provided by everyday life rather than the glass display cases of the high culture museum.

In the volume *Cultural Attractions and European Tourism* (Richards, 2001), we charted the spread of cultural tourism, with a growing range of must-see sights fed by bodies promoting culture for a range of different reasons. As de Haan (1997) noted, the increase in cultural tourism in this period did not reflect increasing cultural interest on the part of consumers so much as a growing tourist market meeting a rising tide of cultural provision. This fed a spiral of cultural tourism growth, where the arrival of visitors to consume new attractions was used to justify the construction of more attractions, therefore stimulating more supply-driven cultural tourism. In the case of Hong Kong, for example, Ng (2002) argues that efforts to diversify the tourism product with new cultural attractions and events led to a 'Cultural Turn of the Tourism Industry', which transformed tourism into a cultural practice.

Growth in cultural tourism was also linked to the shift towards the symbolic economy. Guy Debord (1967) had already announced the advent of the Society of the Spectacle, and spectacular consumption stimulated the growth of cultural destinations. George Ritzer (1999) noted that the means of production had now been transformed into the means of consumption, based on the creation of new 'Cathedrals of Consumption'. Examples of these included the Pompidou Centre in Paris, the Bilbao Guggenheim Museum and the Massachusetts Museum of Contemporary Art (MASS MoCa) in North Adams. The growth of cultural tourism generated more academic analyses of demand for museums and other cultural sites, including studies by Richard Prentice, Duncan Light and Nick Merriman in the UK, Greg Ashworth and Wil Munsters in the Netherlands and Alf Walle in the USA.

Growing research on cultural tourism production and consumption stirred a realization that these processes were intimately linked (Richards, 1996). Gradually, the outlines of what became the experience industry began to be discernible, with the emergence of new 'experience makers', including art historians, journalists, media commentators, gallery owners and cultural tour operators (Richards, Goedhart and Herrijgers, 2001).

The Mobilities Turn

The 1990s saw continued global expansion of tourism and cultural consumption, and by the turn of the Millennium, the volume of international tourism had increased to almost 690 million arrivals, a growth of over 50 per cent compared with 1990. This expansion was supported by increased tourism infrastructure, including airports, hotels and attractions. This generated attention for the growth of 'non-places', including airports and motorways, which are designed for constant motion (Augé, 1995), while Castells (1996) identified the emergence of a global 'space of flows' being created by the network society. It was against this background that John Urry (2000) launched the mobilities paradigm. Some argued that mobilities meant 'the end of tourism' (Gale, 2009), but hindsight suggests the opposite – there were more tourists being more mobile than ever. Cultural tourism also took on a more global dimension, as Boniface and Fowler (2002) described in their analysis of heritage tourism in the 'global village'.

Globalization also drew more attention to cultural differences and their consequences. Cultural diversity, in particular, came to be seen as a stimulus for creativity, innovation and growth. The nascent network of cultural observatories, such as Interarts in Barcelona and Fondazione Fitzcarraldo in Turin, began to chart the consequences of the growing mobility of culture and people, not just in terms of cultural tourism, but also social cohesion, cultural outreach and urban identities. Pioneers such as Eduard Delgado, founder of Interarts, argued for a new vision of cultural plurality and more attention for regional and peripheral cultures, which could also increase their visibility and revive their traditions through cultural tourism (Belda and Laaksonen, 2001). Interarts also convened an international group of researchers to start the discussion that produced the volume *Cultural Tourism: Global and Local Perspectives* (Richards, 2007).

These efforts marked a realization that globalization, seen by authors such as Augé (1995) as erasing culture and difference, was itself creating new forms of local differentiation. This 'glocalization' trend (Robertson, 1994) marked the increasing resistance of local places to the forces of globalization and the eradication of tradition by the forces of modernity. This was part of the process described by Nijman (1999, p. 148) as 'cultural globalization' or 'acceleration in the exchange of cultural symbols among people around the world, to such an extent that it leads to changes in local popular cultures and identities'. Nijman also argued that cultural globalization was dependent on an expanding culture of consumption.

As Richards (2007) observed, the globalization of cultural tourism was part of this process. As culture became the ubiquitous global object of tourism consumption, it also produced a counter movement towards the local. If 'McGuggenheimization' produced an aesthetic of culture as a global branded good, differentiation had to be sought in the local, the everyday. After all, once everywhere had a Guggenheim, what would be the point of going there? A similar trend began to be recognized in the field of intangible culture, with a proliferation of events and festivals around the globe. Places everywhere were suddenly the victims of 'festivalization' (Häussermann and Siebel, 1993).

These shifts produced debates about the meaning of cultural tourism. What could cultural tourism mean in a postmodern world of global cultural brands and copycat events? If we could no longer be sure about the authenticity of places based on appeals to originality, as MacCannell (1976) had suggested, then perhaps the meaning of cultural tourism could be found in a particular style of consumption?

By the turn of the Millennium, there were arguably both grounds for pessimism and optimism (Richards, 2007, p. 293).

> In the view of some, local authenticity is rapidly being replaced by global pastiche, and local communities seem powerless to stop this process. In the view of others, local communities still have the power to create new and authentic forms of culture, which can satisfy the visitor as well as strengthening local identity. This division seems to mirror wider debates about the rise of 'cultural pessimism' .... linked to environmental, moral, intellectual and political narratives of decline in the 'postmodern' world at the end of the 20th century.

The Performative Turn

The performative turn had its origins in the work of Goffman (1959) and Turner (1969). Goffman also influenced the work of MacCannell (1976) on staged authenticity, but the performative turn took a long time to filter through to mainstream tourism studies.

Harwood and El-Manstrly (2012) reviewed the performative turn in tourism, and concluded that it 'attempts to explain practices through the act of something being performed'. They identifed different uses of the term, including transformation, enactment, being, negotiation and efficiency. One of the first extensive studies of cultural tourism performance was Edensor's (1998) research on the Taj Mahal, an iconic World Heritage Site in India. Edensor identified different performance dimensions:

1. Spatial and temporal (for example, the stage on which performances take place);
2. The regulation of the stage (for example, managing boundaries and choreography);
3. The accomplishment of the performance itself (related to the perceptions of the audience and the performers).

This analysis reveals that the interactions between tourists and tourism providers, and between tourists themselves, were becoming central to the performance of tourism. Edensor also distinguished two basic types of performance spaces: homogeneous and heterogeneous. The homogeneous spaces are those produced by or for tourism, which exclude the local (such as hotels and attractions). Heterogeneous spaces, on the other hand, are not specifically designed for tourist use, but shared between residents and visitors, and therefore have disorganized and emergent qualities. Other studies around this time also emphasized the performance qualities of tourism in different contexts, such as backpacking and local gastronomy (Diekmann and Hannam, 2012; Noy, 2008; Ren, 2010). Valtonen and Viejola (2011, p. 176) noted a paradigmatic shift in the conceptualization of agency in tourism, with 'the shift from the gaze to the body..., from authenticity to performatively ..., and from representations to everyday habits and practices'. More attention was paid to material aspects of tourism practices, particularly by those following an actor-network (ANT) approach (van der Duim, 2007). The performative turn has also produced a stronger link between tourism and ritual – a point we return to in Chapters 4 and 5.

Growing attention for performance led tourism scholars to connect cultural tourism more strongly with the everyday, shifting attention away from the symbolic to the embodied and collaborative (Russo and Richards, 2016). Performance and creativity were also highlighted in the 'creative turn'.

The Creative Turn

The creative turn emerged at the end of the 1990s with growing calls from policy makers and consultants to generate economic value from creativity and the rapid growth of the creative industries. Creativity was also important in the development of the experience economy, where the creation of value arguably depended on narrative, theming and performance. Cities and regions began to profile themselves as creative places that could attract the creative class (Florida, 2002). Richards and Wilson (2006) identified three basic forms of creative experiences in tourism – spaces, spectacles and creative tourism. Creative spaces include creative and cultural clusters where creative producers and artisans help provide creative environments for tourism consumption (Marques and Richards, 2014). Creative spectacles include iconic buildings and shows staged by creative companies such as Cirque du Soleil. Creative tourism originally emerged as a concept related to small-scale courses and workshops showcasing the creativity of the destination, but gradually expanded to cover a wider range of practices (see Chapter 5).

Kjær Mansfeldt (2015) characterizes the creative turn as being more pragmatic than the performative or mobilities turn. The creative turn responded to, but also extended, the concept of cultural tourism. The concept of 'creative tourism' (Richards and Raymond, 2000) identified a reaction against standardized and unengaging cultural tourism experiences in the face of globalization and the serial reproduction of culture. At the same time, creative tourism, or the active involvement of tourists in the creative life of the places they were visiting, also provided new possibilities for creative, more fulfilling cultural tourism experiences.

Creative tourism also emphasized relationality, with tourists actively involved in the co-creation of their own experiences, together with producers (Binkhorst and Den Dekker, 2009). Creative tourism incorporates elements of the other tourism turns: emphasizing the everyday, the intangible, the spontaneity of creative experience, and mundane as opposed to specialized tourist spaces. This heralded an important repositioning of the 'local' with respect to tourism – and the local becoming a new arbiter of authenticity (see Chapter 4).

The creative turn marked a growing integration of tourism and creativity, particularly through the growth of the creative economy (OECD, 2014) and increasing references to 'cultural and creative tourism' (Carvalho, Ferreira and Figueira, 2016). Using the creative industries as a means of boosting the economy and attracting visitors arguably had advantages over more traditional cultural tourism strategies (Richards and Wilson, 2007). The creative industries have a more dynamic image than the traditional, staid image of high culture, and they are broader in scope, also encompassing sectors with high knowledge content and levels of innovation. The new Millennium therefore witnessed many developments that integrated tourism and the creative industries. The most prominent of these were the creative districts that sprung up around the world (Marques and Richards, 2014), and which have been developed into mega-attractions in China (see Chapter 3). Value was added to tourism facilities using design, including design hotels (Strannegård and Strannegård, 2012), design districts (Koskinen, 2009) and iconic wineries built by starchitechts (Webb, 2005).

The creative turn helped to drive new spatial distributions of tourism in both cities and rural areas, as described in Chapter 3. It also stimulated the development of new networks and clusters related to creativity and tourism. These included the global Creative Tourism Network (Couret, 2015) and the CREATOUR project in Portugal (Bakas and Duxbury, 2018; Duxbury and Richards, 2019).

The Curatorial Turn

The most recent turn in cultural tourism thinking comes from art. The curatorial turn was first signalled in museum studies in the 1980s (O'Neill, 2007). It represents a shift in the system of artistic value creation away from the traditional intermediation role of the art broker or the gallerist towards the curator, who exercises cultural power by selecting 'the value to come', or sources of future value (Venturi, 2018). In performing the role of the selector, the curator indulges in a process of 'stylistic innovation' (Wijnberg, 2004), or presenting something new in a way that enhances its future value. For the curator, this involves selecting emerging artists whose work is not currently valued (or selected) by others, and essentially betting on their work to increase in value. In tourism, curation is linked to the identification of places or attractions that are currently underrated or undervalued, which can be harnessed to stimulate future tourism growth (such as the 'cool neighbourhoods' identified in Chapter 3).

The art of curation has become essential in the digital age, with its morass of unorganized information. Content curators act as 'trusted guides', helping us to understand the world around us and ourselves: 'Culturally, these curated resources are not just shortcuts to the "essence" of something, but they also shape and define the character, the perimeter of who we are, of what we are interested in, what we like, give value to and seek' (Good, 2017, p. 7).

Good (2017) argues that content curators act as gatekeepers to cultural portals, and as 'multifaceted lighthouses' scanning the digital landscape for places, things and people deemed worthy of attention. In this sense, cultural curation also becomes an act of placemaking, highlighting locations that tourists can identify with and where they can experience meaningful things. Content curation, as a process of ordering information to generate value, is spawning the growth of 'content curation sites' in tourism (Miralbell, Alzua-Sorzabal and Gerrikagoitia, 2013). There are many examples in cultural tourism, such as Culture Trip in the UK, the Cultural Curator, Cultural Tourism DC in Washington and the Creative Tourist platform. The latter features 'creative things to do in Manchester and the North' of England and also advises other destinations on cultural and creative tourism development. These sites create value by ordering information and through their role as selectors. Cultural curation sites highlight the people responsible for the selection, staking their claim to the position of content organizer and gatekeeper. The curatorial turn marks a shift from exchange value to relational value.

The eventification of cultural tourism also allows curators to select specific moments that are significant in cultural consumption. This is most evident in the staging of exhibitions that present 'once in a lifetime' opportunities to see particular works or curated selections of art. But it also underpins selections of festivals to visit or times to be in specific cities and places. The curator, by paying attention to a specific location at a certain time, signals an increase in the value of that place, and hence stimulates visitation to destinations that are 'cool' at a specific moment (Pappalepore, Maitland and Smith, 2014).

The effects of the curatorial moment were charted by Richards (2010) in his dissection of the dilemma posed for Canadian architectural critic Sanford Kwinter in October 1997. Rather than attending the opening of the Bilbao

Guggenheim, he was at the fiftieth anniversary re-enactment of the first super-sonic flight by Chuck Yeager in the Mojave Desert. Kwinter chose the desert:

> because we believe in shock waves, we believe them to be part of the music of modernity, not something to watch a ribbon be cut from, but something to feel with our diaphragms, eardrums, genitals and the soles of our feet. We wanted to be in the desert badlands that day with nothing but the sun, the baked dirt, the pneumatic tremors, and the unbroken horizon. (Kwinter, 2010, p. 89)

Richards explains this in curatorial terms: Kwinter had decided that the Guggenheim represented the past, an event that would attract his fellow critics in droves, whereas the desert represented the value to come. In the end, however, Kwinter's bet on a supersonic future proved a poor one, curtailed less than three years later with the crash of Air France Concorde Flight 4590 near Paris (Richards, 2010). Many cultural tourism curators seem to follow Kwinter's strategy: they look for places that are currently undiscovered, or 'under the radar' of the mass cultural tourist and other selectors, but which are likely to become more popular in future, such as Dundee in Scotland and Tirana in Albania (Lonely Planet, 2018).

Each of the turns outlined above have marked changes in the position and nature of cultural tourism, with concomitant shifts in the actors and structures involved, requiring new research approaches. This book adopts a practice approach as explained in the next section.

TOWARDS NEW APPROACHES TO CULTURAL TOURISM

In recent years, the theory and practice of cultural tourism have undergone significant transformation. From a simple addition of 'culture' and 'tourism' in the 1980s, cultural tourism began to be perceived and analysed as a self-contained field, and perspectives on cultural tourism have also responded to the different turns in social theory. Initial academic interest in the field can be traced back to the cultural turn, with growing attention for the stratification and signification of cultural tourism consumption. The mobilities turn focussed attention on the constant movement of cultural tourists and problematized the original concept of the tourist gaze. The performative turn generated more attention for the agency of the cultural tourist, who was not just a consumer but also a performer of cultural experiences. The creative turn has also highlighted the multiplication of new identities and roles in cultural tourism, and the rise of the 'local' as a category of 'authentic' cultural tourism experience.

The successive academic turns, the expansion of cultural tourism demand, the supply of cultural sites and events and the growing range of actors promoting cultural tourism have also stimulated a growing body of knowledge. From isolated academic studies in the 1980s, the cultural tourism literature has expanded to almost 9000 publications a year in 2019, almost 10 per cent of the total publication output in the field of tourism (Richards, 2018). This growing output covers a number of main themes, including cultural tourism as a form of cultural consumption, motivations for cultural tourism, the economic aspects of cultural tourism, the relationship between tourism and cultural heritage, the growth of the creative economy, and the links between anthropology and cultural tourism.

These studies show a tendency to concentrate either on the consumption of culture (motivation, behaviour) or the production of cultural experiences for tourists (authenticity, satisfaction). However, as the previous discussion has emphasized, it is increasingly difficult to separate consumption and production. In particular, the idea of a relatively passive tourist gazing on the sights offered to them by producers in the tourism industry came under increasing scrutiny. The performative turn shed light on the relatively active role that many tourists have in constructing their own experience (Ek, Larsen, Hornskov and Mansfeldt, 2008). By the turn of the Millennium, there was also more attention for co-creation between producers and consumers to develop tourism experiences (Binkhorst and Den Dekker, 2009; Campos, Mendes, Valle and Scott, 2018). Providers realized they needed to get closer to tourists to understand their needs in fast-moving consumer markets, and that this could be achieved by enlisting them in the experience production process. Vargo and Lusch (2008) outlined similar changes in the emergence of service dominant logic, and the concomitant shift from using operand (tangible resources) to operant (skills and knowledge) resources.

One of the changes that facilitated co-creation was the shift towards intangible cultural resources in tourism experiences (OECD, 2014). This enabled consumers to contribute more of their own knowledge and skills to the experience (Richards and Wilson, 2006). The rise of the Internet and digital technologies also transformed the information flows in tourism from a system of broadcast by producers (Poon, 1993) towards 'new tourists' as co-producers of information. As tourists began providing information to their peers, they also penetrated areas that suppliers had found difficult to reach. Tourists began to consume more areas of 'everyday life', or the elements of the destination that fell outside the framing activities of the tourist industry. The ability of visitors to expand the scope of cultural content produced a more fragmented landscape of cultural tourism demand, with many new niches emerging (Richards, 2011). These were exploited by an army of new cultural and creative intermediaries eager to offer new experiences, leading to innovation and even more fragmentation. This more diverse cultural tourism scene also became more democratized, as the framing power of the tourism industry declined, and new cultural forms began to challenge the previous hegemony of high culture.

The changing nature of cultural tourism consumption and production was recently summarized in the UNWTO *Report on Tourism and Culture Synergies* (2018). This signalled some important shifts in the relationship between tourism and culture:

1. A shift from tangible to intangible heritage in cultural tourism consumption and production;
2. A growing focus on everyday life, or 'living like a local' (Russo and Richards, 2016);
3. Fragmentation of cultural tourism into a series of niches, such as heritage tourism, art tourism, gastronomy tourism, film tourism and music tourism (Richards, 2011);
4. An eventification of cultural tourism supply and demand as a means of generating attention and spreading demand (Richards, 2013);
5. The rise of new intermediaries and systems of curation (Tribe, 2008);
6. A shift from elite to mass culture and the rise of new forms of distinction;
7. A broadening concept of culture as an object of tourism.

This growing complexity means that traditional discipline-based approaches to cultural tourism often fail to capture the nuances of the relationships between the actors and structures in the cultural tourism field. As Bargeman and Richards (2020) have outlined, there is a need to take a broader, more integrated approach to the study of tourism to resolve the actor-structure dichotomy and deal with increasing fragmentation of demand and supply and the rise of co-creation. Such a new approach also needs to deal with the question of how consumers and producers become entrained into practices, such as cultural tourism, and why they maintain or cease their participation.

Three basic moves are enfolded in this practice-based approach. Firstly, a practice view of tourism integrates actor and structure-related factors, seeing practices as routine-based configurations of activities shared by groups of people as part of their everyday life, through which social structures are produced, which in turn guide the actions of participants in the practice. The actors include all those individuals and organizations who can influence or who are influenced by the (cultural tourism) practice. Previous distinctions between producers and consumers in tourism therefore fade: both are enlisted in the creation and maintenance of the practice.

Secondly, we view social practices as a form of interaction ritual (Collins, 2004), which allows us to explain motivations for joining and adhering to tourism practices. Building on studies of leisure practices by scholars from Tilburg University (e.g. van der Poel, 1997), and shaped as a research agenda by Richards (2010), this work has been consolidated and extended by a wider group of researchers also incorporating Breda University of Applied Sciences (e.g. Bargeman, Richards and Govers, 2018; Richards, 2014; Simons, 2019, 2020).

Thirdly, we attempt to address a weakness in Collins' (2004) original view of rituals or practices by paying attention not just to the conditions that produce emotional energy, but also the contexts and the dynamics of practices. Chapter 3 examines the contexts of cultural tourism practices in more detail, highlighting the way in which the locations and times of cultural tourism practices affect, and are affected by, the actors involved. Based on the work of Shove and her collaborators (Shove, Pantzar and Watson, 2012), we also examine how the dynamics of practices evolve through the interaction of competences, materials and meaning.

As Richards (2011) outlines, Shove and Pantzar (2005) argue that a focus on practices produces a new set of research questions, which also apply to the study of cultural tourism:

1. What it means to participate in a practice;
2. How enthusiasms develop and flourish;
3. The demands that practices make of those who follow them;
4. Specific mechanisms of attraction and defection for practitioners;
5. The relationship between individual practitioners and the unfolding entity of the practice.

These are questions that we will also develop through the remainder of the book, seeking to explain how cultural tourism practices come to be through the interactions of actors and structures. Chapter 2 considers the wide range of different actors involved in cultural tourism practices, and how they collaborate and interact to co-create cultural tourism experiences. The actions of these different actors are heavily influenced by social structures (such as markets and regulatory frameworks) and take place in different spatial and temporal contexts. In Chapter 3, we consider how such contexts shape cultural tourism activities, and how they are in turn shaped by the dynamics of cultural tourism. Cultural tourism practices also have a range of consequences or outcomes, both intended and unintended. These include economic benefits to local economies and the cultural system, but also overcrowding at major cultural sites and threats to 'authenticity'. These issues are dealt with in Chapter 4, which also provides a new practice-based definition of cultural tourism. This chapter also develops a model incorporating Collins' (2004) perspectives on interaction rituals, which emphasize relationality and embodiment through physical co-presence and processes of entrainment among groups of actors. Chapter 5 illustrates some of these cultural tourism rituals, including placemaking, creative tourism, photography, gastronomy and eventification, which are often manifested as bundles of practices – in 'new urban tourism', for example. In the final chapter, we look towards the future, sketching emerging research agendas relating to a practice approach. We also pay attention to the issue of interrupted practices: drawing on the experience of the Covid-19 pandemic, which suggests the future of cultural tourism might not be so routine as suggested by traditional practice analysis.

The structure of the text is shown in Figure 1.1, with a progressive focus on different elements of the cultural tourism practice, from actors in Chapter 2 to the contexts of practices in Chapter 3. The interaction of actors and context in the practice serve to generate consequences or effects, which are analysed in Chapter 4. One of the important consequences is the development and maintenance of the practice itself, which are dealt with in the context of Collins' interaction ritual in Chapter 5.

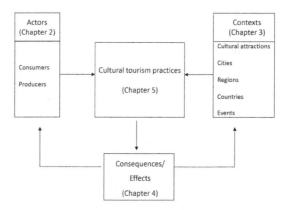

Figure 1.1   Model of cultural tourism practices and structure of the text

REFERENCES

Augé, M. (1995). *Non-places: An Anthropology of Supermodernity*. New York: Verso.

Bakas, F.E. and Duxbury, N. (2018). Development of rural areas and small cities through creative tourism: the CREATOUR project. *Anais Brasileiros de Estudos Turísticos*, *8*(3), 74–84.

Bargeman, B. and Richards, G. (2020). A new approach to understanding tourism practices. *Annals of Tourism Research*, *84*. https://doi.org/10.1016/j.annals.2020.102988.

Bargeman, B., Richards, G., and Govers, E. (2018). Volunteer tourism impacts in Ghana: a practice approach. *Current Issues in Tourism*, *21*(13), 1486–501.

Belda, E. and Laaksonen, A. (2001). *Pyrenne: A European Project to Foster Linguistic Diversity and the Role of Tradition in Contemporary Arts Production*. Barcelona: Fundacio Interarts.

Binkhorst, E. and Den Dekker, T. (2009). Agenda for co-creation tourism experience research. *Journal of Hospitality Marketing & Management, 18*(2–3), 311–27.

Boniface, P. and Fowler, P. (2002). *Heritage and Tourism in the Global Village*. London: Routledge.

Bourdieu, P. (1984). *Distinction: A Social Critique of the Judgement of Taste*. London: Routledge.

Bywater, M. (1993). The market for cultural tourism in Europe. *Travel and Tourism Analyst, 6*, 30–46.

Campos, A.C., Mendes, J., Valle, P.O.D., and Scott, N. (2018). Co-creation of tourist experiences: a literature review. *Current Issues in Tourism, 21*(4), 369–400.

Carvalho, R., Ferreira, A.M., and Figueira, L.M. (2016). Cultural and creative tourism in Portugal. *PASOS. Revista de Turismo y Patrimonio Cultural, 14*(5), 1075–82.

Castells, M. (1996). *The Information Age, Vol. 1: The Rise of the Network Society*. Oxford: Blackwell.

Collins, C. (2004). *Interaction Ritual Chains*. Princeton, NJ: Princeton University Press.

Corner, J. and Harvey, S. (1991). *Enterprise and Heritage: Crosscurrents of National Culture*. London: Routledge.

Couret, C. (2015). Collaboration and partnerships in practice: the creative tourism network®. In D. Gursoy, M. Saayman, and M. Sotiriadis (eds), *Collaboration in Tourism Businesses and Destinations: A Handbook* (pp. 191–203). Bingley: Emerald Group Publishing.

Craik, J. (2002). The culture of tourism. In C. Rojek and J. Urry (eds), *Touring Cultures: Transformations of Travel and Theory* (pp. 123–46). London: Routledge.

Debeş, T. (2011). Cultural tourism: a neglected dimension of tourism industry. *Anatolia, 22*(2), 234–51.

Debord, G. (1967). *The Society of the Spectacle*. New York: Zone Books.

De Haan, J. (1997). *Het Gedeelde Erfgoed*. Den Haag: Sociaal en Cultureel Planbureau.

Diekmann, A. and Hannam, K. (2012). Touristic mobilities in India's slum spaces. *Annals of Tourism Research, 39*(3), 1315–36.

Duxbury, N. and Richards, G. (2019). *A Research Agenda for Creative Tourism*. Cheltenham, UK and Northampton, MA, USA: Edward Elgar Publishing.

Edensor, T. (1998). *Tourists at the Taj: Performance and Meaning at a Symbolic Site*. London: Routledge.

Ek, R., Larsen, J., Hornskov, S.B., and Mansfeldt, O.K. (2008). A dynamic framework of tourist experiences: space-time and performances in the experience economy. *Scandinavian Journal of Hospitality and Tourism, 8*(2), 122–40.

Florida, R. (2002). *The Rise of the Creative Class*. New York: Basic Books.

Gale, T. (2009). Urban beaches, virtual worlds and 'the end of tourism'. *Mobilities, 4*(1), 119–38.

Goffman, E. (1959). *The Presentation of Self in Everyday Life*. New York: Anchor Books.

Good, R. (2017). Content curation & cultural heritage: the social value of selecting and organizing existing content. https://medium.com/content-curation-official-guide/content-curation-cultural-heritage-5cb602d066af (accessed 18 December 2020).

Gratton, C. and Richards, G. (1996). The economic context of cultural tourism. In G. Richards (ed.), *Cultural Tourism in Europe* (pp. 71–87). Wallingford: CABI.

Halewood, C. and Hannam, K. (2001). Viking heritage tourism: authenticity and commodification. *Annals of Tourism Research, 28*(3), 565–80.

Harwood, S. and El-Manstrly, D. (2012). The performativity turn in tourism. *University of Edinburgh Business School Working Paper Series, 12*(05), University of Edinburgh Business School.

Häussermann, H. and Siebel, W. (1993). Die Politik der Festivalisierung und die Festivalisierung der Politik. In H. Häussermann (ed.), *Festivalisierung der Stadtpolitik: Stadtentwicklung durch große Projekte* (pp. 7–31). Wiesbaden: VS Verlag für Sozialwissenschaften.

Hewison, R. (1987). *The Heritage Industry: Britain in a Climate of Decline*. London: Methuen.

Hitchcock, M. and King, V.T. (2003). Discourses with the past: tourism and heritage in South-East Asia. *Indonesia and the Malay World, 31*(89), 3–15.

Jansen-Verbeke, M. and Van Rekom, J. (1996). Scanning museum visitors: urban tourism marketing. *Annals of Tourism Research, 23*(2), 364–75.

Kirshenblatt-Gimblett, B. (1998). *Destination Culture: Tourism, Museums, and Heritage*. Davis, LA: University of California Press.

Kjær Mansfeldt, O. (2015). The inbetweenness of tourist experiences. PhD thesis, Royal Danish Academy of Fine Arts, Copenhagen.

Koskinen, I. (2009). Design districts. *Design Issues, 25*(4), 3–12.

Kwinter, S. (2010). Mach 1 (and other mystic visitations). In A.K. Sykes (ed.), *Constructing a New Agenda: Architectural Theory 1993–2009* (pp. 80–9). New York: Princeton Architectural Press.

Lonely Planet (2018). Best in Europe 2018. https://www.lonelyplanet.com/articles/best-in-europe-2018 (accessed 18 December 2020).

MacCannell, D. (1976). *The Tourist: A New Theory of the Leisure Class*. Davis, CA: University of California Press.

MacLeod, N. (2013). Cultural routes, trails and the experience of place. In M. Smith and G. Richards (eds), *The Routledge Handbook of Cultural Tourism* (pp. 390–5). London: Routledge.

Maitland, R. (2007). Tourists, the creative class and distinctive areas in major cities: the roles of visitors and residents in developing new tourism areas. In G. Richards and J. Wilson (eds), *Tourism, Creativity and Development* (pp. 95–108). London: Routledge.

Marques, L. and Richards, G. (2014). *Creative Districts Around the World*. http://creativedistricts.imem.nl/articles/36/00_Marques_Richards_Creative_Districts_complete_book.pdf (accessed 18 December 2020).

McDonald, S. (1998). *The Politics of Display: Museums, Science, Culture*. London: Routledge.

Miralbell, O., Alzua-Sorzabal, A., and Gerrikagoitia, J.K. (2013). Content curation and narrative tourism marketing. In Z. Xiang and I. Tussyadiah (eds), *Information and Communication Technologies in Tourism 2014: Proceedings of the International Conference in Dublin, Ireland, January 21–24, 2014* (pp. 187–99). Cham: Springer Science & Business Media.

Ng, M.K. (2002). From a 'cultural desert' to a 'cultural supermarket': tourism promotion in Hong Kong. In W.B. Kim and J.Y. Yoo (eds), *Culture, Economy and Place: Asia-Pacific Perspectives* (pp. 179–218). Anyang: Korea Research Institute for Human Settlements.

Nijman, J. (1999). Cultural globalization and the identity of place: the reconstruction of Amsterdam. *Ecumene, 6*, 146–64.

Noy, C. (2008). Traversing hegemony: gender, body, and identity in the narratives of Israeli female backpackers. *Tourism Review International, 12*(2), 93–114.

OECD (2014). *Tourism and the Creative Economy*. Paris: OECD.

O'Neill, P. (2007). The curatorial turn: from practice to discourse. In J. Rugg and M. Sedgwick (eds), *Issues in Curating Contemporary Art and Performance* (pp. 13–28). Bristol: Intellect Books.

Pappalepore, I., Maitland, R., and Smith, A. (2014). Prosuming creative urban areas. Evidence from East London. *Annals of Tourism Research, 44,* 227–40.

Pickel-Chevalier, S., Violier, P., and Sari, N.P.S. (2016). Tourism and globalisation: vectors of cultural homogenisation? (the case study of Bali). In A.M. Morrison, A.G. Abdullah, and S. Leo (eds), *Proceedings of the Asia Tourism Forum, 2016 'A New Approach of Tourism'* (pp. 452–7). Paris: Atlantis Press.

Poon, A. (1993). *Tourism, Technology and Competitive Strategies*. Wallingford: CABI.

Ren, C. (2010). Assembling the socio-material destination: an actor-network approach to cultural tourism studies. In G. Richards and W. Munsters (eds), *Cultural Tourism Research Methods* (pp. 199–208). Wallingford: CABI.

Richards, G. (1996). Production and consumption of European cultural tourism. *Annals of Tourism Research, 23*(2), 261–83.

Richards, G. (2001). *Cultural Attractions and European Tourism*. Wallingford: CABI.

Richards, G. (2007). *Cultural Tourism: Global and Local Perspectives*. New York: Haworth Press.

Richards, G. (2010). *Leisure in the Network Society: From Pseudo-events to Hyperfestivity?* https://www.academia.edu/1271795/Leisure_in_the_Network _Society (accessed 18 December 2020).

Richards, G. (2011). Rethinking niche tourism in the network society. Paper presented at the ATLAS Annual Conference in Cyprus, November 2011. https:// www.academia.edu/1868914/Rethinking_niche_tourism_in_the_network_society (accessed 18 December 2020).

Richards, G. (2013). Events and the means of attention. *Journal of Tourism Research & Hospitality, 2*(2). http://www.scitechnol.com/2324-8807/2324-8807-2-118.pdf (accessed 18 December 2020).

Richards, G. (2014). Imagineering events as interaction ritual chains. In G. Richards, L. Marques, and K. Mein (eds), *Event Design: Social Perspectives and Practices* (pp. 14–24). London: Routledge.

Richards, G. (2018). Cultural tourism: a review of recent research and trends. *Journal of Hospitality and Tourism Management, 36,* 12–21.

Richards, G. and Raymond, C. (2000). Creative tourism. *ATLAS news, 23*(8), 16–20.

Richards, G. and Wilson, J. (2006). Developing creativity in tourist experiences: a solution to the serial reproduction of culture? *Tourism Management, 27,* 1209–23.

Richards, G. and Wilson, J. (2007). *Tourism, Creativity and Development*. London: Routledge.

Richards, G., Goedhart, S., and Herrijgers, C. (2001). The cultural attraction distribution system. In G. Richards (ed.), *Cultural Attractions and European Tourism* (pp. 71–89). Wallingford: CABI.

Ritzer, G. (1999). *Enchanting a Disenchanted World: Revolutionizing the Means of Consumption*. Thousand Oaks, CA: Pine Forge Press.

Robertson, R. (1994). Globalisation or glocalisation? *Journal of International Communication, 1*(1), 33–52.

Russo, A.P. and Richards, G. (2016). *Reinventing the Local in Tourism: Producing, Consuming and Negotiating Place*. Bristol: Channel View Publications.

Shove, E. and Pantzar, M. (2005). Consumers, producers and practices: understanding the invention and reinvention of Nordic walking. *Journal of Consumer Culture*, 5(1), 43–64.

Shove, E., Pantzar, M., and Watson, M. (2012). *The Dynamics of Social Practice: Everyday Life and How It Changes*. London: Sage.

Silberberg, T. (1995). Cultural tourism and business opportunities for museums and heritage sites. *Tourism Management*, 16(5), 361–5.

Simons, I. (2019). Events and online interaction: the construction of hybrid event communities. *Leisure Studies*, 38(2), 145–59.

Simons, I. (2020). Changing identities through collective performance at events: the case of the Redhead Days. *Leisure Studies*, 1–17.

Smith, M.K. (ed.). (2007). *Tourism, Culture and Regeneration*. Wallingford: CABI.

Strannegård, L. and Strannegård, M. (2012). Works of art: aesthetic ambitions in design hotels. *Annals of Tourism Research*, 39(4), 1995–2012.

Tribe, J. (2008). The art of tourism. *Annals of Tourism Research*, 35(4), 924–44.

Turner, V. (1969). *The Ritual Process: Structure and Anti-structure*. Piscataway, NJ: Transaction Publishers.

UNWTO (2018). *Report on Tourism and Culture Synergies*. Madrid: UNWTO.

Urry, J. (1990). *The Tourist Gaze*. London: Sage.

Urry, J. (2000). *Beyond Societies: Mobilities for the Twenty-first Century*. London: Routledge.

Valtonen, A. and Veijola, S. (2011). Sleep in tourism. *Annals of Tourism Research*, 38(1), 175–92.

Van der Duim, R. (2007). Tourismscapes: an actor-network perspective. *Annals of Tourism Research*, 34(4), 961–76.

Van der Poel, H. (1997). Leisure and the modularization of daily life. *Time & Society*, 6(2–3), 171–94.

Vargo, S.L. and Lusch, R.F. (2008). Service-dominant logic: continuing the evolution. *Journal of the Academy of Marketing Science*, 36(1), 1–10.

Veblen, T. (1899). *Theory of the Leisure Class: An Economic Study in the Evolution of Institutions*. New York: Macmillan.

Venturi, F. (2018). Curating music, articulating value: towards a definition of the curatorial within live new music. https://www.academia.edu/42055917/Curating_Music _Articulating_Value_Towards_a_definition_of_the_curatorial_value_of_live_new _music (accessed 18 December 2020).

Webb, M. (2005). *Adventurous Wine Architecture*. Melbourne: Images Publishing.

Wijnberg, N.M. (2004). Innovation and organization: value and competition in selection systems. *Organization Studies*, 25(8), 1413–33.

Zukin, S. (1995). *Culture of Cities*. Oxford: Blackwell.

2.   Actors in cultural tourism practices

INTRODUCTION

The cultural tourism field unites many actors, individuals and organizations, encompassing tourism, culture and many other areas. The culture and tourism fields are very different in terms of their modes of operation, their values and objectives. Bringing these fields together is difficult, because they speak different languages (OECD, 2009). Actors in the cultural sector tend to have a discourse related to autonomy, artistic quality and creativity (Kaare Nielsen, 2003), whereas the discourse of the tourism sector is related to economic value and efficiency. The report produced by the UNWTO (2018) on synergies between tourism and culture shows that cultural tourism experts see differences in objectives between the sectors as the main challenge for tourism and culture collaboration.

Traditional analyses of cultural tourism have tended to focus on particular groups of actors, such as consumers or producers. Cultural tourism is often seen as an experience produced by tourism and/or cultural actors and consumed by tourists. In a practice approach, however, the focus shifts to how actors interact with one another and with the structures that encompass the practice. In seeking to resolve the duality of actors and structures, our focus shifts from the behaviour and motivations of actors, or the structures that bound their actions, towards the recursive nature of actor-structure relationships. Whereas previous studies of cultural tourism have concentrated on the influence of structures such as class or education in determining action, we argue that actions shape the structures that in turn influence action. In this chapter, we concentrate on the actors who produce and reproduce cultural tourism practices, and in Chapter 3, we focus on the 'field' or context that these practices support, shape and constitute.

The division between supply and demand, or between producers and consumers, is a common duality in tourism studies. This stems from the economic or management basis of much tourism analysis, which in the past treated the tourism industry as the supplier of products to the tourist, or consumer. During the 1990s, approaches emerged that began to challenge the basic division of supply and demand. For example, Smith's (1994) model of the generic tourism product highlighted the role that consumers play in the creation of tourism services, through freedom of choice and involvement. Such ideas began to crystallize with the emergence of the experience economy (Pine and Gilmore, 1998), in which their original 'first generation' conception of experiences still gave basic control of the experience to the producer (Boswijk, Thijssen and Peelen, 2006). Subsequent studies underlined the increasing co-creation of experiences (Binkhorst and Den Dekker, 2009) in which tourists were included in the experience creation process.

Over time, there has been growing attention for agency in (cultural) tourism. The actors able to exert agency include the tourists and experience producers and other actors related to the development and supply of experiential opportunities, such as cultural organizations and tour operators. Because of the important public value generated by culture (Holden, 2006), cultural tourism also has a significant element of public sector involvement.

The range of cultural tourism actors is also expanding, as Gravari-Barbas (2018) notes, partly due to globalization processes. Because of the constantly expanding constellation of individual and organizational actors in cultural tourism, we focus not so much on the actors themselves, but on their actions, interactions and relationalities. Drawing on our model of cultural tourism practices in Chapter 1 (Figure 1.1), we see that actor-related factors include not just socio-demographic characteristics such as education, age and class, or individual motivations, which are extensively dealt with in the cultural tourism literature, but also on co-creation processes, and the role of previous experiences, skills, knowledge and emotions, which have more recently received attention.

MOTIVATIONS FOR CULTURAL TOURISM

According to Richards and Munsters (2010, p. 2), 'the search for cultural experiences has become one of the leading motivations for people to travel' and this 'has attracted the attention of a growing number of researchers and policy makers, vastly increasing the scope of cultural tourism research'. Motivation is key to conceptualizing cultural tourism and is the basis of most definitions. Richards (2018, p. 13) proposed a definition of cultural tourism based on motivational factors: 'Cultural tourism is a type of tourism activity in which the visitor's essential motivation is to learn, discover, experience and consume the tangible and intangible cultural attractions/products in a tourism destination.' Not all visitors to cultural sites have a cultural motivation, however, and therefore arguably should not be categorized as cultural tourists (Richards, 2001). This is important from the perspective of policy, since tourists who are motivated by culture will react to cultural tourism marketing and development initiatives, whereas visitors with other motivations may not.

Much previous research has focussed on what motivates people to engage in cultural tourism, and the extent to which this behaviour is driven by cultural motivations. Early studies by the Association for Tourism and Leisure Research and Education (ATLAS) revealed that cultural visitors indicated learning new things and experiencing the 'atmosphere' of the cultural site as their most important motivations (Richards, 1996). The importance of learning as a driver for cultural tourism was also more recently confirmed by Falk, Ballantyne, Packer and Benckendorff (2012) and Chen and Rahman (2018). The ATLAS research also distinguished between tourists with a specific cultural motivation, related to seeing a specific site or cultural artefact, and a general cultural motivation where culture was not a specific objective of the trip.

The distinction between general and specific cultural motivations has also been underlined in other studies, for example, by Bywater (1993), who distinguished between tourists with a cultural motivation, those who were culturally inspired and those attracted by culture. The varying 'depth' of desired cultural experience was confirmed as an important distinction between cultural tourist types by McKercher and du Cros (2002), and Galí-Espelt (2012) also categorized tourists in terms of the degree of 'culturedness', which she related to the length of visit and the cultural content of the experience.

Richards (2002) confirmed the important role of cultural attractions in stimulating travel, with data from the ATLAS research providing strong support for Leiper's (1990) idea that tourists are 'pushed' towards attractions by their motivations rather than being drawn by the magnetic 'pulling power' implied by the term 'attraction' (Gunn, 1988). Cultural visitation was shown to be strongly related to motivation and the resulting use of attraction markers. The ATLAS research also indicated that those with stronger cultural motivations experienced higher levels of satisfaction, indicating a link between the antecedents and outcomes of cultural tourism behaviour (Richards, 2002).

Bond and Falk (2013) presented a theoretical model of identity-related tourism motivation, arguing that how tourists see themselves is important in motivating cultural visits as opposed to other forms of tourism.

> There is evidence to suggest that core identity attributes may be a primary motivation for certain types of tourism (such as cultural or heritage tourism); however, it is unlikely that a person's cultural or religious identity is the primary motivator behind a visit to a zoo or a theme park. (p. 432)

One of the differences between visiting cultural and other types of sites may also be related to people's self-identifying as 'cultural tourists'. Figures from the ATLAS research in the Albanian city of Vlora in 2018, for example, indicate that just over 23 per cent of tourists identified themselves as cultural tourists (Richards, 2019).

Important motivations for cultural tourism include the desire to learn and nostalgia. Cultural tourism has been connected with learning since antiquity (Ivanovic, 2008) and this link was strengthened during the Grand Tour, which educated the upper classes about history, literature and art through travel to countries such as Italy, France and Germany (Towner, 1985). The link to learning remained even after the democratization of travel in the 20th century, because inquisitiveness about other people, places and histories have remained important travel motivations.

Learning was seen as an important element of the motivation of cultural tourists by McKercher and du Cros (2002), who argued that cultural tourists for whom culture was a central motivation would also see learning about the culture of the destination as a major reason for visiting. Lynch, Duinker, Sheehan and Chute (2011) examined tourist interest in Mi'kmaw Aboriginal cultural tourism in Nova Scotia, Canada. They found that 'most respondents were motivated to participate in Mi'kmaw cultural tourism for reasons of education, learning, and gaining a better understanding of Mi'kmaw culture' (p. 981). There was also a strong link between education level and cultural tourism participation and interest. International tourists had a particularly strong desire to participate in cultural learning activities, which was related to the longer distances travelled. Lynch et al. also emphasized that the learning process applied not just to the tourists, but also the host community, which used the visitor centres as meeting places and as an opportunity to learn more about their own culture.

McIntosh (2004) argued that tourists in New Zealand wanted to learn about contemporary Maori life as well as historical elements of their culture. She interviewed international tourists arriving and departing from Christchurch International Airport and found that most respondents had 'learnt something new' about Maori culture. Learning was primarily informal, through meeting and talking to Maori people. However, she found that this learning was shallow, and covered different aspects of Maori history, traditional lifestyle, Maori legends and stories and customs. Most tourists had little prior knowledge of Maori culture, and they held traditional stereotypical impressions, but they gained an increased understanding and appreciation for Maori culture from their visit. Moscardo and Pearce (1999) studied visitors to an Aboriginal cultural park in Australia and identified different groups in terms of their desire to learn about indigenous culture. The Passive Cultural Learning Group accounted for just under a quarter of respondents, exhibiting high levels of interest in ethnic tourism, particularly focussed on cultural learning rather than direct contact experiences.

It is noticeable that many early studies of learning in cultural tourism were conducted in the context of indigenous cultures, which have long been under threat from the forces of modernity. The position of indigenous groups reflects an interest in ways of life that are disappearing, which is also linked to feelings of nostalgia about the past. In an Australian context, Trotter (1999) argued that nostalgia is integral to the development of cultural tourism. In tracing the historical development of views on nostalgia, he compares David Lowenthal's *The Past is a Foreign Country* (1985) and Robert Hewison's *The Heritage Industry* (1987). Lowenthal's epic panorama of the past sees some merit in nostalgia, which he argued can help to render the present familiar and help create group and individual identities. Hewison, on the other hand, treats nostalgia as a 'social pathology' that helped Britain adjust to crisis. Trotter argues that 'nostalgia is a natural ally for tourism: both offer a means of "escape"; one to another time, the other to another place' (p. 23). He further suggested such escapes to the past are not necessarily a bad thing, because they legitimize individual and group memory alongside institutional history-making, and they give satisfaction, connecting people and enriching the present. Other commentators have taken a more negative stance, arguing that heritage tourism commodifies the past and plays on nostalgia to generate tourism. Shaw (1992) saw the 'economics of nostalgia' behind the growth of heritage tourism in the UK, and Dann (1995) referred to tourism as 'the nostalgia industry of the future'.

It is clear that the actors in the cultural tourism practice are not just the tourists, but the whole range of people and institutions that facilitate cultural tourism experiences. Studies have therefore begun to dissect the motivations of the providers of cultural tourism experiences, which can range from profit to education, to lifestyle, to a desire to share culture with others. More recently, the motivations of both consumers and producers to create experiences together has been analysed under the banner of co-creation. This trajectory has also been based on the increased agency attributed to tourists. There is evidence of growing attention for reflexivity on the part of tourists, and a parallel development in the desire of producers to get closer to and learn from the consumer (Feighery, 2006).

SEGMENTING THE CULTURAL TOURISM AUDIENCE

The profile of cultural tourists has been extensively researched, primarily because of the value of segmentation for marketing purposes (McKercher, Ho, du Cros and So-Ming, 2002). Market segmentation can be based on different variables (Dolničar, 2004; Kotler and Armstrong, 2018) including: geographic factors; demographics; psychographics; and behavioural variables. In the field of cultural tourism, the main segmentation variables have tended to be psychographic and behavioural, particularly focussing on levels of cultural interest and motives for cultural visitation.

Motivational Segmentation

Motivation is often seen as the key to defining and understanding cultural tourism. However, as Howard Hughes (2002) notes: 'confusion has arisen because all tourists at cultural attractions are often regarded as cultural tourists' (p. 172), regardless of their motivation. More recently, Brida, Dalle Nogare and Scuderi (2016, p. 261) observed that 'Tourists who occasionally consume cultural services while on holiday are often mistaken for agents whose main motivation in choosing a holiday destination is to experience the destination's rich supply of cultural services.'

Much current motivational segmentation can be traced back to a pioneering paper by Silberberg (1995). He proposed a segmentation based on the degree of motivation to experience culture, ranging from those who were 'greatly motivated' by culture (15 per cent), in part motivated by culture (30 per cent), those for whom culture was an 'adjunct' to their visit (20 per cent) and the 'accidental cultural tourist' (20 per cent), who did not intend to consume culture at all, but encountered it anyway, and a final 20 per cent of tourists who would not consume culture 'under any circumstances'. The distribution of tourists between these different groups was not based on empirical research, but rather estimates.

Subsequent empirical work has confirmed differences in motivation and behaviour in the cultural tourism audience. Howard Hughes (2002) distinguished 'culture-core' and 'culture-peripheral' tourists. Those in the culture-core choose to travel to experience a particular aspect of the culture. This group can in turn be divided into two groups: the primary culture-core, whose main purpose in travelling is to visit a specific cultural site, and multi-primary culture core, for whom different cultural attractions are of equal importance as a reason for visiting. The culture-periphery group does not have culture as a central motivation for their visit. These visitors can also be divided between the 'incidental' culture-peripheral tourists, for whom culture was a secondary reason for the visit (equivalent to Silberberg's 'adjunct'), and 'accidental' culture-peripheral tourists for whom culture does not feature at all in the decision to visit, but who still consume culture in some form during their trip.

Based on surveys of visitors to Hong Kong, McKercher and du Cros (2002) produced a similar motivational segmentation of cultural tourists, combining the desired depth of cultural experience and the importance of cultural motivations in the decision to visit. Based on these two dimensions, they propose five different types of tourist: serendipitous; purposeful; incidental; casual; and sightseeing. Özel and Kozak (2012) used cluster analysis to identify five distinct groups, labelled: 'Relaxation Seekers', 'Sports Seekers', 'Family Oriented', 'Escapists', and 'Achievement and Autonomy Seekers'. The division between those seeking culture and those using it as a form of escape is highlighted by Correia, Kozak and Ferradeira (2013). They identified push and pull satisfaction factors in visits to Lisbon, including the intrinsic desire to learn about aspects of culture (such as *Fado* music) and a search for novelty.

Over time, studies have employed increasingly sophisticated segmentation techniques. In their analysis of the Spoleto Festival in Italy, Formica and Uysal (1998) used motivational segmentation based on factor and cluster analysis. Spoleto is a small city northeast of Rome, with a rich cultural heritage. Visitors to the annual festival exhibited six motivational factors labelled: (1) Socialization and Entertainment, (2) Event Attraction and Excitement, (3) Group Togetherness, (4) Cultural/Historical, (5) Family Togetherness, and (6) Site Novelty. Two clusters of visitors could be identified – Moderates and Enthusiasts. The Enthusiasts were thirsty for a variety of cultural experiences, enjoyed the mix of culture and history and mixing with the festival crowds. The Moderates were less interested in the festival content and were particularly attracted by the uniqueness of the event. The Moderates showed little interest in interacting with other visitors and tended to avoid festival crowds.

Brida et al. (2016) identified two dimensions of cultural consumption among tourists with Multiple Correspondence Analysis, which they labelled 'light consumption' and 'hard consumption'. The former they link to a more recreational motivation, and the latter with a more intellectual motive. They see the former type as occasional cultural tourists, for whom cultural tourism behaviour is the consequence of a temporarily large amount of leisure time combined with a lack of alternatives, in an unfamiliar environment. This recreational motivation tends to result in fewer visits to museums than those with an intellectual motivation.

In recent years, however, the vaguer boundaries between high and popular culture, and the mixing of educational and other motives have produced more complex motivations. Moreno Gil and Ritchie (2009) examined the relationship between motivation and satisfaction of cultural tourists at museums in Gran Canaria, and they found that 'to learn' and 'to be entertained' combined in a single dimension, which they termed 'rich experience' (or edutainment).

Demographic Segmentation

Empirical evidence from different countries suggests that all age groups are represented in the cultural tourism audience. The ATLAS research has consistently indicated that the most frequent respondents at cultural sites and events tend to be aged 20–29. Richards (2001) argues that participation of younger cultural tourists is stimulated by rising higher education levels as well as the expansion of cultural tourism supply into popular and contemporary culture. In Macau, Vong (2016) also found that cultural tourists tended to be younger, mainly between 15 and 34 years old. Interestingly, in this research, serendipitous cultural tourists reported the highest visitation to heritage sites, even surpassing the purposeful cultural tourists. However, there is also evidence that points to an older profile, as Brida et al. (2016) found that museum attendance increases with age, also for tourists. Eurostat (2015) statistics also indicate that older people (aged 65 to 74 years) in the European Union (EU) were more likely to visit cultural sites than attend live performances or go to the cinema.

Richards and Van der Ark (2013) suggested that cultural tourists may develop a cultural 'travel career', as younger visitors tend to consume more contemporary art, creativity and modern architecture, whereas older visitors are more prevalent at more traditional monuments and museums. This may represent a generational shift, or a preference for contemporary culture among the young. Establishing if this is a cohort or age-related effect will be important in assessing future patterns of cultural tourism demand.

Cultural tourists are also often characterized as relatively wealthy travellers, which in turn makes them attractive for tourism firms, cultural organizations and policy makers. ATLAS data confirm that cultural tourists have higher average incomes than most other types of tourists (Richards, 2001, 2015). In addition, Santos (2020) shows that cultural tourism firms extract higher average profits, although they also appear more vulnerable to periods of crisis and expansion than other tourism firms.

Behavioural Segmentation

As studies progressed, the segmentation methods employed also evolved to become more multi-dimensional and more advanced statistical techniques were adopted, allowing more complex patterns of behaviour to be analysed. For example, van der Ark and Richards (2006) used latent class analysis (LCA) to differentiate between cultural tourists based on frequency of visit and perceived attractiveness of 19 European cities. They found three classes of cultural tourists, corresponding broadly to specific cultural tourists, general cultural tourists, and infrequent visitors with a preference for popular culture and entertainment.

Pulido-Fernández and Sánchez-Rivero (2010) adopted a LCA approach to cultural tourism, surveying 2983 visitors to medium-sized towns of Andalusia. They found three groups of cultural tourists: Museum culturophiles (49 per cent of the total) with a high level of museum visits; Roaming culturophiles (20 per cent) who were more likely to visit cultural events; and Culturally inactives (31 per cent) with a low level of cultural visitation. They also concluded that cultural tourism practices are largely determined by age and income, with older, more wealthy people engaging more often in cultural tourism.

Richards and Van der Ark (2013) employed multi-dimensional scaling (MDS) to analyse the ATLAS surveys from different countries, identifying not just different groups of cultural tourists, but also the types of cultural attractions they visited. They found that cultural tourists differ significantly in their consumption of cultural attractions, with high levels of cultural capital being related to consumption of more 'complex' and less 'popular' cultural sites. In general, increasing cultural capital is related to higher levels of visits to museums and historical sites.

From a qualitative perspective, Stylianou-Lambert (2011) studied the different 'gazes' in cultural tourism, showing that tourists visiting art museums use different types of 'perceptual filters' that influence their gaze. She found several different filters and resulting gazes (professional, art-loving, self-exploration, cultural tourism, social visitation, romantic, rejection, and indifference), and she argued that these perceptions, rather than individuals, could be categorized.

It has been observed that some groups of cultural consumers exhibit 'omnivorous' consumption, tending to mix different forms of culture and being more frequent consumers of culture in general (Peterson, 2005). Research has demonstrated a causal relationship between cultural omnivorousness, and participation in cultural events, visiting cultural sites and discovering exotic cultures (Toivonen, 2005). The implications of this for cultural tourism research are clear: individual site visits should not be viewed in isolation. There is a need to trace the behaviour of people over the course of a whole trip (the 'destination journey', according to Richards, King and Yeung, 2020) and also in their holiday time in relation to time spent at home.

GENDER IN CULTURAL TOURISM

Demographic segmentation indicates that cultural tourism consumption is more prevalent among women, which reflects cultural consumption patterns in general (Eurostat, 2015). More recently, the role of gender has been explored as an important aspect of the power and agency of actors in cultural tourism. Gender roles can be both strengthened and challenged by cultural tourism, depending on the context. The cultural turn in tourism studies led to a conceptualization of tourism spaces as political and contested, with more attention for the position of women (Pritchard, 2004). Women occupy a specific role not just in terms of their consumption of culture as tourists, but also in terms of how they are represented as objects of cultural tourism consumption.

Aitchison (1999) offered a critique of gendered representations of heritage and their role in the creation of gendered cultural tourism spaces in Scotland. She analysed the masculinization of heritage in the city of Stirling, which used the films *Braveheart*, *The Bruce* and *Rob Roy* for tourism promotion. She argued that the city used images of masculinism, militarism and nationalism to create gendered spaces, places and landscapes. Tucker's (2007) research in the Turkish region of Cappadocia indicated that women became more present in tourism-related work. In the 1990s, few women worked in tourism and they were also confined to the 'backstage'. By 2005, many more women were visibly engaged in cultural tourism activities, inviting tourists to view their cave-houses and selling handicrafts. The role of women in tourism was also strengthened by female tourists coming to the village and then staying as residents, changing the attitudes of local women, and forging new gender roles. These changes enabled women to negotiate new spatial and moral boundaries to find a role for themselves in the tourism economic realm.

Much work on cultural tourism and women has been in emerging economy contexts. Babb's (2012) study of gender and race in cultural tourism in Peru and Mexico revealed that although gender inequality is still prevalent in society, indigenous females can generate new cultural capital in the form of appearance, dress, language, artistic ability and everyday practices, which may bring economic advantage. Analysing cultural and experiential tourism (*turismo vivencial*) in Peru, Babb found that visitors want to know about the lives and culture of the indigenous Quechua-speaking people. The descriptions of the experiences emphasize the value of staying with or meeting a craftsman, a beekeeper, a musician, a weaver or a toolmaker – all men. Only men attended workshops where they were taught how to receive guests and interact with them. Women are behind the scenes or serving food, 'men are the designated hosts and play the leading public role in experiential tourism in the community, women are critically important to its success' (p. 43). In Chiapas, in Mexico, Babb found that tourists do not recognize the diversity of local indigenous peoples, seeing them as essentialized Indians. However, indigenous women are seen by tourists as being 'culturally authentic', giving them an economic advantage in tourism. Women have been empowered by artisan cooperatives where they control production and marketing, enabling them to be 'cultural standard bearers'. Babb notes that tourists often seek to interact with indigenous women, bringing the women into more active engagement with tourism. Ironically, increased engagement may reduce the apparent authenticity that attracts tourists in the first place. Female identities are shifting in response to tourism, creating both challenges and opportunities for historically marginalized groups. Arguably, the short-term gains offered by cultural tourism can advance the more strategic individual and collective interests of women: 'In times and places where women recognize the need to assert their rights, they clearly tend to have a more prominent role both in political mobilization and in tourism development' (p. 47).

In Northern Tanzania, Bayno and Jani (2018) argue that cultural tourism activities occupy much of women's time as well as being more valuable to them as a source of income. Within cultural tourism activities, dancing, tour guiding and warrior fighting are relatively dominated by males, whereas women devote more time to making and selling souvenirs. Women had both more positive and negative attitudes to cultural tourism compared to men, perhaps reflecting a greater awareness of the impacts. Having higher education levels raises the chances of both women and men having a more positive attitude towards cultural tourism.

Moswete and Lacey (2015) analysed cultural tourism in rural Botswana, which remains a patriarchal society with serious discrimination towards women. Government cultural tourism policies generated a sense of female empowerment, which gave them more freedom from economic dependence on men and their families. Women became actively involved in culture-related tourism ventures, which gave them more freedom to 'make choices, purchase land, build homes, pursue additional business interests, provide for their families, educate their children, travel, and engage socially with a wide range of people including foreign tourists' (p. 614).

In Bali, Long and Kindon (2005) found that women were considered particularly well suited for work in cultural tourism because:

1. Women are socialized to be sensitive to the needs of others.
2. Women are reputed to be verbally better than men at language acquisition so they can learn foreign language easier.
3. Women are considered caring and good at routine jobs.
4. Women are considered more attractive than men.

However, these supposed advantages are not matched by a significant female role in tourism production.

Many other potential areas of research on the role of women as actors in cultural tourism also remain. These include the relative under-representation of women in cultural institutions, which does not reflect their dominance as consumers of culture or their representation in art. The representation of female artists in major museums has hardly changed over the past couple of decades, for example, Guerrilla Girls, 2020.

CULTURAL TOURISM AS SKILLED CONSUMPTION

Social practices, as Shove, Pantzar and Watson (2012) emphasize, involve actors acquiring and developing skills and competences. Consuming culture while on holiday can be an educational process, usually through informal skill acquisition. Bourdieu (1984) examined how different groups acquired cultural capital, or skills in deciphering culture, from their cultural consumption, for example by visiting art museums. One of Bourdieu's key observations was that some cultural intermediaries used their increased cultural capital as a means of increasing their economic capital. By gaining expertise in particular forms of culture, they could sell their skills in the growing market for symbolic consumption. A specific cultural tourism example was the increasing number of guides and specialized tour operators related to art history. From the 1980s onwards, as cultural tourism became a mass market, art historians and other culture buffs began to earn a living by developing cultural tourism products and tours (Richards, Goedhart and Herrigers, 2001). At that time, Destination Marketing Organizations (DMOs) were just discovering the potential of cultural tourism for increasing spending and reducing seasonality. They supported theme years, such as the Van Gogh Year in the Netherlands in 1990, and increasingly tried to attract events related to the European Capital of Culture and other cultural labels (Richards, 1999). In the pre-Internet age, cultural tourism products were mainly distributed by intermediaries such as tour operators and DMOs. Cultural tourism specialists such as the German company Studiosus (founded in 1954) had a particularly important role as producers of tour packages. With the advent of the Internet in the 1990s, many companies and networks moved online, and created websites featuring cultural tourism destinations and experiences. For example, the Art Cities in Europe network spawned the arttourist.com website, a curated listing of 'Experience Culture', including art, theatre, dance, jazz, new music, photography, film, design and literature in a wide range of destinations throughout Europe. The providers of cultural experiences, often centred on cities, were keen to establish their role as experts in both high culture and local culture, underlined by their ability to arrange tickets for important cultural events as well as providing 'insider tips' (Welk, 2004) on culture.

Cultural capital or cultural consumption skills were of course also essential for the cultural tourist. Without the requisite capital it would be impossible to appreciate or enjoy the cultural experiences on offer. As expanding leisure time and rising incomes also made it possible to spend more time and travel further and more frequently to consume culture, so the fledgling cultural tourists were able to indulge in what Scitovsky (1976) dubbed 'skilled consumption'.

Scitovsky argued that people either seek or avoid stimulation. Boredom is related to a lack of stimulation, spurring a search for greater stimulation, whereas stress represents an overload of stimuli, leading to stimulus avoidance. However, not all tourism activities provide the same level of stimulation. Low-skill activities, such as beach holidays or theme park visitation, can be stimulating when tried for the first time, but can quickly become boring when repeated. Attractions such as theme parks, which are based on 'unskilled consumption' therefore need to innovate frequently to add new sources of stimulation for the unskilled consumer. Activities such as cultural tourism are based on 'skilled consumption' and offer opportunities for participants to learn and develop new skills, which in turn stimulates repeat consumption (Richards, 1996).

Scitovsky (1976, p. 226) considered culture as knowledge, more specifically the knowledge required to make stimulation enjoyable: 'Culture is the preliminary information we must have to enjoy the processing of further information.' In this sense, Scitovsky adds to the motivation of securing economic capital outlined by Bourdieu (1984), also considering the importance of intrinsic motivations. Scitovsky further argues that this explains why some cultural activities are more highly regarded than others – a person is considered 'cultured' because their consumption involves more skills, which take more time and effort to acquire.

Higher levels of education, resulting in greater consumption skills, drove growth in cultural tourism from the 1990s onwards (Richards, 2001). Tourism shifted away from sun, sea and sand destinations towards urban and cultural sites. Cities have become hubs for cultural tourism production and consumption, driven by regeneration strategies and the growing attractiveness and popularity of city centres. Cultural tourism became a major focus for many destinations, based in part on forecasts of enormous growth. For example, Bywater (1993) reported that cultural tourism would grow by an average 15 per cent a year, well above the long-term global average of around 4 per cent per annum.

Skilled consumption also linked cultural tourism consumers and producers. Research by ATLAS revealed that just under 30 per cent of cultural tourists had a cultural occupation (Richards, 2015). For those directly involved in the production of cultural experiences, such as those employed in museums or working as cultural tour operators, the experience of being a tourist helped them to gain more cultural skills and at the same time learn more about how culture was being produced for and consumed by tourists. As in the case of Bourdieu's (1984) new cultural intermediaries, therefore, cultural capital was transformed into economic capital.

More recently, the intertwining of consumption and production skills has been linked to the concept of co-creation, which Binkhorst (2007) defined as the involvement of individuals in designing or co-creating, undergoing and evaluating their own experiences. This is increasingly evident in cultural tourism, and particularly in creative tourism (Richards, 2011). Producers and consumers come together at particular touchpoints, or 'consumption junctions' (Spaargaren, Weenink and Lamers, 2016), but as Tan, Lim, Tan and Kok (2020) note, producers can also co-evolve with consumers. In the context of creative tourism, they argue that interaction allows consumers to value the skill of the producer as they develop their own skills. This can lead to a change in the meaning of crafts, from an association with the artisan (lower status) to 'entrepreneur/creator/artist' (higher status). The role of artists in shaping places and contributing to tourism attractiveness was also examined by Slak Valec (2020) for artists in residence in Abu Dhabi. She found that artists in residence derive 'working pleasure' from their stay, inspired by the new setting and landscapes, particularly the experience of the desert. This inspires them to promote the destination through their future work and via social media.

Cultural tourism has therefore shifted from a simple meeting of supply and demand, into a system in which producers and consumers contribute skills and knowledge to actively collaborate in co-creating value. The close relationship of consumption and production challenges Scitovsky's (1976, p. 226) assertion that 'Consumption skills, therefore, are part of culture, while production skills are not.' For Scitovsky, culture is enjoyment, which can only come from consumption. In fact, consumption skills are increasingly an important raw material in the production of cultural experiences – as producers need to know what it means to consume an experience in order to make it engaging.

DIVERSITY AND IDENTITY

Cultural diversity is an important element in cultural tourism development, with destinations vying to emphasize their cultural and creative diversity to woo visitors. The importance of diversity as an element of urban development increased significantly with the publication of Richard Florida's *The Rise of the Creative Class* in 2002. Florida argued that creative people were attracted to diverse, tolerant places, and that this helped to make places attractive for others, including tourists (Richards and Wilson, 2007).

Tolerance of different forms of diversity is becoming an increasingly important issue. As people from diverse backgrounds travel, they also want to feel welcome and safe in the destination. The problems faced by, for example, LGBT travellers have long been the subject of research. Visser (2003) describes the confluence of gay spaces and cultural tourism in De Waterkant area of Cape Town, 'Africa's gay tourist capital', while Hodes, Vork and Gerritsma (2007) examined tourism related to the gay scene in Amsterdam.

Diversity is also seen as being particularly important in the face of globalization, often argued to be homogenizing cultures (Zukin, 2004). Consumption of difference and the search for new experiences makes diversity a big issue in cultural tourism, because many cultural sites and events depend on cultural diversity for their very existence. Places are also keen to use different types of diversity to distinguish and profile themselves, and people travel to confirm their own identity, as well as consuming the symbols of other people's identity.

In cultural tourism, more attention is also being paid to the role of indigenous peoples, whose very way of life is often under threat from modernization and economic development (Richards, 2018). Indigenous communities have been exploited for cultural tourism development, often without having control over how their resources are used or represented. Ochoa Zuluaga (2015) studied cultural tourism in the Colombian Amazon, showing that indigenous participation in tourism is marked by strong historical power relationships. Indigenous populations were incorporated as part of the tourism product from the beginning of the tourism industry, which mirrored patterns of transnational domination of commodity exploitation. The participation of indigenous communities in tourism is organized at the level of individuals, families and solidarity groups, rather than the whole community, and this principle also applies to the distribution of the benefits from tourism. Tourism has provided indigenous people in the Amazon with higher incomes, but it also changes their relationship to the environment, promoting new forms of work, and encouraging people to seek individual benefits. Profit becomes the aim of exchange, undermining traditional social relations and the community as a whole. This mirrors the argument of Korstanje (2012) that indigenous tourism helps maintain neo-colonialist attitudes, generating ethnocentric treatment of indigenous populations, who are 'protected' for tourist consumption.

Many internal and external actors now link indigenous and Aboriginal populations and tourists, and there are increasing moves by these communities to exert control over tourism development. For example, in Canada, the Indigenous Tourism Association of Canada (ITAC) brings together associations, organizations, government departments and industry leaders to promote and develop 'authentic' indigenous experiences. ITAC is helping different regions of Canada with their indigenous tourism development plans, including Alberta (Indigenous Tourism Alberta, 2019; Indigenous Tourism Association of Canada, 2019). The strategy was based on discussions with Alberta indigenous cultural tourism stakeholders, including in-person discussions and written feedback and surveys. The resulting vision is to develop: 'A thriving Indigenous tourism economy sharing authentic, memorable and enriching experiences.' The strategy also seeks to improve the socio-economic situation of indigenous people by promoting economic development, supporting professional development and engaging in advocacy, leadership and representation.

The use of race as a source of differentiation also highlights the important role of identity in cultural tourism. Lanfant, Allcock and Bruner (1995) describe the development of cultural tourism in Bali as a process of identity preservation. Faced with the growth of mass tourism, Bali acquired an identity bestowed by outsiders. The apparent solution was to develop 'the doctrine of "cultural tourism", which reconciled apparently contradictory objectives of tourism and local culture, by developing "tourist culture", as the Balinese themselves termed it. By means of this device Balinese identity could be preserved' (p. 11).

Cultural tourism has long been a means of strengthening national identity, but increasingly also about local or regional or conflicting identities. The growth of museums in recent decades to some extent reflects this need to claim cultural identity. For example, the emergence of new nation states in post-Soviet Eastern and Central Europe saw the opening or renovation of many museums and monuments. In the Netherlands, the idea of a museum of national history has been the subject of debate for many years. Proponents argue that it is important to have an institution that projects the cultural history and identity of the nation, while opponents link it to the recent rise in national-ist and populist sentiment. This development is linked by van de Laar (2009) to the 'emotional turn' in the Netherlands and the influence of new media on the contemporary concept of the museum. The founding of new museums by the state also points to the fact that these developments are effectively statements of power. New states find themselves with the power to assert a new identity, and do this through the creation of new institutions. In many countries, there are also ongoing discussions about who has the power to represent national or regional or local identities.

Ethnic diversity also constitutes a cultural tourism resource in major cities. Rath (2007) describes how ethnic quarters became an interesting tool for urban tourism authorities. Framing ethnic differences in concrete places in the city becomes a means of attracting attention to diversity and developing concentra-tions of ethnic entrepreneurs who can arguably increase levels of innovation. Shaw (2007) examines the development of ethnic enclaves for tourism in London (Banglatown) and Montreal (Chinatown), and suggests that these can provide new identities for cities previously reliant on national or colonial stereotypes. In Sydney, Australia, Collins and Kunz (2007) analyse the role of ethnic entrepreneurs and ethnic precincts into tourism circuits. They found many conflicts arising from the contested authenticity of the ethnic theming of the precincts, as well as a disconnect between the place marketing of Sydney as a contemporary global cultural hub and the ethnic difference reflected in the various precincts.

As Oliveira (2019) describes in Lisbon, ethnic entrepreneurs are now much more engaged actors in the production of tourism than previous generations. Rather than being concerned to maintain links with home, or settling with their compatriots, some entrepreneurs from ethnic minorities are more eager to indentify new opportunities, wherever they may be. Oliveira recounts how a Bangladeshi entrepreneur based himself in Lisbon, because it was easier than opening a business in the other locations he researched in London and Germany. These developments are appearing in many cities around the world. Diekmann and Smith (2015) edited a volume exploring *Ethnic and Minority Cultures as Tourist Attractions*, which features examples from Hungary, Belgium, Australia, South Africa and Brazil. There is also a special issue of the *Journal of Tourism and Cultural Change* dedicated to the relationship between ethnic minorities and tourism (Timothy, 2019).

EMOTIONS

Recent years have arguably seen an 'emotional turn' (Cohen and Cohen, 2012) in the social sciences, which has also stimulated more research on the emotional dimensions of cultural tourism. For example, Pérez-Gálvez, Gomez-Casero, Tito and Alba (2019) identified four groups of tourists at the Oruro Carnival in Bolivia, an event designated as UNESCO intangible heritage. One group were identified as 'emotional tourists', who had a strong emotional connection to the event, generating high levels of satisfaction. A further study in the city of Sucre, Bolivia (Pérez-Gálvez, Fuentes Jiménez, Medina-Viruel and González Santa Cruz, 2020) also identified an emotional tourist segment, which comprised 26.5 per cent of the tourists surveyed.

The growing emotional content of cultural tourism experiences also implies an increasing amount of emotional labour from actors involved with cultural resources (Richards, 2018). For example, Smith and Zátori (2016) analyse the presentation of alternative tours in Budapest, finding a focus on surprise and novelty and self-development in terms of the presentation and content of the tours. The element of surprise is created by framing the 'everyday' and the 'local' in new ways for the visitors. The (re)production of the everyday for tourists involves a lot of emotional labour on the part of tourist guides and others involved in the production and consumption of such spaces. Zátori, Smith and Puczko (2018) further examined the role of producers of guided tours in Budapest in providing engaging experiences and found that interaction between the producers and consumers was the most important influence on experience-involvement.

Richards (2014) describes an example of expat tourism entrepreneurship in Hidden City Tours, a social enterprise offering walking tours of the gothic quarter in Barcelona, guided by homeless people. The founder is an expat: Lisa Grace, a market research consultant who has been living in Barcelona since 2004. She explained: 'I felt I had spent far too many years helping the global food, drink and cosmetic giants flog more of their products'. While looking for voluntary work in the spring of 2013, Lisa stumbled across Secret City Tours, a social enterprise in Bath offering homeless walking tours, and decided to copy paste the concept to Barcelona.

Homeless guided walking tours therefore provide another example of the global circulation of cultural tourism concepts. The concept can now be found in London (Unseen Tours, founded in 2010), Prague (Pragulic, 2012), Berlin (Querstadtein, 2013), Amsterdam (Amsterdam Underground, 2015), Ljubljana (Nevid(e)na Lublana, 2015), Vienna (Shades Tours, 2015), Athens (Shedia Invisible Tours, 2016), Edinburgh (Invisible Edinburgh, 2016). The rapid spread of the concept can partly be explained by the fact that a number of these projects are linked to homeless newspapers, which also have an international dissemination. However, there is also evidence of these ideas circulating via mobile actors, often expats with an extensive travel history.

For example, Invisible Edinburgh was founded in 2016 by French Zakia Malouaoui, who was first inspired by the Invisible Tours in Athens.

> Originally from the South of France, Zakia moved to Scotland when she was 21 years old. For several years, she was Director of International Partner Development at the Homeless World Cup Foundation, a global network of street soccer projects. After her health took a bad turn and she had to fight bowel cancer, she decided to take a break to travel. At the end of 2015, she spent time in Greece and volunteered in a refugee camp on Lesvos Island. It is when she returned that she decided to set-up her own social enterprise: Invisible Cities. (invisible-cities.org)

Invisible Cities now runs homeless walking tours in Edinburgh, York, Manchester, Glasgow and Cardiff.

These new cultural tourism experiences are capitalizing on previously hidden intangible resources in cities, and using emotional capital to grab attention and create new relationalities in the tourism field. Many of these actors are also involved in the curation of experiences offered to tourists.

THE ROLE OF THE CURATOR

As outlined in Chapter 1, the curatorial turn has had a significant effect on cultural tourism practices, permitting entry for a range of new actors. A key distinguishing feature of curation is the idea of selection, which generates exclusiveness. Curated experiences are often counterposed to mass tourism, as the Justraveling manifesto outlines:

> *Be wise and shy away from the sirens of mass tourism*, avoid the typical tourist hotspots and opt for alternative destinations instead. Always take the road less traveled instead of the well-beaten path, follow the byways (and your instinct). Forget about 'must-see' attractions and *be your own guide*. Consider staying at home as the best option at 'peak season'. Avoid global chains, tourist traps, and dangerous places. *Never pay for what you can get for free*. (www.justraveling.com/alternative -travel-manifesto/)

The ethos promoted by Justraveling emphasizes getting away from mass tourism, avoiding tourist traps and commodification and finding authenticity. The curator, in this case the website and its many content contributors, provides a selection of experiences that will take the onus of difficult decisions away from you – ironically providing an anti-tourism experience using tried and trusted tourist techniques.

The rise of new modes and moderators of authenticity also lends itself to the curation of cultural tourism experiences. Culture Trip, a UK-based travel content company, curates a vast store of cultural experiences gathered from a team of freelance content creators around the globe. Each of these creators is an expert, not necessarily on culture, but in the interpretation and transmission of cultural experiences. Combining these stories with analysis of their social media platform allows Culture Trip to identify gaps in the cultural tourism market. For example, they identified a growing demand for street art experiences (see Chapter 3), which were being well served by a wide range of experience content and tours in London, but was lacking in Berlin, which also has a rich supply of street art. This enabled them to commission new pieces of content highlighting Berlin graffiti, effectively strengthening a new cultural tourism niche in the city.

The curatorial turn has brought a range of new actors into cultural tourism practices, including platforms and 'switchers' who can link different forms of content together in the global space of flows, down to individual creatives and expats who can weave a story from local elements of the space of places.

SHIFTING POWER RELATIONS IN CULTURAL TOURISM

In the past, tourism services have often been government regulated and supplied by professionals. This is evident in cultural tourism in the case of tour guiding, for example. As Dahles (2002) reported in the case of Indonesia, official tour guides were licensed by the state, and their professional status was dependent on taking specific qualifications in approved schools. These included approved narratives about national history and culture, and state ideology, enforced by direct and indirect control. In many other countries, the guiding profession was also controlled by government to ensure that locally trained guides would be employed ahead of outsiders.

In recent years, however, neo-liberal policies have undermined such systems of professionalization, and guides have found new ways to access their clients and express themselves. Also in the case of Indonesia, Salazar (2005) identified the 'glocalization' of guide discourses in the city of Yogyakarta, with licensed guides adapting their stories to the needs of different audiences rather than following the official script. With the changing role of government in many places towards a broader system of governance, there has been greater involvement of non-governmental actors in the development of policies and actions for cultural tourism. Broader governance systems can encourage the involvement of non-governmental organizations (NGOs), cultural and heritage bodies, commercial organizations and residents in the development of cultural tourism policies. Such systems can also facilitate cross-border cooperation

(Stoffelen, Ioannides and Vanneste, 2017). Governance systems can also help in the framing of different forms of cultural content for place marketing purposes (Piñeiro-Naval and Serra, 2019).

The flattening of hierarchies has allowed collaborative economy platforms such as Airbnb to carve out a powerful position in the curation of cultural experiences. The development of such platforms has transformed power relations in cultural tourism. In the 1970s, Nolan (1976) found that American tourists were most likely to trust guidebooks and government information sources in finding their travel information. The guidebook in particular provided trusted information and became an extension of the identity of the user. At the same time, the discourse of the guidebook exerts power over the decision-making processes of the user (Mazor-Tregerman, Mansfeld and Elyada, 2017). The new digital platforms appear to offer choice and convenience, but actually present information in ways that benefit their own operation. For example, the algorithms used by Airbnb promote the choice of particular accommodation or experiences, even though the user is presented with what seems to be an objective selection (Bialski, 2016). This type of manipulation by digital platforms can counter the 'power of the user', which is increasingly seen as crucial in the marketing of cultural tourism destinations (Serra and Piñeiro-Naval, 2019).

The shift towards intangible and everyday culture noted in Chapter 1 also means that local communities are enlisted, knowingly or unknowingly, as providers of cultural experiences. In addition to living their daily lives as an input to tourist consumption, local communities also have an important relationship to cultural heritage. By inhabiting a place, which becomes a destination, we are all part of the culture consumed by other tourists. We play a role in the reproduction of tourism simply by being there (see Chapter 5). But our daily lives also include the maintenance of the communities and places we live in, including the use and preservation of heritage. In the book *After Heritage: Critical Perspectives on Heritage from Below*, Muzaini and Minca (2018) issue a call to develop more collective heritage processes and practices, critiquing 'the blind-sights of scholarship' generated by authorized heritage discourse (AHD).

AHD, which privileges the view of experts, is contrasted with the social production of heritage. Taken in this way, 'heritage' can be anything and everything. Popular understandings of heritage are never fixed but are constantly reinterpreted and rejuvenated by actors who produce and reproduce 'living heritage' through use. 'Heritage' is seen as anything valuable that can be preserved in the present for the benefit of current and future generations. Heritage is therefore a process of selection, or curation – establishing the future value of the past. The range of actors who negotiate these values is also increasing. As Coombe and Weiss (2015, p. 43) note, neo-liberal policies have caused a shift from state protection of heritage to new, diverse assemblages of governmental regulation. Government heritage policy therefore relies increas-ingly on 'citizens and self-organized communities in marketized relationships which position cultural heritage as a resource'.

The growing reliance on self-organized communities and governance regimes highlights the fact that many decisions related to culture and heritage are taken outside government. Shehade and Stylianou-Lambert (2020) high-light that the selection of heritage sites and our perceptions of authenticity related to these are influenced by powerful, non-governmental actors such as UNESCO.

Heritage is made in the present and created through a process of selection by different actors. Sung (2020) argues that heritage is not just everything old, but the elements of the past which have been filtered by a selection process drawing on the past and the present which determines what we should remem-ber, and why. This becomes part of a discourse constructed for the local com-munity (which elements of the past are worth preserving?), but also for those who visit it (which elements of heritage are worth visiting, and why?). The construction of heritage for tourism is therefore a co-creation between local actors and tourists, in which, as Augé (2004) suggests, there is collective for-getting and the active cultivation of some memories at the expense of others. Augé notes: 'Remembering or forgetting is doing gardener's work, selecting, pruning. Memories are like plants: there are those that need to be quickly eliminated to help the others burgeon, transform, flower. Indeed, memories are crafted by oblivion as the outlines of the shore are created by the sea' (Augé, 2004, p. 20). Römhild (1990) takes a slightly different tack, suggesting that tourism can contribute to cultural revitalization in the sense of 'intercultural communication readiness'. She argues that 'dead' cultural elements that have no fixed place in the everyday and festive life context can probably only be reactivated if their qualities are rediscovered by contemporary actors (such as tourists) and modified by the inhabitants according to their current needs.

This provides us with an interesting new perspective on practices. Because routine has an important role in the maintenance of practices, the focus of researchers often lies with continuity. There is far less attention for practices that are interrupted, or which cease to exist. But the fact that some practices die away suggests an important role for forgetting, as Scitovsky (1976) suggests. We pay more attention to disrupted and discarded practices in Chapter 5.

A raft of new actors has been recruited into cultural tourism as a result of the growth of tangible and intangible heritage, covering the public, private and voluntary sectors. The range of actors has expanded in all these fields, as we can see in the case of China. Liu (2020) argues the expansion of public sector intervention has grown significantly in China in recent years. In 2010, the Ministry of Culture and the National Tourism Administration announced that a theme year of cultural tourism would be launched every four years, and an international cultural tourism festival every two years, supported by local cultural tourism events. The preservation of traditional villages would be assured by the Traditional Village Protection and Development Expert Committee, which drew up the first list of 646 traditional Chinese villages with conservation value.

A relatively top-down approach by the public sector in China is noted by Zhang, Zhang, Law, Chen and Wang (2020), who review the many different bodies involved in the reproduction of heritage related to brocade (Nanjing Yunjin) in the Chinese city of Nanjing. These have different functions, including production of cloth (Yunjin's weaving department), management, protection, communication and research. Similarly, in the Chinese city of Tianjin, Chauffert-Yvart, Ged, Lu, Mengin and Rousseau (2020) describe a 'superposition of heritage actors in an evolving system', which involves the Tianjin Municipal Administration of Cultural Heritage, the Tianjin Planning Bureau, the Tianjin Municipal Bureau of Land Resources and Housing Administration and the Tianjin Historic Architecture Conservation Committee, under the Tianjin Municipal Bureau of Land Resources and Housing Administration. Contradictory or parallel strategies for heritage protection are emerging, with mixed results. The display of a heritage protection policy masks the existence of various approaches. They overlap, sometimes conflict, correspond to different practices and influences, and are related to initiatives linked to individuals much more than to a political strategy established at the national level. For example, the former Italian concession in Tianjin has been developed into the New I-Style Town. The remodelling of the concession took place in the context of developing trade relations between China and Italy, providing a showcase for Italian industry in the city. Private sector actors are also active in the Chinese cultural tourism market, as Thibault Paquin (2014) reports in relation to the development of 'Cultural Tourism Cities', which refers to new urban centres 'where cultural elements such as museums, shows, themed attractions and restaurants, lifestyle retail, etc are forming an attractive and creative environment – branded as a destination – for the enjoyment of visitors, both locals and tourists'. Developer Sunac plans a series of Cultural Tourism City projects in Wuhan, Harbin, Nanchang, Hefei, Qingdao, Wuxi and Guilin. Designed to attract millions of visitors a year, they feature theme park features such as roller coaster rises, as well as live shows and other cultural content.

As Condevaux, Djament-Tran and Gravari-Barbas (2016) argue, in relation to 'off-the-beaten-track' tourism, it is difficult to create a clear demarcation between civil society actors and tourism professionals, political decision-makers and economic actors. There is also growing participation from voluntary sector associations, particularly in cities such as Berlin, where tourism has become a generalized social issue. Such moves are facilitated through social media platforms, which as Gombault argues, 'result in ... major democratisation of creation to the extent that the boundaries are blurred between the creators and the consumers, and traditional creators are forced to find new business models that trivialise creation and its diffusion' (2011, p. 22).

NON-HUMAN ACTORS IN CULTURAL TOURISM

Growing attention for nature has been reflected in increased research on non-human actors in tourism and other practices. These include the different objects or 'things' that act in cultural tourism, which are seen as integral to social practices by Shove et al. (2012) as materials which are then given meaning by actors and their application of competences. There are also more active, natural elements of cultural tourism practices as well. As Paul Cloke (2007) argues, nature itself is creative. The creative turn in rural tourism means that tourists interact with the creativity of nature. This is increasingly facilitated by walking routes and sightseeing tours, such as whale watching at Kaikoura on New Zealand's South Island, where visitors can appreciate the blowing and fluting of whales and acrobatics of dolphins. In the case of natural settings, plants and animals may be unwitting creative performers for cultural tourists. In other cases, however, animals often form part of cultural displays, including horses used in parades, camels and elephants used for rides, animals integrated into agricultural settings, and the recent emergence of 'cat cafes' in major cities. According to Wikipedia, the world's first cat cafe was the 'Cat Flower Garden' in Taipei, Taiwan, which opened in 1998. This also attracted Japanese tourists, and the concept was widely copied in Japan (Plourde, 2014), and since 2014 the concept has been globalized.

However, not all encounters between animals and tourists are positive, as Malchrowicz-Mośko, Munsters, Korzeniewska-Nowakowska and Gravelle (2020) emphasize. They propose a typology of cultural tourism experiences related to the abuse of animals, which includes animals in contests, animal slaughter (for example, sacrifices) and animals as tourist commodities (for example, a means of transport). They link the demand for experiences related to animals with cultural omnivorousness, which 'makes tourists sensation-seeking, which contributes to the rise, development and perpetuation of controversial forms of tourism such as the abuse of animals featuring in tourist attractions or cultural and sports events' (p. 27).

Nature is also present in many events through the presence of plants, including tree festivals, flower shows, and events related to food derived from plants, such as Chili Festivals and Garlic Festivals. Such food and agriculture-based events stimulate cultural tourism in rural areas (Lee and Arcodia, 2011) and the presence of such materials influence where and how cultural tourists move, and they provide opportunities for action.

The growing popularity of Actor Network Theory enables us to gain a better understanding of the tangled relationships between people and things, even though, in the context of cultural tourism, this can become 'messy' (Ren, 2010). It provides a focus on relationality, and how actors and things become ordered and assembled through relational practices. For example, Ren traces the relational contexts of *oscypek* cheese in the Polish city of Zakopane. This locally produced smoked sheep's cheese is a highly visible part of cultural tourism practices, with stands selling the cheese located in the main shopping street of the town. Domestic Polish tourists see buying the cheese as an almost compulsory part of their trip, with many conversations between tourists and cheese sellers revolving around issues of provenance and authenticity. Ren argues that the cheese acts as an agent conveying traditional work practices and helping to shape the tourism networks of the region. She describes the 'cheese discourses' surrounding the inclusion of oscypek on the EU list of regional products. There were fears that the hygiene regulations attached to this would affect the traditional production processes and reduce the authenticity of the cheese. The cheese became an actor linking global and European debates with regional branding strategies and local politics.

CONCLUSIONS

This chapter has reviewed the wide range of different actors – public and private, individual and collective, tourism and cultural – which have a capacity to act in the field of cultural tourism. These actors are driven by a wide range of motivations, including a desire to learn, a search for meaningful experiences or economic motives. One important implication of adopting a practice approach to cultural tourism is that the previous divide between 'consumers' and 'producers' fades, opening up a field of co-creation, in which both consumers and producers are involved in the development of experiences. All these different actors come together in the field of cultural tourism, and jostle for position according to their motivations, their resources and skills.

We can see power struggles emerging between actors, for example, over the control of cultural assets, or the ability to claim particular resources as 'cultural heritage'. These struggles intensify as globalization reduces the friction of geography and government, and liberalization and democratization have given a bigger role to non-governmental actors in the fields of culture and heritage. The weakening hierarchies of culture and tourism have also facilitated an expansion of the field of cultural tourism, moving away from the authorized discourse of traditional cultural institutions towards bottom-up and self-organized cultural forms. This has also expanded the range of contexts, locations and times in which cultural tourism can be produced and consumed, as we discuss in the following chapter.

REFERENCES

Aitchison, C. (1999). Heritage and nationalism: gender and the performance of power. In D. Crouch (ed.), *Leisure/Tourism Geographies: Practices and Geographical Knowledge* (pp. 59–73). London: Routledge.

Augé, M. (2004). *Oblivion*. London and Minneapolis: University of Minnesota Press.

Babb, F.E. (2012). Theorizing gender, race, and cultural tourism in Latin America: a view from Peru and Mexico. *Latin American Perspectives, 39*(6), 36–50.

Bayno, P.M. and Jani, D. (2018). Residents' attitudes on the contribution of cultural tourism in Tanzania. *Journal of Tourism and Cultural Change, 16*(1), 41–56.

Bialski, P. (2016). Authority and authorship: uncovering the socio-technical regimes of peer-to-peer tourism. In A.P. Russo and G. Richards (eds), *Reinventing the Local in Tourism: Producing, Consuming and Negotiating Place* (pp. 35–48). Bristol: Channel View.

Binkhorst, E. (2007). Creativity in tourism experiences: the case of Sitges. In G. Richards and J. Wilson (eds), *Tourism, Creativity and Development* (pp. 147–66). London: Routledge.

Binkhorst, E. and Den Dekker, T. (2009). Agenda for co-creation tourism experience research. *Journal of Hospitality Marketing & Management, 18*(2–3), 311–27.

Bond, N. and Falk, J. (2013). Tourism and identity-related motivations: why am I here (and not there)? *International Journal of Tourism Research, 15*(5), 430–42.

Boswijk, A., Thijssen, T., and Peelen, E. (2006). *A New Perspective on the Experience Economy*. Bilthoven, the Netherlands: The European Centre for the Experience Economy.

Bourdieu, P. (1984). *Distinction: A Social Critique of the Judgement of Taste*. London: Routledge.

Brida, J.G., Dalle Nogare, C., and Scuderi, R. (2016). Frequency of museum attendance: motivation matters. *Journal of Cultural Economics, 40*(3), 261–83.

Bywater, M. (1993). The market for cultural tourism in Europe. *Travel and Tourism Analyst, 6*, 30–46.

Chauffert-Yvart, B., Ged, F., Lu, Y., Mengin, C., and Rousseau, É. (2020). Tourism and heritage in the enhancement of Tianjin. *Built Heritage, 4*(1), 1–20.

Chen, H. and Rahman, I. (2018). Cultural tourism: an analysis of engagement, cultural contact, memorable tourism experience and destination loyalty. *Tourism Management Perspectives, 26*, 153–63.

Cloke, P.L. (2007). Creativity and tourism in rural environments. In G. Richards and J. Wilson (eds), *Tourism, Creativity and Development* (pp. 37–47). London: Routledge.

Cohen, E. and Cohen, S.A. (2012). Current sociological theories and issues in tourism. *Annals of Tourism Research, 39*(4), 2177–202.

Collins, J. and Kunz, P. (2007). Ethnic entrepreneurs, ethnic precincts and tourism: the case of Sydney, Australia. In G. Richards and J. Wilson (eds), *Tourism, Creativity and Development* (pp. 201–14). London: Routledge.

Condevaux, A., Djament-Tran, G., and Gravari-Barbas, M. (2016). Before and after tourism(s). The trajectories of tourist destinations and the role of actors involved in 'off-the-beaten-track' tourism: a literature review. *Via Tourism Review, 9*. https://doi.org/10.4000/viatourism.413.

Coombe, R.J. and Weiss, L.M. (2015). Neoliberalism, heritage regimes, and cultural rights. In L. Meskell (ed.), *Global Heritage: A Reader* (pp. 43–69). Hoboken, NJ: Wiley-Blackwell.

Correia, A., Kozak, M., and Ferradeira, J. (2013). From tourist motivations to tourist satisfaction. *International Journal of Culture, Tourism and Hospitality Research, 7*(4), 411–24.

Dahles, H. (2002). The politics of tour guiding: image management in Indonesia. *Annals of Tourism Research, 29*(3), 783–800.

Dann, G.M. (1995). Tourism: the nostalgia industry of the future. In W.F. Theobald (ed.), *Global Tourism: The Next Decade* (pp. 55–67). London: Routledge.

Diekmann, A. and Smith, M.K. (eds) (2015). *Ethnic and Minority Cultures as Tourist Attractions*. Bristol: Channel View.

Dolničar, S. (2004). Beyond 'commonsense segmentation': a systematics of segmentation approaches in tourism. *Journal of Travel Research, 42*(3), 244–50.

Eurostat (2015). Culture statistics – cultural participation. https://ec.europa.eu/eurostat/ statistics-explained/index.php?title=Culture_statistics_-_cultural_participation #Cultural_participation_by_sex (accessed 18 December 2020).

Falk, J.H., Ballantyne, R., Packer, J., and Benckendorff, P. (2012). Travel and learning: a neglected tourism research area. *Annals of Tourism Research, 39*(2), 908–27.

Feighery, W. (2006). Reflexivity and tourism research: telling an (other) story. *Current Issues in Tourism, 9*(3), 269.

Florida, R. (2002). *The Rise of the Creative Class.* New York: Basic Books.

Formica, S. and Uysal, M. (1998). Market segmentation of an international cultural-historical event in Italy. *Journal of Travel Research, 36*(4), 16–24.

Galí-Espelt, N. (2012). Identifying cultural tourism: a theoretical methodological proposal. *Journal of Heritage Tourism, 7*(1), 45–58.

Gombault, A. (2011). Tourisme et création: les hypermodernes. *Mondes du tourisme, 4*, 18–35.

Gravari-Barbas, M. (2018). Tourism as a heritage producing machine. *Tourism Management Perspectives, 25*, 173–6.

Guerrilla Girls (2020). Do women still have to be naked to get into the Met. Museum? https://www.guerrillagirls.com/naked-through-the-ages (accessed 18 December 2020).

Gunn, C.A. (1988). *Vacationscape: Designing Tourist Regions*. New York: Van Nostrand Reinhold.

Hewison, R. (1987). *The Heritage Industry: Britain in a Climate of Decline*. London: Methuen.

Hodes, S., Vork, J., and Gerritsma, R. (2007). Amsterdam as a gay tourism destination in the twenty-first century. In G. Richards and J. Wilson (eds), *Tourism, Creativity and Development* (pp. 200–10). London: Routledge.

Holden, J. (2006). *Cultural Value and the Crisis of Legitimacy*. London: Demos.

Hughes, H.L. (2002). Culture and tourism: a framework for further analysis. *Managing Leisure, 7*(3), 164–75.

Indigenous Tourism Alberta (2019). Indigenous Tourism Alberta Strategy 2019–2024. https://indigenoustourism.ca/corporate/wp-content/uploads/2019/04/ITA-Strategy -2019-2024-FINAL-EDIT-1.pdf (accessed 18 December 2020).

Indigenous Tourism Association of Canada (2019). 2018–2019 Annual Report. https:// indigenoustourism.ca/corporate/wp-content/uploads/2019/11/ITAC-Annual-Report -2018-19.pdf (accessed 18 December 2020).

Ivanovic, M. (2008). *Cultural Tourism*. Cape Town: Juta and Company.

Kaare Nielsen, H. (2003). Cultural policy and evaluation of quality. *International Journal of Cultural Policy*, *9*(3), 237–45.

Korstanje, M. (2012). Reconsidering cultural tourism: an anthropologist's perspective. *Journal of Heritage Tourism*, *7*(2), 179–84.

Kotler, P. and Armstrong, G. (2018). *Principles of Marketing*. Harlow: Pearson.

Lanfant, M.F., Allcock, J.B., and Bruner, E.M. (eds) (1995). *International Tourism: Identity and Change*. London: Sage.

Lee, I. and Arcodia, C. (2011). The role of regional food festivals for destination branding. *International Journal of Tourism Research*, *13*(4), 355–67.

Leiper, N. (1990). Tourist attraction systems. *Annals of Tourism Research*, *17*(3), 367–84.

Liu, S. (2020). Cultural tourism policies and digital transition of ancient village heritage conservation in China. In *Cultural and Tourism Innovation in the Digital Era* (pp. 37–51). Cham: Springer.

Long, V.H. and Kindon, S.L. (2005). Gender and tourism development in Balinese villages. In M.T. Sinclair (ed.), *Gender, Work and Tourism* (pp. 99–128). London: Routledge.

Lowenthal, D. (1985). *The Past is a Foreign Country*. Cambridge: Cambridge University Press.

Lynch, M.F., Duinker, P.N., Sheehan, L.R., and Chute, J.E. (2011). The demand for Mi'kmaw cultural tourism: tourist perspectives. *Tourism Management*, *32*(5), 977–86.

Malchrowicz-Mośko, E., Munsters, W., Korzeniewska-Nowakowska, P., and Gravelle, F. (2020). Controversial animal tourism considered from a cultural perspective. *Turyzm/Tourism*, *30*(1), 21–30.

Mazor-Tregerman, M., Mansfeld, Y., and Elyada, O. (2017). Travel guidebooks and the construction of tourist identity. *Journal of Tourism and Cultural Change*, *15*(1), 80–98.

McIntosh, A.J. (2004). Tourists' appreciation of Maori culture in New Zealand. *Tourism Management*, 25(1), 1–15.

McKercher, B. and du Cros, H. (2002). *Cultural Tourism: The Partnership between Tourism and Cultural Heritage Management*. Binghamton, NY: Haworth Press.

McKercher, B., Ho, P.S., Du Cros, H.D., and So-Ming, B.C. (2002). Activities-based segmentation of the cultural tourism market. *Journal of Travel & Tourism Marketing*, *12*(1), 23–46.

Moreno Gil, S. and Ritchie, J.B. (2009). Understanding the museum image formation process: a comparison of residents and tourists. *Journal of Travel Research*, *47*(4), 480–93.

Moscardo, G. and Pearce, P.L. (1999). Understanding ethnic tourists. *Annals of Tourism Research*, *26*(2), 416–34.

Moswete, N. and Lacey, G. (2015). 'Women cannot lead': empowering women through cultural tourism in Botswana. *Journal of Sustainable Tourism*, *23*(4), 600–17.

Muzaini, H. and Minca, C. (2018). *After Heritage: Critical Perspectives on Heritage from Below*. Cheltenham, UK and Northampton, MA, USA: Edward Elgar Publishing.

Nolan Jr, S.D. (1976). Tourists' use and evaluation of travel information sources: summary and conclusions. *Journal of Travel Research*, *14*(3), 6–8.

Ochoa Zuluaga, G. (2015). Global tourism chains and local development in the Amazon: implications for community wellbeing. PhD, Tilburg University.

OECD (2009). *Culture and Tourism*. Paris: OECD.

Oliveira, N. (2019). A Lisboa cosmopolita e o fascínio da diversidade. *Cidades. Comunidades e Territórios, 39*, 115–28.

Özel, Ç.H., and Kozak, N. (2012). Motive based segmentation of the cultural tourism market: a study of Turkish domestic tourists. *Journal of Quality Assurance in Hospitality & Tourism, 13*(3), 165–86.

Paquin, T. (2014). The growth of the cultural tourism city: China's new model lifestyle/urban centre. https://blooloop.com/features/the-growth-of-the-cultural-tourism-city-chinas-new-model-lifestyleurban-centre/ (accessed 18 December 2020).

Pérez-Gálvez, J.C., Fuentes Jiménez, P.A., Medina-Viruel, M.J., and González Santa Cruz, F. (2020). Cultural interest and emotional perception of tourists in WHS. *Journal of Quality Assurance in Hospitality & Tourism*, 1–22.

Pérez-Gálvez, J.C., Gomez-Casero, G., Tito, J.C., and Alba, C.A.J. (2019). Segmentation in intangible heritage of humanity (ICH) events: the Oruro Carnival. *International Journal of Event and Festival Management, 10*(2), 81–94.

Peterson, R.A. (2005). Problems in comparative research: the example of omnivorousness. *Poetics, 33*(5–6), 257–82.

Pine, B.J. and Gilmore, J.H. (1998). Welcome to the experience economy. *Harvard Business Review, 76*, 97–105.

Piñeiro-Naval, V. and Serra, P. (2019). How do destinations frame cultural heritage? Content analysis of Portugal's municipal websites. *Sustainability, 11*(4), 947.

Plourde, L. (2014). Cat cafés, affective labor, and the healing boom in Japan. *Japanese Studies, 34*(2), 115–33.

Pritchard, A. (2004). Gender and sexuality in tourism research. In A.A. Lew, C.M. Hall, and A.M. Williams (eds), *A Companion to Tourism* (pp. 316–26). London: Wiley.

Pulido-Fernández, J.I. and Sánchez-Rivero, M. (2010). Attitudes of the cultural tourist: a latent segmentation approach. *Journal of Cultural Economics, 34*(2), 111–29.

Rath, J. (ed.) (2007). *Tourism, Ethnic Diversity and the City*. London: Routledge.

Ren, C. (2010). Assembling the socio-material destination: an actor-network approach to cultural tourism studies. In G. Richards and W. Munsters (eds), *Cultural Tourism Research Methods* (pp. 199–208). Wallingford: CABI.

Richards, G. (1996). *Cultural Tourism in Europe*. Wallingford: CABI.

Richards, G. (1999). Cultural capital or cultural capitals? In L. Nystrom (ed.), *City and Culture: Cultural Processes and Urban Sustainability* (pp. 403–14). Stockholm: Swedish Urban Environment Council.

Richards, G. (2001). *Cultural Attractions and European Tourism*. Wallingford: CABI.

Richards, G. (2002). Tourism attraction systems: exploring cultural behavior. *Annals of Tourism Research, 29*(4), 1048–64.

Richards, G. (2011). Creativity and tourism: the state of the art. *Annals of Tourism Research, 38*(4), 1225–53.

Richards, G. (2014). Tourism and creativity in the city. *Current Issues in Tourism, 17*, 119–44.

Richards, G. (2015). *ATLAS Cultural Tourism Research Project: Research Report 2008–2013*. Arnhem: ATLAS.

Richards, G. (2018). Cultural tourism: a review of recent research and trends. *Journal of Hospitality and Tourism Management, 36*, 12–21.

Richards, G. (2019). ATLAS Cultural Tourism Group Report 2019. In T. Duncan, L. Onderwater, and J. Veldman (eds), *Tourism Transformations: ATLAS Reflections 2019* (pp. 19–20). Arnhem: ATLAS.

Richards, G. and Munsters, W. (2010). *Cultural Tourism Research Methods*. Wallingford: CABI.

Richards, G. and Van der Ark, A. (2013). Dimensions of cultural consumption among tourists: multiple correspondence analysis. *Tourism Management, 37*, 71–6.

Richards, G. and Wilson, J. (2006). Developing creativity in tourist experiences: a solution to the serial reproduction of culture? *Tourism Management, 27*, 1209–23.

Richards, G. and Wilson, J. (2007). *Tourism, Creativity and Development*. London: Routledge.

Richards, G., Goedhart, S., and Herrijgers, C. (2001). The cultural attraction distribution system. In G. Richards (ed.), *Cultural Attractions and European Tourism* (pp. 71–89). Wallingford: CABI.

Richards, G., King, B., and Yeung, E. (2020). Experiencing culture in attractions, events and tour settings. *Tourism Management*. https://doi.org/10.1016/j.tourman.2020.104104.

Römhild, R. (1990). *Histourismus: Fremdenverkehr und lokale Selbstbehauptung*. Frankfurt am Main: Inst. Für Kulturanthropologie und Europäische Ethnologie.

Salazar, N.B. (2005). Tourism and glocalization 'local' tour guiding. *Annals of Tourism Research, 32*(3), 628–46.

Santos, E. (2020). Do cultural tourism firms perform better than their rivals? In Á. Rocha, A. Abreu, J. de Carvalho, D. Liberato, E. González, and P. Liberato (eds), *Advances in Tourism, Technology and Smart Systems. Smart Innovation, Systems and Technologies* (pp. 383–93). Singapore: Springer.

Scitovsky, T. (1976). *The Joyless Economy: An Inquiry into Human Satisfaction and Consumer Dissatisfaction*. Oxford: Oxford University Press.

Serra, P. and Piñeiro-Naval, V. (2019). Algumas questões e controvérsias atuais sobre o turismo cultural. In V. Piñeiro-Naval and P. Serra (eds), *Cultura, Património e Turismo na Sociedade Digital (Vol. 2): Diálogos interdisciplinares* (pp. 1–16). Covilhã: Editora LabCom.IFP.

Shaw, G. (1992). Culture and tourism: the economics of nostalgia. *World Futures: Journal of General Evolution, 33*(1–3), 199–212.

Shaw, S. (2007). Ethnic quarters in the cosmopolitan-creative city. In G. Richards and J. Wilson (eds), *Tourism, Creativity and Development* (pp. 189–200). London: Routledge.

Shehade, M. and Stylianou-Lambert, T. (2020). Revisiting authenticity in the age of the digital transformation of cultural tourism. In V. Katsoni and T. Spyriadis (eds), *Cultural and Tourism Innovation in the Digital Era* (pp. 3–16). Cham: Springer.

Shove, E., Pantzar, M., and Watson, M. (2012). *The Dynamics of Social Practice: Everyday Life and How It Changes*. London: Sage.

Silberberg, T. (1995). Cultural tourism and business opportunities for museums and heritage sites. *Tourism Management, 16*(5), 361–5.

Slak Valek, N. (2020). Word-of-art: contribution of artists-in-residence to a creative tourism destination. *Journal of Tourism and Cultural Change, 18*(2), 81–95.

Smith, M.K. and Zátori, A. (2016). Re-thinking host-guest relationships in the context of urban ethnic tourism. In A.P. Russo and G. Richards (eds), *Reinventing the Local in Tourism: Producing, Consuming and Negotiating Place* (pp. 129–50). Clevedon: Channel View.

Smith, S.L. (1994). The tourism product. *Annals of Tourism Research, 21*(3), 582–95.

Spaargaren, G., Weenink, D., and Lamers, M. (2016). Introduction: using practice theory to research social life. In G. Spaargaren, D. Weenink, and M. Lamers (eds), *Practice Theory and Research: Exploring the Dynamics of Social Life* (pp. 3–27). New York: Routledge.

Stoffelen, A., Ioannides, D., and Vanneste, D. (2017). Obstacles to achieving cross-border tourism governance: a multi-scalar approach focusing on the German-Czech borderlands. *Annals of Tourism Research, 64*, 126–38.

Stylianou-Lambert, T. (2011). Gazing from home: cultural tourism and art museums. *Annals of Tourism Research, 38*(2), 403–21.

Sung, Y.Y. (2020). Cultural tourism and social resilience: discourse of historic cities in East Germany, the case of Gotha and Eisenach. PhD thesis, Bauhaus University, Weimar.

Tan, S.K., Lim, H.H., Tan, S.H., and Kok, Y.S. (2020). A cultural creativity framework for the sustainability of intangible cultural heritage. *Journal of Hospitality & Tourism Research, 44*(3), 439–71.

Timothy, T. (2019). Special Issue: Ethnic minorities and global tourism. *Journal of Tourism and Cultural Change, 17*(1), 377–561.

Toivonen, T. (2005). Omnivorousness in cultural tourism: an international comparison. ATLAS Cultural Tourism Research Project. https://www.researchgate.net/ publication/347463490_Omnivorousness_in_cultural_tourism_An_inter-national _comparison_ATLAS_Cultural_Tourism_Research_Project (accessed 18 December 2020).

Towner, J. (1985). The Grand Tour: a key phase in the history of tourism. *Annals of Tourism Research, 12*(3), 297–333.

Trotter, R. (1999). Nostalgia and the construction of an Australian dreaming. *Journal of Australian Studies, 23*(61), 19–26.

Tucker, H. (2007). Undoing shame: tourism and women's work in Turkey. *Journal of Tourism and Cultural Change, 5*(2), 87–105.

UNWTO (2018). *Report on Tourism and Culture Synergies*. Madrid: UNWTO.

Van der Ark, L.A. and Richards, G. (2006). Attractiveness of cultural activities in European cities: a latent class approach. *Tourism Management, 27*(6), 1408–13.

van de Laar, P. (2009). Het Nationaal Historisch Museum en de emotional turn. *BMGN – Low Countries Historical Review, 124*(3), 431–7.

Visser, G. (2003). Gay men, tourism and urban space: reflections on Africa's 'gay capital'. *Tourism Geographies, 5*(2), 168–89.

Vong, F. (2016). Application of cultural tourist typology in a gaming destination – Macao. *Current Issues in Tourism, 19*(9), 949–65.

Welk, P. (2004). The beaten track: anti-tourism as an element of backpacker identity construction. In G. Richards and J. Wilson (eds), *The Global Nomad: Backpacker Travel in Theory and Practice* (pp. 77–91). Bristol: Channel View.

Zátori, A., Smith, M.K., and Puczko, L. (2018). Experience-involvement, memorability and authenticity: the service provider's effect on tourist experience. *Tourism Management, 67*, 111–26.

Zhang, K., Zhang, M., Law, R., Chen, X., and Wang, Q. (2020). Impact model of tourism production and consumption in Nanjing Yunjin: the perspective of cultural heritage reproduction. *Sustainability, 12*(8), 3430.

Zukin, S. (2004). Dialogue on urban cultures: globalisation and culture in an urbanizing world. Paper presented at the UN-Habitat World Urban Forum, Barcelona, 13–17 September.

3. The changing contexts of cultural tourism

INTRODUCTION

The practice approach recognizes that actions are both enabled and constrained by a range of structures. These structures are socially constructed, so actors also help maintain the structures that affect their own behaviour. This is essentially the logic of the 'field', as developed by Bourdieu (1984). This is a particularly useful starting point for our analysis of cultural tourism contexts, since Bourdieu's field analysis centred on culture. We build on this using Warde's (2004) reconceptualization of the relationship between practices and the field.

We will first review the wider field in which cultural tourism practices take place, and then the more specific contexts of these practices. We follow the logic of Packer and Ballantyne (2016) in viewing the experience of cultural tourism as a result of both the antecedents of the consumer and the context, or environment provided by the producers and/or other consumers. As discussed in Chapter 2, the cultural tourism practice is co-created by a range of different actors, who perform contextualized actions that are shaped in interaction with a specific setting (Simons, 2020).

Russo and Richards (2016) argue that as increasing mobility has spread tourism physically, the performative turn has departed from a critique of MacCannell (1976) to emphasize that tourism can be performed by anyone, anywhere. The creative turn also repositions cultural tourism as encounter, relationship and negotiation within the symbolic domain of tourist destinations, ceasing to be an activity undertaken by 'tourists' in specific 'tourist spaces' at specific times. It is now a mobilized, de-differentiated process of meaning construction engaged in by large numbers of producers and consumers. One result of this is the emergence of 'new localities' in tourism, non-traditional tourism places shaped by recent tourism trends (Russo and Richards, 2016). In the field of cultural tourism, these include cultural and creative clusters (Marques and Richards, 2014), postmodern museums (Franklin, 2017) and festivals and events. This chapter conceptualizes cultural tourism as a co-created social practice occurring in a constantly changing cultural field, featuring a rapidly developing cast of actors.

THE CULTURAL FIELD

Bourdieu conceptualized practices as being performed in a 'field', such as sport, music, food, politics or language (Warde, 2004). Each field has specific features that provide possibilities for distinction. Bourdieu argued that the field concept provided a representation of the relational nature of social organization, supported by a systematic set of concepts, such as capital, investment and interest, that allowed the positions of actors in the field to be analysed.

> A field is a relatively structured autonomous domain or space, which has been socially instituted, thus having a definable but contingent history of development. One condition of the emergence of a field is that agents refer to its history. (Warde, 2004, p.12)

Each field is a site of struggle for capital, and the legitimation of different types of capital is vital to this process. The dynamics of the field arise from the positions and position-taking of agents with different resources and dispositions, which are reliant on their habitus and capital acquired through experience. The field, explains Warde (2004), operates as a game, in which actors adopt different strategies, which may include redefining and expanding the field. The boundaries of the field are therefore constantly changing. For example, eating out is seen by Warde as an identifiable practice, or a coordinated entity, recognizable through doings and sayings, and reproduced through performances, based on a nexus of shared understandings, competences and reasons for engagement.

The features of a field are summarized by Warde as follows:

1. Some particular stakes and commitment to their value.
2. A structured set of positions.
3. A set of strategic and competitive orientations.
4. A set of agents endowed with resources and dispositions.

Cultural tourism also arguably represents such a field. What is at stake in cultural tourism is the representation of culture and the value this generates. Many actors have adopted positions in this field, as we saw in Chapter 2, and they have strategic and competitive orientations. For example, cities compete to attract cultural tourists by framing their cultural assets, and museums compete through staging attractive exhibitions. These different agents use their resources and dispositions (such as knowledge, contacts and cultural capital) to compete in the cultural tourism field.

The conceptualization of cultural tourism as a field of practices helps us to understand the expansion of cultural tourism in recent decades. In the past, cultural tourism was a relatively elite practice, dominated by highly educated and wealthy individuals consuming high culture, but the recent cultural tourism boom has been fed by a raft of new forms of culture being integrated into the field (such as street art and gastronomy), and new intermediaries who have secured their position using cultural capital related to these new forms (such as street artists or chefs). The boundaries of the field are constantly moving because of the strategic positions adopted by these actors, and constantly debated in terms of legitimacy. Should we, for example, consider street art a legitimate target of the cultural tourism practice? This is a question we return to later in the chapter.

Discussions about what might legitimately be considered as 'culture' are continually pushing the boundaries of the field. This conceptual expansion creates challenges for the study of cultural tourism. On the one hand, over-claiming the boundaries of culture may result, as the UNWTO once remarked, in all tourism becoming cultural tourism (Richards, 1996). On the other hand, a rigid definition of the field, for example restricting it to high culture, may lead to an elitist, euro-centric conceptualization that ignores the emergence of new cultural forms.

To what extent can we view cultural tourism as a coherent field? Bourdieu (1984) conceived of the cultural field as a collection of social practices through which 'creators' develop a cultural product, such as works of art or literature. In cultural tourism, there are many different cultural fields contributing products or experiences, such as architecture, painting, sculpture, literature, street art and so on. As the field expands and develops, actors from these different backgrounds jostle for position, and seek to capitalize on their knowledge and skills by developing new orientations that will appeal to the market.

Bourdieu saw the field as being structured by the actions of producers, and he did not consider consumers as part of the field itself. More recent readings of relational economies, however, would suggest consumers also play a role in the field, because they co-create value together with cultural producers. The reactions of the audience are ultimately crucial in determining the positions and strategies of producers. Cultural audiences range from connoisseurs to the mass public, including tourists. The relationship between cultural products and audiences is maintained by a multiplicity of institutions, including museums, art galleries, the media, knowledge institutions and funding bodies. The role of institutions in influencing and structuring the cultural field was examined by Cohendet, Grandadam and Simon (2010) in the context of creative cities. They divided the field of the city into the cultural Upperground, Middleground and Underground. The Upperground is the preserve of the elite cultural institutions, such as museums, which are also bastions of cultural tourism. The

Underground, in contrast, represents the dense fabric of small cultural enterprises that generate cultural products and experiences which support the local buzz. The Middleground links the Upperground with the Underground, most importantly through events and programmes that bring the small players in the Underground to the attention of the gatekeepers of the Upperground.

The structuring of the cultural field within places also feeds competition between these places, as Bathelt, Malmberg and Maskell (2004) indicated. Successful cities use the Underground, Middleground and Upperground to develop their 'local buzz' of cultural activity, which is then linked to global markets through 'pipelines'. If we combine the perspectives of Cohendet et al. (2010) on the function of the cultural field within a city with the insights of Bathelt et al. (2004) on the links between cities, we have a much more powerful explanation of how specific cultural tourism destinations develop and compete with each other. Places need to be culturally attractive, and Cohendet et al. (2010) see this depending on the collaboration of different levels of the cultural system. However, cultural tourism is also highly dependent on the relative attractiveness of cultural destinations. The comparative perspective offered by Bathelt et al. (2004) provides an important additional dimension to understanding the operation of the cultural tourism field.

Because the field of cultural tourism conflates tourism and culture, it is important to understand how both sectors operate. Culture rarely relies on tourism, and generally makes little reference to it. This is arguably because the conceptions of value of the cultural and tourism fields, and thus their languages, are fundamentally different (UNWTO, 2018). But tourism influences the cultural field because it represents an increasingly important source of external capital – for example, through admission fees for museums or the purchase of works of art to develop a collection attractive to visitors (see the Bosch500 example in Chapter 5). In the architecture field, spectacular buildings that will attract visitors to a city are also increasingly important as commissions for 'starchitechts'.

The production of value in the cultural field has been extensively studied by economists. Throsby (2001), for example, argued that the cultural field provides two types of value: economic and cultural. He proposed a concentric circles model in which the cultural content of the output of the cultural industries declines as one moves outwards from the core. The value created by the 'core creative arts' (literature, music, performing arts, visual arts) is mainly cultural, whereas the outer rings of 'other core cultural industries' (film, museums, galleries, libraries), the 'wider cultural industries' (heritage services, the media, digital content) and the peripheral 'related industries' (advertising, architecture, design, fashion) rely successively less on culture. Throsby (2008) empirically tested this model using employment data from Australia, Canada, New Zealand, the UK and the USA (all English speaking!), showing that creative employment progressively declined from the core creative arts to the peripheral related industries. Hesmondhalgh (2002) also developed a model working outwards from the 'core cultural industries', which he saw as creating social meaning through the production and circulation of texts. These include broadcasting, film, music media, digital games, advertising and web design. These industries compete for resources, limited amounts of disposable consumer income and consumption time. This also explains why the cultural industries have entered the tourism field in their search for additional resources.

A key issue raised in these conceptions of the cultural industries, and in the study of cultural tourism, is the definition of 'culture'. Because culture is such a multifaceted, dynamic and ambivalent concept, we should arguably approach it in a flexible way, so that the distinction between the cultural and the non-cultural is seen as 'porous, provisional and relative' (Hesmondhalgh, 2002). Such approaches have been slow to penetrate tourism studies, where most definitions of cultural tourism are still based on a fixed list of cultural resources consumed by tourists (see below).

A challenge in using concepts from cultural sociology and cultural economics in studying cultural tourism is their high level of abstraction. For example, a criticism of Bourdieu is that he abstracts the social from other realms, including space (Hanquinet, Savage and Callier, 2012). Such approaches are limiting, because the boundaries between culture and economy have become increasingly vague, to the point where many now refer to a 'cultural economy' in which value is determined by symbolic worth (Lash and Urry, 1994). These changes also have real spatial implications, such as the reformulation of urban space into new hybrid forms, such as the concept of 'holistic dining' developed by the Alchemist restaurant in Copenhagen:

> Holistic dining is per definition multi-layered. It draws upon elements from the world of gastronomy, theatre and art, as well as science, technology and design, in order to create an all-encompassing and dramaturgically driven sensory experience. (https://alchemist.dk/holistic-cuisine/)

The dynamism of the cultural field is also reflected in the development of cultural tourism.

THE EVOLVING FIELD OF CULTURAL TOURISM

Looking at Warde's criteria cited above, it seems reasonable to refer to cultural tourism as a field. Cultural tourism has a particular stake as a 'good' and desirable form of tourism, both for tourists and the places they visit. It is characterized by many set positions, such as the cultural institutions that receive visitors and the intermediaries that direct tourists to particular places. These actors also compete for tourism business, and they utilize the resources they have, in terms of brand equity and networks, to attract attention and visitors.

The dynamics of the cultural tourism field are influenced by shifts in both culture and tourism. Richards (2014a) analysed the development of cultural tourism using Pier Luigi Sacco's (2011) conceptualization of the evolution of culture. In this model, Culture 1.0 represents the origins of public culture in the modern era, with museums funded by rich industrial patrons, and later embraced by the state as symbols of national power (Table 3.1). If the wealth generated by other industries fuelled the early development of culture, it was the recognition of culture itself as an industry that heralded the arrival of Culture 2.0. Culture began to be seen as a source of jobs and income, and as a means of attracting tourists to cities and regions. From the turn of the Millennium, however, the diversification of cultural taste, the fragmentation of cultural production and access to new technologies and media undermined the mass production of culture under Culture 2.0. Alongside economic value, culture came to be seen as a means of creating identity, stimulating social cohesion and supporting creativity (Culture 3.0). The development of culture was also shaped by the evolution of cities, from the industrial city (City 1.0) to the rise of cities as consumption spaces (City 2.0) and the emergence of creativity and 'critical infrastructure' as drivers of urban development (City 3.0), as Landry (2014) suggests.

The changes in culture and cities provided new contexts for tourism, with the elite Grand Tour that marked Culture 1.0 being supplanted by mass cultural tourism flooding the new museums and other temples of Culture 2.0, and finally under Culture 3.0 new forms of cultural tourism emerge, such as creative tourism, gastronomic tourism and street art (Duxbury and Richards, 2019). These changes also reflected shifts in the urban contexts that were becoming predominant in cultural tourism around the turn of the Millennium (City 2.0 to 3.0).

The diminishing barriers between the cultural, economic and digital fields produce new contexts for cultural tourism, which are increasingly linked together in the network society. De Andrade (2018) argues that the work of Sacco and Richards takes insufficient account of emerging complex phenomena, such as digital social networks. De Andrade proposes the concept of 'cultural e-tourism', which takes place in urban, cultural and digital networks. In this situation, mobile citizens, immigrants and tourists co-produce their own discourse through travel, facilitated by TripAdvisor and other platforms. The social semantic city emerges as a globalized place where networks are used to produce mobile urban cultures and 'urban and tourist communication', in Culture/City/Cultural tourism 4.0.

Table 3.1   *Phases in the development of culture, cities and cultural tourism*

Phase	Culture	City	Cultural tourism
1.0	*Culture 1.0:* culture as by-product of industrial growth. Wealthy merchants and industrialists invested in culture as a means of polishing their image and/or doing good for the community.	*City 1.0:* large factories and mass production; the mental model is the city as a machine.	*Cultural tourism 1.0:* Grand Tour, cultural consumption by a small elite.
2.0	*Culture 2.0:* culture as industry. With industrialization and the growth of the culture industries, culture became an economic field, invested in by the public sector to stimulate growth and jobs.	*City 2.0:* spectacularization, the rise of consumption and the creative industries. Mobility, physical connectivity and inclusion.	*Cultural tourism 2.0:* mass cultural tourism, development of cultural resources as tourist attractions.
3.0	*Culture 3.0:* culture as a source of new value(s). The diversification of cultural taste, the fragmentation of cultural production and access to new technologies and media challenges the monolithic production of culture under Culture 2.0. Alongside economic value, culture is also seen as a means of creating identity, stimulating social cohesion and supporting creativity.	*City 3.0:* the 'social semantic city', harnessing the collective imagination and intelligence of citizens in making, shaping and co-creating their city. 'Soft urbanism', based on digital connectivity.	*Cultural tourism 3.0:* culture as a value platform for tourism (and vice versa), increasing integration of tourism and everyday life.
4.0	Culture/City/Cultural Tourism 4.0 Hybrid, creolized contexts and e-cultural tourism actors		

Source: de Andrade (2018); Landry (2014); Richards (2014a); Sacco (2011).

Similar processes are described in the context of China by Liu (2020), who traces four stages in China's tourism development.

1.   Before 1980, tourism was mainly used for national diplomacy.

2. From 1980 to 2009, modern tourism was developed, with cultural exhibitions and sightseeing.
3. From 2009 to 2018, a transition from tourism to cultural tourism. The first policy on cultural tourism was developed by the Ministry of Culture and China National Tourism Administration in 2009.
4. After 2018, with the development of the 5G mobile network, the digital transformation of cultural tourism (or cultural tourism +). This also marked the merging of the Ministry of Culture and the National Tourism Administration into a single Ministry of Culture and Tourism.

The development of cultural tourism in China has also been marked by the 'heritage turn' (Ludwig, Wang and Walton, 2020, p. 15), in which: 'The Chinese state employs modes of heritage governance to construct new modernities/identities in support of both its political legitimacy and its claim to status as an international superpower.' The global spread of western ideas about heritage has had significant implications for heritage management and cultural tourism, and now the Chinese 'turn' has introduced a new range of actors at the intersections of heritage, culture and tourism. As de Andrade (2018) suggests, the development of cultural tourism in China has also seen a significant integration of new technologies and a move towards smart tourism.

Although much attention has been focussed on urban cultural economy, rural areas have also offered many new opportunities for cultural tourism because of economic restructuring, changing rural lifestyles and the expansion of second residences. Low population density and lack of agglomeration advantages are often seen as barriers to the development of rural cultural economies (Farole, Rodríguez-Pose and Storper, 2011), but as Brouder (2012, 2019) shows, even in very sparsely populated regions such as the Swedish or Canadian Arctic, successful cultural and creative tourism development can occur. The convergence of tourists seeking rural tranquillity and cultural difference and locals using tourism as a new coping strategy has produced a surge in rural cultural tourism, particularly with the Covid-19 pandemic.

As Bessière (2012, p. 27) remarked, 'rural space, the land, now represents a place that is dreamt of, imagined, chosen, having been pushed aside, rejected and denigrated for so long'. There is now a stream of new cultural routes, heritage and crafts centres and niche museums in rural areas, a trend that parallels the growth of urban cultural attractions in the 1990s. Some of these attractions are adapted to the rural setting through their small scale, relying on enhancing the landscape through intangible culture and storytelling. Museums such as the Museum of Icelandic Sorcery and Witchcraft, the Icelandic Sea Monster Museum and the Icelandic Seal Centre have opened in very small communities in Iceland, for example (Aquino and Burns, 2020). In their analysis of the tiny Museum of Icelandic Sorcery and Witchcraft, Jóhannesson and Lund (2018) highlight the storytelling skills of the museum's Director, Sigurður Atlason, but also the emotional appeal of his cat, Mr Hippopotamus.

Storytelling is also facilitated by cultural routes and trails (Timothy, 2018). Cultural routes link cultural resources together, often themed around particular periods or styles of cultural production (Puczkó and Ratz, 2007). In Europe, for example, the European Cultural Routes include the famous *Camino de Santiago*, and also routes dedicated to architecture, food, historical periods and famous individuals, including Vikings, Jewish heritage, olive trees, the Phoenicians, ceramics, art nouveau, Le Corbusier, the Reformation, Robert Louis Stevenson and Napoleon. Briedenhann and Wickens (2004) explored the creation of cultural routes in southern Africa, where the African Dream project created 32 routes in four countries, covering a distance of 11,623 kilometres. In this context, Lourens (2007) analysed the experience of the Midlands Meander in South Africa as a route tourism destination offering of arts and crafts in a scenic rural environment in KwaZulu-Natal.

The links made by cultural routes depend greatly on institutional actors. The creation of cultural routes is one of the most frequent actions undertaken by national tourism administrations in the development of cultural tourism (OECD, 2009). However, after establishing such routes, public administrations often struggle to maintain them. In Brazil, de Pádua Carrieri, Luz and Pereira (2014) analyse the experience of the *Estrada Real* (Royal Road), and show that although the route has increased tourism to hotels along the route, it suffers from patchy support and coordination from local government(s).

This review indicates that the field of cultural tourism grows and shifts in a fluid way that was not imagined by Bourdieu in his conception of the cultural field. Cultural tourism has grown in terms of demand and production, which have dialectically responded to each other. The jostling between actors not only reorders the actors in the field, but also expands the field itself.

THE GROWING ATTRACTIONS OF CULTURE

In spite of the growing diversity of cultural attractions, museums and monuments continue to be the mainstay of cultural tourism. The big advantage of museums and monuments is that they tend to be permanent and readily accessible, unlike events and other ephemera. Many museums and monuments are also elevated in terms of cultural and social status so that they become 'must see sights' (MacCannell, 1976). Guidebooks indicate the sights that tourists should see, or make a detour for, producing a hierarchy of cultural value. This was graphically illustrated in the Second World War, when the so-called 'Baedeker Raids' by the German Airforce targeted UK cities listed as being of particular cultural value in the Baedeker guidebooks (Rothnie, 1992). Less often mentioned is the fact that the Allies later used Baedeker guidebooks in their bombing of German cities (Hohn, 1994).

Cultural institutions such as museums and monuments in the Upperground (Cohendet et al., 2010) serve as platforms that focus global flows of attention on specific places and themes (Richards, 2020a). Placing objects in a museum raises their cultural value, and draws the attention of different publics, including tourists. The UNESCO (1972) *Convention on World Heritage* gives a definition of cultural heritage, which includes monuments (architecture, monumental sculpture and painting, archaeological sites), groups of buildings and individual sites, which are of 'outstanding universal value' in historical, aesthetic, ethnological or anthropological terms. This has since been expanded to intangible heritage, but the UNESCO view is generally conservative, and largely ignores new and emergent cultural forms.

In early cultural tourism research, identifying and enumerating cultural tourism attractions was a means of charting the scale and scope of the practice. In Canada, Ritchie and Zins (1978) identified 12 main types of cultural attractions, including Handicrafts; Language; Tradition; Food; Art and music; Local history; Local work traditions and technology; Architecture; Religion; Educational systems; Dress; and Local events and leisure activities. Even this comprehensive listing omits some areas included in later classifications. Typologies developed in a European context tended to distinguish more categories of built heritage, such as the European Centre for Traditional and Regional Cultures (ECTARC) listing in 1989, which also included archaeological sites and museums and divided architecture into different types (ruins, famous buildings, whole towns).

Later typologies by Munsters (1994) and Smith (2015) progressively covered a wider range of cultural settings related to tangible and intangible heritage, attractions and events, and high and popular culture. For example, Smith (2015, p. 17) included Industry and commerce; Modern popular culture and Special interest activities. Richards (2001) broadened the view of cultural tourism settings by conceptualizing a field delineated by the form and function of cultural attractions (Figure 3.1). These ranged from a more classic concept of cultural tourism being based on artefacts from the past that have an educational function (for example, museums and monuments), to those which also seek to entertain, for example through animation and re-enactment, to attractions based on contemporary culture, with an educational focus, such as arts and languages, or primarily focussed on entertainment, such as theme parks or musicals.

The development of static lists of cultural attractions into the more dynamic concept of a cultural attraction field mirrored the shift from a view of culture as fixed and immutable towards more diverse and fluid conceptualizations of culture. Cultural tourism also began to include a more diverse range of sites

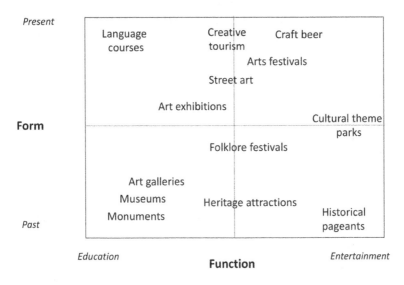

Source: After Richards (2001).

Figure 3.1   The field of cultural tourism attractions

and attractions, driven by the desire to reflect a wider view of the culture(s) of the places visited by tourists, and by the increasing cultural diversity of tourists themselves. Many studies highlighted 'new' forms of cultural tourism related to popular culture (McKercher, Ho and Du Cros, 2004), events (McHone and Rungeling, 1999), cultural routes (González and Medina, 2003), popular music (Gibson and Connell, 2003), everyday life (Ooi, 2002) and indigenous culture (Zeppel, 2002). This expansion demonstrates that the act of cultural tourism defined structures and contexts that were being created or redefined by the growing practice of cultural tourism. This focussed much research on the (new) spaces being occupied by cultural tourism as part of general processes of 'commodification' or 'heritagization'.

Rodríguez, Vecslir, Rubio Vaca and Molina Restrepo (2020) analyse how Buenos Aires and Bogotá have created new spaces for cultural tourism, based on the daily life of the inhabitants. This includes promotion of street art, local festivals and spaces that frame local activities. The spatial distribution of cultural tourism has extended in these cities, and neighbourhoods such as Palermo Soho in Buenos Aires and Usaquén in Bogotá have been transformed into new tourist products. These areas have a 'bohemian' character, attractive for the local and mobile creative class (Florida, 2002). The aestheticization of public space allows entrepreneurs to capitalize on the authenticity of these neighbourhoods to distinguish themselves from the rest of the city. As Zukin (2010, p. xiii) argued in the case of New York, authenticity became a framing device utilized in struggles over the use of urban space.

> the idea of authenticity has an undeniable cultural power. It has a real effect on our attachment to our neighborhood, on the stores where we like to shop, on the way we see some places as interesting and others as unworthy of our attention as cultural consumers.

Growing commodification has also been linked to the privatization of public space (Minton, 2006) and the 'festivalization' of the city (Häussermann and Siebel, 1993). Such debates have grown in recent years as the number of events staged in public space has grown. For example, Smith (2015) catalogues the growing number of events being held in the Royal Parks in London, detailing how public space is being acquired by private companies for profit. Other research has highlighted the ability of grassroots movements to reclaim or create new cultural spaces in opposition to neo-liberal policies. Novy and Colomb (2013) highlight the development of clubs and alternative cultural spaces in Berlin and Hamburg. In Rome, the emergence of bottom-up cultural spaces has been highlighted by Bragaglia and Krähmer (2018) and Galdini (2020), often linked to alternative cultures and squatter movements.

THE HERITAGE INDUSTRY AND THE RECYCLING OF OLD CONTEXTS

In both rural and urban contexts, the growth of tourism has been boosted by the extension of cultural heritage. Robert Hewison (1987) signalled the dramatic growth of heritage that emerged in the late 1970s and early 1980s. He argued that heritage represents a past that never existed; a manufactured version of history, made palatable and accessible for consumers. Writing about the UK, Hewison linked this development to Thatcherism, and a climate of decline caused by economic restructuring, de-industrialization and nostalgia for a lost empire. In fact, one can identify similar developments taking place around the same time in North America and continental Europe, which were also affected by economic recession and a loss of manufacturing industry. Looking to the past became a means of coping with contemporary adversity and giving a new purpose and meaning to post-industrial areas.

Tourism was an important means of valorizing heritage, and as Gravari-Barbas (2018, p. 173) argues, tourism became a 'a heritage producing machine', in which 'Heritage development encourages tourism, which in turn contributes to heritage development, which encourages tourism, and so on ...' Tourists are important to heritage production because they give value to objects abandoned by the host society, including old factories that become museums, old markets repurposed as food courts or former banks and jails that become hotels. Heritage is also actively produced by tourists through their practices, such as photography. Susan Sontag (2001, p. 68) in *On Photography* remarks that today, fewer people have old objects that have attained a patina, and instead they use the camera as a 'featherweight pocket museum', using photographs to turn the past into a consumable object.

The heritagization process has also extended beyond specific sites to include whole cultural landscapes, 'leisurescapes' and 'tourismscapes'. Whole countries and regions have been created and inhabited by heritage, including literary landscapes such as Shakespeare Country and Bronte Country in the UK (Philips, 2011), and heritage landscapes such as the Hanseatic League network of medieval ports in northern Europe (Michelson and Paadam, 2016). Van der Duim (2007) defines tourismscapes as actor-network assemblages that order people and material objects into products suitable for tourism consumption. A tourismscape unites a variety of networked actors: firstly people, secondly objects, media, machines and technologies, and finally spaces. Van der Duim's research on the Spanish island of Lanzarote shows how the artist César Manrique pioneered sustainable tourism development, based on the 'Manrique model', a philosophy of limited growth and respect for local architecture in which tourism, nature and culture are integrated (van der Duim, 2007). Making the model work, in the face of global economic forces and national planning structures, required creativity, and the supranational resources of the European Union.

The creation of new contexts for cultural and heritage tourism is driven not just by the transformation of history into contemporary heritage, but also by the growth of tourism itself. Empirical evidence for the synergies between tourism demand and heritage supply was provided by de Haan (1997), who demonstrated that cultural tourism was growing through an increased supply of heritage sites to visit. Richards (1996, p. 278) observed that 'The supply of cultural attractions ... grew much more strongly in the 1980s with the result that average attendance per heritage attraction actually fell in some countries during this period.'

In the Netherlands, the number of museums climbed steadily from 150 in 1945 to 873 in 2001 (Huysmans, van den Broek and de Haan, 2005), indicating possible overcapacity, driven by 'illusory expectations of the future'. There are also more monuments in the Netherlands, up from 44,000 in 1990 to 61,863 in 2017 (+40 per cent). In recent years, increased attendance and revenue have depended to a large extent on tourism. Foreign visits to museums totalled 4 million in 1999, rising to 9.7 million visits in 2016. Tourists contributed 15 per cent of total museum visits in 2009 and 28 per cent in 2016 (CBS, 2016).

In China, cultural infrastructure has also expanded in what Xue, Sun and Zhang (2020) refer to as the 'heat of cultural buildings'. More than 360 grand theatres were constructed between 1998 and 2015 exceeding the total built in Europe over the past 70 years. Wang and Liu (2019) also note the growth of museums in China, which by 2018 had 5354 national museums, attracting 1.126 billion visits. At a global level, UNESCO figures indicate that between 2012 and 2019, the number of museums globally increased by almost 60 per cent to about 95,000 institutions (UNESCO, 2020). This is a much greater increase than international tourism, which rose by 35 per cent over the same period.

Of course, not all of this growth in heritage is attributable to tourists. Tourists represent just one part of the flows of global mobility, information, communication and cultural exchange that stimulate what Gravari-Barbas (2018) terms 'heritage globalization' (*patrimondialisation*). These processes are together responsible for a considerable extension of the objects deemed worthy of consideration as cultural objects (Richards, 1996, 2001). Attracting global flows is also part of a global power game of cultural labels, such as the UNESCO World Heritage designation. As Huang, Tsaur and Yang (2012) state: 'The idea that having World Heritage Sites (WHS) can promote tourism seems to be a common belief.' At a global level, the UNWTO (2018) reports a strong positive correlation between the number of WHS and the number of cultural tourists reported by different countries.

The imbalance in WHS locations makes the supply-driven nature of cultural tourism potentially problematic. Steiner and Frey (2012) note that 46 per cent of WHS are in Europe, and only 9 per cent are in Africa. In 1994, the UNESCO World Heritage Committee launched the *Global Strategy for a Balanced, Representative and Credible World Heritage List*. However, the distribution of sites has become even more imbalanced since the Global Strategy was intro-duced. The share of Cultural WHS relative to Natural WHS has also continued to increase.

At the national level, there has also been a debate on whether WHS generate more visitation. For domestic tourism in Italy, Patuelli, Mussoni and Candela (2013) found a positive effect on tourism flows to regions with WHS, and a negative impact of WHS on visits to surrounding areas (as much as −13 per cent), indicating significant spatial competition for cultural tourists. Yang, Lin and Han (2010) found that cultural WHS were significant attractors of inter-national tourists, although the effects varied by origin country. In the case of Macau, China, Huang, Tsaur and Yang (2012) used econometric modelling to measure the impact of the WHS designation of the 'Historic Centre of Macau' in 2005 on visitation. They found no overall increase in tourism because of the designation, although they also concluded that the effects vary between different origin countries.

The UNWTO (2018) has signalled a shift in the focus of national cultural tourism policies from tangible heritage (national and World Heritage Sites, monuments, historic places and buildings) to intangible heritage (handicrafts, gastronomy, traditional festivals, traditional music, oral traditions and religion). Almost all national tourism organizations included tangible heritage and intangible heritage in their definition of cultural tourism, and over 80 per cent also include contemporary culture (for example, film, performing arts, design, fashion, new media). Tangible heritage was rated the most important element of cultural tourism, followed by intangible heritage and then contemporary culture. A mix of tangible and intangible heritage with contemporary culture was also seen as imparting uniqueness to the cultural tourism product of a destination, since this mix cannot be experienced elsewhere. The shift to intangible heritage and contemporary culture has other important consequences, such as growing integration of culture, tourism and technology; the expansion of audiences for cultural and creative content; and increased consumption of everyday culture (Richards, 2011; UNWTO, 2018). This changes the experience of cultural tourism, as Turgeon (2014, p. 8) observes:

> While for a long time visitors were content to marvel at the physical presence and symbolic power of objects presented in the museum space, they now require that the interpretative process be enhanced with information about the objects' fabrication, use and meaning. Further, they want the museum experience to enable them to access the intangibility of heritage, to feel the force of its affects. They wish to observe real people and live performances in a state of heightened reality, to feel the emotions they convey.

Greater use of intangible heritage in museums means that rather than viewing objects, the visitor is encouraged to play a more active role in the staging of experiential heritage (Williams, 2018). As the idea of history comes closer to the present (Richards, 2001), it is also more likely that visitors will consume experiences based on their own past and emotional connections. For example, one of the most successful events during the European Capital of Culture (ECOC) in Rotterdam in 2001 was an exhibition on the 20th century history of the city, which attracted many older Rotterdammers (Richards, Hitters and Fernandes, 2002). As a result of such shifts, not just styles of cultural tourism production and consumption are changing, but also the spaces in which they take place.

THE NEW SPACES OF CULTURAL TOURISM

One of the major recent themes of cultural tourism research has been the identification and analysis of new spaces of cultural tourism production, consumption and co-creation. Many of these new spaces are linked to intangible culture, rather than the tangible heritage resources typical of traditional forms of cultural tourism. Cities have long sought to develop new areas for tourism, away from crowded central cultural sites. For example, in 2001 Sydney launched a campaign to develop cultural tourism in gentrifying suburbs outside the city centre (Wirth and Freestone, 2003).

New tourist areas (NTAs) were originally identified by Maitland (2007) in his work on inner London. He found well-educated visitors, many of whom had made previous visits to London, discovering areas previously avoided by mainstream tourists. This coincided with efforts by outlying areas of London to develop tourism products that would help them profit from the growing numbers of visitors to the centre of the city. The recent growth of urban tourism has facilitated the incorporation of previously marginal areas into mainstream cultural tourism, particularly as repeat visitors seek out new experiences (Mayor of London, 2017).

In East London, Pappalepore (2010) examined different creative tourism clusters and found that new areas were being incorporated into mainstream tourism through processes of gentrification and art-led regeneration. She found 'trendsetters' who were in search of new creative experiences. They tended to be employed in the creative sector (especially media, fashion and arts), and they play a key role in starting new fashion trends, acquiring distinction through insider knowledge about niche artists and musicians, latest alternative fashion trends and counter-cultural venues. They seek out marginal areas undiscovered by the masses, but they are quickly joined by 'coolseekers' eager to soak up the trendy atmosphere of NTAs. Eventually, they are joined by 'accidental cultural tourists' who stumble across areas newly connected to mainstream tourism. This is also the development trajectory followed by areas of London such as Spitalfields, which was a marginal and degraded area in the 1980s (Shaw, 2007), but is now an established destination that attracts mainstream tourists with its alternative 'atmosphere' provided by independent shops, young artists, new fashions and cultural diversity (Pappalepore, 2010).

If the NTAs were previously in the inner city, now they are often suburban (Maitland, 2017). Visitors seeking the 'real London' are now pointed towards areas such as Muswell Hill, which has no attractions of note and no tube station to bring hordes of visitors. Often these suburbs are discovered by accidental cultural tourists, but they can also be lured with new projects and developments. Šebová, Peter Džupka and Urbancíková (2014) analyse the SPOTS project in Košice in Slovakia, which aimed to decentralize culture to suburban areas by converting former heat exchange stations into small cultural centres in residential areas of the city. This has motivated cultural tourists to visit suburban areas of the city due to their unconventional designs with climbing walls, graffiti and skate tracks. Chatzinakos (2020) also examines suburban communities in Manchester, focussing on suburban festivals as a means of placemaking in seemingly unlikely cultural destinations.

Barrera-Fernández and Hernández-Escampa (2017) chart spatial changes in the Mexican city of Oaxaca as a result of a shift from cultural to creative tourism. New creative tourism businesses are emerging in the city, responding to travellers who want to mix with locals. These include experiences based on local arts and crafts, traditional cuisine and local products such as coffee, chocolate, *mezcal* and *mole*. These experiences are much more widely spread than the cultural tourism activities concentrated on the historic centre. The creative tourists initially discovered these facilities, and new establishments then opened to cater for the increased demand. The research shows that traditional cultural tourism relates directly with gentrification in specific urban areas, whereas creative tourism activities articulate more widely with the city. Creative tourists arguably get more knowledge and a deeper experience, and they spread their expenditure over a larger number of businesses. The 'discovery' by creative tourists of neighbourhoods previously considered as uninteresting has also attracted attention from policy makers, and these areas have subsequently benefitted from regeneration and improvement. Barrera-Fernández and Hernández-Escampa (2017) therefore argue that creative tourism styles produce greater social and economic sustainability.

Cities are now actively using these trends, positioning neighbourhoods that are currently 'off the beaten track' as cool places for tourists to find locals. As *Time Out* explains in the introduction to 'The 50 coolest neighbourhoods in the world' (Manning, 2019):

> It's easier than ever to travel like a local these days: we stay in homes instead of hotel rooms, we never get lost, we can hail a cab anywhere and translate any language in seconds. But in the best cities in the world, there's still one big difference between visitors and residents: location. Experiencing a city like a local means getting off the tourist trail and discovering the places where clued-up residents actually hang out.

This aligns with Maitland's (2017) argument that tourists increasingly need to seek out the real city, the places where the locals are and other tourists are not (yet). The *Time Out* coolest neighbourhoods were selected on 'uniqueness, timeliness, geographic diversity, and cultural brilliance'. There is no objective basis for this curation of cultural tourism destinations: it is a list developed by critics and experts, people in the know, tastemakers, coolhunters and switchers. For each neighbourhood, the basic attractions are 'EAT, DRINK, DO, STAY and LOCALS SAY'. For example, what locals say about the Number 1 coolest neighbourhood in the world, Arroios in Lisbon, is: 'There are lots of independent things happening, young people, artists and people from all over the world. A neighbourhood that people used to be afraid of is now Lisbon's dynamic, intercultural hub.' As Oliveira (2019) notes, the top billing for Arroios is linked to the fact that the City of Lisbon has placed cultural diversity at the heart of its urban development policies, which is reflected in the *Time Out* description:

> A neighbourhood of contrasts, Arroios stands out from the other parishes of Lisbon for the multiculturalism of its people and places. Cradle of Amália, the greatest Portuguese fado singer of all time, and home to almost a hundred nationalities, Arroios is the largest parish in central Lisbon, though you can walk across it in half an hour. More than a neighbourhood, it's a world in itself, and its many impressive kilometres of streets are packed with open-air galleries, restaurants from all corners of the world, public services, cultural and sporting venues. (Dias da Silva, 2019)

The production of such lists is an act of curation. The new cultural intermediaries responsible for these lists (usually journalists and bloggers) are essentially identifying neighbourhoods with future value – their time is still to come, and few tourists have discovered them. Other, more established neighbourhoods, such as London's Shoreditch, Barcelona's Gràcia or Amsterdam's Jordaan, don't make the top 50 list because they are now overvalued.

Time Out itself has progressed from a simple London listings magazine to global experience producer – another interesting indicator of how urban cultural tourism has changed. Originally aimed at residents, as tourism grew it started catering to visitors, and more recently to locals aspiring to be 'tourists in their own city' (Richards, 2017). *Time Out* started as a London-only publication in 1968 and has since expanded its editorial recommendations to 315 cities in 58 countries worldwide. The magazine produced its first guidebook in 1972, but sales peaked in 2006 and *Time Out* stopped producing them in 2016. *Time Out* has not only analysed the growth of 'cool' places, but has also guided people to them and developed its own cool experiences. A food and cultural experience, Time Out Market, was launched in Lisbon, Portugal, in 2014, followed by Miami, New York, Boston, Montréal and Chicago. New Time Out Markets are set to open in Dubai (2020), London (2021) and Prague. In 2018, 3.9 million visitors came to the Lisbon market to experience the 32 restaurants and kiosks, eight bars and cafes, five shops and cooking workshops and other events. *Time Out* has essentially capitalized on its own roles as a curator and trendsetter, which enable it to identify and bet on sources of future value.

The fact that markets are now generating many new forms of value creation besides selling food ingredients has been noticed by others as well. In many cities, markets have become new spaces of tourism, as in Barcelona in Spain (Dimitrovski and Crespi Vallbona, 2018), Auckland in New Zealand (Kikuchi and Ryan, 2007) and in Taiwan (Hsieh and Chang, 2006). Revamped markets are ideal spaces for tourists seeking the local. They usually focus the flow of different people through the neighbourhood and the city and represent points at which bundles of practices come together. In the case of Florence, Palomares Alarcón (2017) contrasts the liveliness of the San Lorenzo Market with the 'city museum':

> Most … who live in the city centre seem to be living in something similar to a Renaissance theme park or a shopping centre. You can still feel the most daily relationships as buying on the Sant`Ambrogio market. There, life in the city feels beyond the numerous tourists who visit Florence just for one day. (p. 723)

However, San Lorenzo Market has become a carefully managed multifunctional space, which combines the essence of the market with leisure functions in a beautiful 19th century building. The market is oriented to people from the neighbourhood, but also to Florentine residents in general.

Such developments are often stimulated by public authorities keen to kick-start economic development in run-down areas. Markwick (2018) analyses the metamorphosis of Strait Street, the former prostitution hub of Valletta, capital city of Malta. Valletta's hosting of the ECOC in 2018 was linked to a strategy to develop more cultural tourism to an island previously dominated by beach tourism. The city had an ageing population and declining economic activity and cultural facilities. The ECOC was an opportunity to reverse these trends by attracting more high-spending cultural visitors to Valletta. The Maltese Tourism Organization indicated that only about 14 per cent of tourists were 'culture and heritage' tourists (Markwick, 2018), and the ECOC was an opportunity to change this by positioning Valletta as a short break cultural destination. Following the drafting of a new National Cultural Policy, a cultural development emphasis was given to the Valletta 2018 programme. As well as the tangible heritage attractions of the island, attention was also given to contemporary culture and intangible cultural heritage. This included the development of small creative clusters, including Strait Street. The development of theatres, exhibitions, burlesque and jazz bars and themed restaurants was supposed to enliven the night-time ambiance of the area, particularly to cater for a younger, cultural omnivore audience. As Munsters (2011) points out, this is challenging given the overwhelming weight of traditional cultural heritage in Malta. But many new developments have helped to progress the creativity of the old city, including improvements to Strait Street, such as the regeneration of the covered market and the old civil abattoir and luxury apartments for tourists.

FROM GRAFFITI TO STREET ART

New spaces for intangible cultural tourism have been created by the global growth of street art, or urban art. Street art began life as the illegal practice of graffiti, spawned by the hip hop culture in North American cities, where dereliction also provided an expansive canvas (Young, 2013). Over time, graffiti developed into an artform, with leading exponents becoming global superstars. The *Contemporary Art Market Report*'s (2017) ranking of contemporary artists in 2016 included four street artists in the top 10 (Keith Haring, Shepard Fairey, Banksy and Kaws). Banksy murals attract swarms of visitors, and there are many open-air street art museums (Amsterdam, St Petersburg, Berlin), as well as the Modern Contemporary (Moco) Museum in Amsterdam that showcases this artform. In New York, The Museum of Street Art (MoSA) in the CitizenM hotel in the Bowery has recreated the art from the original 5 Pointz site in Queens, a graffiti landmark painted over in 2013. In this case, street art was literally salvaged by tourism.

Street art has been linked to tourism (Campos and Sequeira, 2019) and is also increasingly analysed by cultural tourism scholars (for example, Skinner and Jolliffe, 2017). Graffiti was first embraced and then actively encouraged by cities keen to stimulate street culture and attract attention from mobile consumers. Campos and Sequeira (2019) analysed the street art scene in Lisbon, and identified the 'touristification of urban art', which they link to a set of social actors. The transition of street art or graffiti from a criminal activity to a lucrative art market has been marked by the increasing fame of street art superstars. The growing use of the city as a giant canvas links to the creative city concept, and the increasing popularity of everyday culture. Many other street art destinations have sprung up, including Penang in Malaysia and Chamanus in Canada, as well as those highlighting 'mural tourism' (Skinner and Jolliffe, 2017). Centres for mural art tourism include locations of separatist struggles, such as Northern Ireland and Sardinia, and cities like Los Angeles, where African-American murals are being showcased (de Miguel Molina, de Miguel Molina and Santamarina Campos, 2020). The presence of street art is often framed through the creation of festivals, with Upfest in Bristol being hailed by *Lonely Planet* as the largest street and urban art festival in Europe.

The touristification of urban art influences the tourist offer of the city, but also the relations and interactions between actors such as tour operators and guides, tourists, artists, institutions and local communities. In Lisbon, the public authorities play a crucial role in authorizing and supporting artists and artworks. Touristification was preceded by a political process of valorization. In 2008, the Municipality launched the *Galeria de Arte Urbana* (Gallery of Urban Art – GAU) to combat illegal graffiti. Panels were installed in the popular Bairro Alto District, using an exhibit space managed by GAU. This legitimated street art, and in 2009, GAU developed a strategy aimed at promoting urban art. This was supported by the organization of exhibitions and a festival of street art, Muro Urban Art Festival. GAU also promotes internationalization of urban art, working with other cities in the International Network for Urban Creativity. One of GAU's principles is 'ephemerality', in which street art has a limited life span before it is naturally 'erased'. This contributes to rotation of artworks and the rejuvenation of the urban landscape. This basic principle also links with the eventification of the city (see below), and the need to develop new cultural tourism attractions to cater to repeat visitors. The flexibility of street art makes it easy to (re)direct the flow of visitors. GAU points artists to places where it is permitted to paint, and this spreads street art to new spaces in the city – also those with few tourists.

There are now many street art tours in Lisbon, and Visit Portugal (2020) even has a web page dedicated to Street Art in Portugal, classified as 'art and culture' (Campos and Sequeira, 2019). Increasing attention also attracts members of the scene, who open street art businesses. These include the urban art shop/cafe/working space Underdogs Public Art store and Stupido 1/1, an Urban Art Bar curated by Portuguese artist Vhils. This 'creative crowd' (Den Dekker and Tabbers, 2012) organizes experiences linking street art with tourists, including the Lisbon Street Art App, a *Lisbon Street Art* photobook (Wilkinson, 2015), a street art map supported by the Municipality (Street Art Lisbon, 2017), an international conference (Soares Neves and de Freitas Simões, 2015) and regular contributions to blogs and formal media. Lisbon was declared the best street art city in the world by the *Guardian* newspaper (Dixon, 2011), and features high on other rankings, such as the Best Street Art Cities by the *Huffington Post*. Artists are also looking for the best spots to paint, so they are also attracted by a buzzing scene. This in turn will generate more activity and business, strengthening the street art scene.

Tourists are also attracted by this local buzz (Bathelt et al., 2004), fed by global media pipelines. Campos and Sequeira (2019) argue that street art tours promote 'touristification' in Lisbon, and Andron (2018) identifies similar processes in London. Street art tours serve to construct and legitimate the 'scene' in Lisbon, and the attribution to a specific artist becomes an important element in authorization and authentication. There is also evidence that the audience is becoming more specialized and skilled, creating a dialectic relationship between producers and consumers, who develop in tandem through co-creation (Tan, Luh and Kung, 2014). Street art tours attract two basic types of tourists: the curious tourist, less familiar with the scene, and the specialized tourist skilled in urban art. The recent increase in skilled consumption leads to the development of more open, co-created tours in peripheral areas. Campos and Sequeira (2019) argue that the tour guides contribute to configuring the urban art scene, which is also becoming a cultural tourism scene. The guides help to commodify urban art for tourism, but also help to increase the visibility of the scene, which in turn increases their economic capital. The more knowledgeable guides also mediate between artists and potential foreign buyers. The discourse of urban art in Lisbon also highlights authenticity being created through viewing the 'alternative city' or 'unknown city', far from the beaten paths of mass tourism. In this way, urban art in Lisbon matches the desire of the Municipality to project Lisbon as an open, cosmopolitan city, and to spread tourism beyond the crowded centre (Richards and Marques, 2018). Street art actors therefore become enlisted into a ritual practice which extends itself throughout the city, at least in part driven by tourism (see Figure 4.2).

One of the challenges for street art destinations is creating economic value from artworks that are essentially openly accessible for all. If a city becomes more attractive because of the quality of street art, this generates indirect value in terms of tourism volumes, and potentially new residents and businesses. Such processes are clearly visible in *Beco de Batman* (Batman's Alley) in São Paulo, Brazil, which started with a single Batman figure and now boasts a dense covering of images that are constantly renewed, and which attract many visitors. The crowds in turn attract street vendors, coffee shops and art galleries. Most tourists take numerous pictures of the artworks, which also generate content for social media sites and websites, attracting still more visitors.

The original attraction of cities for many street artists is the availability of large painting surfaces, particularly where there are derelict buildings, which are easier to paint. In Lisbon and other cities, deprived areas have often been at the leading edge of street art production. But as street art helps to raise the profile of these places, it also stimulates redevelopment and rising property prices, which in the long run reduces the opportunities to make art.

CLUSTERS – SPATIAL AGGLOMERATION AND FRAMING

Formal clusters have their roots in classic economic theory (Marshall, 1919), which extols the advantages of locating close to other producers, promoting knowledge spillover effects and innovation. This is also the logic of cultural and creative clusters, or cultural districts (Sacco and Blessi, 2007). Bathelt et al. (2004) emphasize the value of clusters as places that stimulate face-to-face interaction, promoting the exchange of ideas and therefore stimulating innovation.

The development of local clusters can also be seen as a counter movement to globalization, valorizing the local as a source of difference and innovation (Russo and Richards, 2016). In cultural tourism, glocalization processes are evident in the framing of local culture for consumption by global audiences, which also represents a turn from productive arguments for clustering to consumption-based rationales (Richards and Tomor, 2012). Cultural clusters or precincts (Hayllar, Griffin and Edwards, 2010) are often designed to present local culture and creativity in a palatable form for a broad audience, providing a cultural theming of an area or district.

Clusters frame places as sites of cultural production and consumption, and therefore as cultural tourism destinations. Governments have actively stimulated this process, identifying areas suitable for cultural and creative activities, giving support to businesses located there and sometimes actively managing the cluster. Brooks and Kushner (2001, p. 5) defined a cultural district as 'a designated area of a city in which arts and culture facilities serve as the primary attraction'. They developed a typology related to the extent of public sector intervention, ranging from simple designation or labelling to domination, where the public sector controls all aspects of the cluster. Bertacchini and Re (2017, p. 21) note that 'a cultural district model is particularly suited to address cultural tourism demand', because they concentrate the supply of cultural and tourism services and support the production of craft goods and material culture.

There are three main themes in cultural tourism cluster research: the use of former productive spaces as sites of tourism consumption; the use of ethnic minorities as a creative anchor for clusters; and the use of creative activities as a means of valorizing specific spaces, both urban and rural (Brouder, 2012; Diekmann and Smith, 2015; Shaw, 2007). Clusters are often designated in a top-down fashion, aiming to support economic activity through tourism. In China, as the OECD (2014) reports, cultural clusters in Shanghai attracted over 5 million visitors a year, many of these being tourists. O'Connor and Gu (2014, p. 6) analysed the development of creative clusters in Shanghai, where they identified many 'bounded, gated and officially recognized entities concerned with industrial development; ... aesthetically refurbished old factories set to provide culturally inflected retail/leisure destinations linked to a "creative atmosphere" or "buzz".' They suggest that the 'Chinese government wrapped the commercial appeal of the creative industries into its project of "soft power"', adopting the hybrid label 'cultural creative industry cluster'. Yuan Yuan (2020) reviews the development of Cultural-Creative Industries Parks in the cities of Shenzhen and Guangzhou, and McCarthy and Wang (2016) analysed the development of the 798 Art Zone in Beijing, which they argue has been important in terms of city branding and tourism, but which has also generated gentrification. They identify an increasing emphasis on mainstream tourism and consumption-based activities in the Zone, and surveys indicated that visitors were attracted both by the art as well as the overall cultural atmosphere. Reports indicate that the 798 Art District had become the third most visited tourist destination in Beijing, after the Forbidden City and the Great Wall (Sun, 2014).

Zhou, Tang and Zou (2019) also describe the growth of 'urban villages' in China as engines of redevelopment in cities such as Shanghai, Beijing and Guangzhou, largely with a top-down approach. Other, more bottom-up approaches tended to be less successful. In the case of Wuhan, government involvement in cultural creative urban villages increased when the city staged the 7th Military World Games in 2019. Residents were shown to have a positive attitude towards the development of creative cultural tourism in the villages, even though 50 per cent of the houses are now occupied by artists and entrepreneurs, who have replaced the original inhabitants.

Hitters and Richards (2002) compared the operation of top-down designated and managed clusters and more informal creative cluster development in the Netherlands. In the case of the Witte de With cluster in Rotterdam, a creative district emerged through the activity of local entrepreneurs. The success of the cluster attracted more visitors and the attention of the Municipality, which integrated the area into its tourism planning and promotion. Over the years, the cluster has become less creative and more commercial, as creative workshops and artist studios have been displaced by higher rents, with a shift towards cafes, restaurants and hotels.

Arguably, such creative clusters have abandoned their origins as productive creative spaces, and become hubs for consumption, tourism and leisure. This can undermine the creative 'scene economies' (Kühn, 2015a) which made them popular with hipsters, Bohemians and creative tourists. Scene economies are characterized by small-entrepreneurial infrastructures (clubs, shops, media, creative producers and distributors) with a value creation chain embedded in a subcultural aesthetic. The scene economy is often held together by alternative and oppositional ideologies, which in the case of Berlin has helped the city to become 'the capital city of the underground' (Kühn, 2015b, p. 64). Such scenes are effectively strategic positions in a field taken by actors who wish to underline their own independence and alternative orientation. Colomb (2012) describes how the vibrant Berlin club and music scene originally thrived in vacant spaces in the city but suffered as it was harnessed to promote Berlin's image as an international creative hub. Tourism is seen as one force that drives commodification of these alternative clusters and brings them into the mainstream.

EVENTIFICATION

Events can mark out a 'special time' in a place, stimulating people to visit, also through Fear of Missing Out (FOMO). You only get one opportunity to visit an event, because every edition provides a different experience. The growth of events has therefore fed off modern experience hunger (de Cauter, 1995) and the need of places to attract attention. Eventification has long been ignored by researchers, who generally privilege space over time: as tourists are seen to travel in space, the spatial aspects of their behaviour are often viewed as paramount. However, as Iribas (2004, p. 143) argues, 'Time is the key to tourist consumption, as in the rest of our daily lives: space has become a mere instrument for selling time.'

Taking a broad definition of cultural tourism as participation in cultural experiences, all tourists visiting cultural events are cultural tourists. Major cultural events such as the ECOC are therefore seen as good opportunities to develop the cultural tourism market. On average, the ECOC increased the level of overnight tourism to the host city by just under 12 per cent in the period 1985 to 2002, and individual cities have recorded far greater tourism growth. Weimar (ECOC in 1999) increased overnight visitor numbers by 56 per cent and Graz (ECOC in 2003) by 23 per cent (Richards and Palmer, 2010).

Other 'blockbuster events' are now regularly organized to attract tourists, although they did not begin this way. In Australia, Berryman (2013) argues that the first blockbuster exhibitions in the 1970s were organized for reasons of cultural diplomacy rather than tourism. But in the 1990s, the rationale changed to stimulating the local economy as cities saw increasing tourism revenues being generated. However, some cities found to their cost that block-busters could also fail financially. The exhibition *Masterpieces from Paris: Post-Impressionism from the Musee d'Orsay*, a blockbuster at the National Gallery of Australia in 2010, attracted 480,000 visitors, but still had a shortfall of AU$5.4 million. These problems encouraged more cities and museums to seek financial guarantees from the government (Berryman, 2013). As Gorchakova (2017) found in a review of exhibitions in Melbourne, Canberra, Auckland and Wellington, there are also non-economic advantages of staging blockbuster events, such as expanding the experiential dimension of the city's tourism offer, improving the tourism mix, strengthening the brand and helping to achieve long-term marketing objectives.

At a smaller scale, eventification has seen the emergence of pop-up spaces, often found in major city centres (Richards, 2014b), supporting what Pasquinelli (2015) terms 'temporary urbanism'. Pasquinelli (2015) argues pop-up attrac-tions heighten the dispersed nature of urban tourism, allowing new spaces to be animated in different parts of a city quickly. Wynn (2016) analyses the temporary urbanism generated by music festivals that create a hybrid 'music/city'. Analysing music festivals in the American cities of Austin, Nashville and Newport, he identifies 'citadel', 'core' and 'confetti' patterns of music events, with increasing levels of integration into the urban fabric. These events attract cultural tourists and develop the cultural fabric of the city. Music festivals have helped Austin to grow its economy as well as supporting the creative sector, in a positive, synergistic process that Wynn (2016) terms 'festivalization'. Music-friendly policies stimulated Austin festivals, which in turn put the city on the map as the 'Live Music Capital of the World'. Richards (2020b) reports that the flagship SXSW festival attracted 289,000 visitors in 2018, generating US$350 million in economic impact. However, growth in music consumption is set against a shrinking music industry, which could undermine the long-term sustainability of Austin's music economy.

De Andrade (2018) argues that the integration of culture, tourism and new media (phase 4.0 in Table 3.1) is producing a combination of a mobile cyberspace and cybertime. In the public cybertime/spaces of the city, the idea of a particular place or time for cultural tourism has been replaced by hybrid notions of 'creolized consumption'. This integration of time and space in cultural tourism practices reflects the fact that choosing a space to visit is also choosing a particular time to be there. This integration of space and time is also evident in the buzz or atmosphere attached to certain places at particular times. Eventification provides the software that enables the synchronization of social agendas, so that groups of consumers will meet in particular places at specific times, providing new structures for the 24/7 cultural economy.

Many places have used eventfulness strategies to generate liveliness and movement and provide links to the space of flows. Events are a particularly useful tool for cultural, creative and economic development, being flexible, relatively cheap and amenable to policy direction. As Richards and Palmer (2010) note, eventful cities aim to increase 'eventfulness', or a feeling of activity and animation that helps to increase a sense of well-being and connection with the city. Culture often forms a cornerstone of eventfulness, providing significant moments that can be celebrated and framed to generate positive outcomes (see Chapter 5). Events provide temporal contexts in which actors can come together and 'make things happen' (Bærenholdt, 2017).

BUZZ AND PIPELINES

The buzz provided by groups of actors coming together in specific places at particular times provides an important stimulus for cultural tourism. Many experiences depend on particular space/time relationships through which a mix of specific capitals is deployed and encountered. A key finding of research on cultural tourism experiences is the importance of 'atmosphere'. This is a difficult term to define: we can't describe the atmosphere of a place, but we know when we are in a place with a good atmosphere. Atmosphere is sometimes linked with terms such as 'ambiance' or 'buzz'. For example, Vanolo (2008, p. 372) emphasizes the importance of social buzz in the creative city concept, which he links to scenes with diverse groups of people meeting and chatting.

For Bathelt et al. (2004, p. 38) buzz refers to the 'information and communication ecology created by face-to-face contacts, co-presence and co-location of people', vital to the conducting of business, but which also underpins social interaction. The local buzz based on physical co-presence also feeds off distant interaction with other 'scenes', linked together by global pipelines. Places constitute temporary clusters that sustain local buzz and which support global pipelines, allowing communities to position themselves both at local and global levels (Bathelt and Schuldt, 2010). Pipelines to the space of flows are fed by business, the media, and the movement of people, including tourists. Tourists inject life and reputational capital into the cultural scene of the places they visit, and they expand the consumer base from which the local cultural industries can draw support (Richards and Marques, 2018). Cultural tourists therefore become an important part of the attention economy of places, helping to put them on the map for other tourists, and eventually also businesses and investors.

In the case of Berlin, the relationship between buzz and pipelines became very clear in the 1990s, as the city developed a booming music and arts scene, which also attracted growing numbers of cultural tourists. Visit Berlin maintains that more than half of the city's visitors come for art and culture:

> The three most important reasons given for a trip to the German capital are the sights, the art and culture scene as well as the cityscape and architecture. Over the past year, the art and culture scene under the title 'BERLIN 365/24' has been successfully marketed throughout the world by *visitBerlin* in cooperation with Kulturprojekte Berlin. (Visit Berlin, 2017)

Picaud (2019) compared Berlin with its DIY venues and relatively unprofessionalized and unsubsidized music scene with the more classic cultural capital, Paris. Whereas Paris has always emphasized high culture, Berlin was 'poor but sexy', its branding linked to 'youth and club cultures' (Picaud, 2019, p. 37). In recent years, Berlin has been building the cultural tourism market by renovating old museums, building new ones and attracting cultural talent. The latest addition to the high culture scene is the Humboldtforum, which will occupy a reconstructed royal palace on Museum Island, with 30,000 square metres of space. The €595 million museum houses Berlin's ethnological and Asian art collections and was launched digitally in December 2020 due to coronavirus restrictions. Tim Renner, Berlin's cultural affairs secretary, stated 'Cultural tourism is an important economic factor for our city, that's why we're exerting a big effort to make the cultural offerings even more attractive for international visitors' (Fahmy, 2015).

Berlin attracts not just high cultural visitors, but also those attracted by the local buzz. Rapp (2009) identified the 'Easyjetsetters' as partygoers who fly to

Berlin for one night, with no interest in the traditional cultural offer. Instead, they came for the cultural scene attached to the night-time economy:

> public authorities soon realized that this 'subcultural capital' was instrumental in redefining the way their capital was perceived abroad. In Berlin as in Paris, night-life is instrumental to touristic and urban policies, which are linked to the city's economic development. In Berlin, territorial marketing has been used to develop a 'creative' city. (Picaud, 2019, p. 46)

However, Picaud (2019) charts the complaints of music club owners that tourism and gentrification were destroying the alternative feeling of neigh-bourhoods such as Kreuzberg.

The experience of Berlin and other cities highlights the role of different elements of the cultural infrastructure of cities in supporting cultural tourism. This also reflects the distinction discussed earlier between the Upperground, Middleground and Underground of the cultural city (Cohendet et al., 2010). The buzz of the underground has long been used to develop (cultural) tourism, as in 'Swinging London' in the 1960s (Truman, 2010). In the past, the profile of the Underground was raised by the intermediaries in the Middleground to support more formalized cultural activity and to generate cultural content. Today, the tourism sector and other non-cultural intermediaries are also involved in the exploitation and dissemination of local buzz, as we saw in the case of street art.

FROM CATHEDRALS OF CONSUMPTION TO NICHE MUSEUMS

In major cities the cultural power of the Upperground is demonstrated by the new 'cathedrals of consumption' – spectacular museums and monuments designed for cultural consumption as well as display. Following the opening of the Pompidou Centre in Paris in 1977, numerous other cities followed suit, with the Bilbao Guggenheim, the Tate Modern in London, the San Francisco Museum of Modern Art (SFMOMA) and the Louvre in Abu Dhabi.

The Bilbao Guggenheim has attracted particular attention, arguably because it transformed the once dreary, smelly port of Bilbao into a postmodern cultural tourism mecca. Beatriz Plaza followed the development of the museum and the city over two decades, mapping the economic, social and cultural effects of the Guggenheim. She emphasized the success of the project in generating cultural tourism to Bilbao (Plaza, 2000), causing significant economic impacts. The scale and effects of the economic impulse was the subject of much debate, however (for example, Gómez and González, 2001), and over time, Plaza also began to reflect on the challenge of the museum in balancing embeddedness in the Basque region with global networking. Plaza and Haarich (2015) see the role of the Guggenheim in developing the tourism sector in the Basque Country as an important aspect of local embeddedness. The Guggenheim is increasingly involved in local and regional planning processes and is central to a tourism strategy 'based on culture, architecture and urban aesthetics, haute cuisine and traditional Basque gastronomy' (p. 1467). The international diffusion of the 'Bilbao effect' is a reflection of the international networking of the museum and the Municipality, which generated a global flow of policy makers coming to learn from the city (González, 2011). Plaza and Haarich (2015) argue that the Guggenheim 'can be seen as an atypical multinational enterprise as it combines the characteristics of a MNC and a local cultural tourism attraction' (p. 1473).

The 'Bilbao Effect' suggests that any city with enough money could attract cultural tourists. This message was seized upon by many, and a long waiting list of wannabe Guggenheim cities emerged, at one stage with 60 hopeful candidates (Richards, 2000). Other major museums followed similar expansion strategies, with the Tate now having four branches (the Tate Britain and Tate Modern in London, the Tate Liverpool and Tate St. Ives in Cornwall), the Louvre opening subsidiaries in Lens and Abu Dhabi, and the Hermitage expanding to Amsterdam and partnering with the Guggenheim to open an exhibition centre in Las Vegas. Evidence is now beginning to emerge of resistance to this cultural colonialism, with Helsinki having decided not to pursue the development of a Guggenheim Museum following protests from the cultural sector, and the municipality of Barcelona fighting plans to build a Hermitage franchise next to the city's cruise terminal (Richards and Marques, 2018).

The new cathedrals of consumption rooted in the Upperground are also being challenged by newcomers, as enthusiastic art collectors themselves are now building their own art museums (Franklin, 2017). Franklin estimates there are now 317 of these institutions globally with active, living collector-founders. Of these, 70 per cent were built after 2000, and many more are anticipated. 'They have opened museums of contemporary art in many more countries and regions where once there were none, resulting from a massive global expansion of private contemporary art collecting' (p. 997). The case study used by Franklin, the opening of the Museum of Old and New Art (MONA) in Hobart, Australia in 2011, has developed a considerable stream of cultural tourists to this provincial city. Franklin (2017) reports that numbers of tourists to Tasmania indicating they had visited MONA increased by 30 per cent between 2011 and 2014. By 2013, the *Lonely Planet Guide* had ranked Hobart number seven in their list of top cities to visit and was listed sixth on *Time Out*'s top 50 neighbourhoods list in 2019.

CONCLUSIONS

The contextual field of cultural tourism shapes possibilities for actors, and in turn is shaped by their actions. New actors and cultural forms need to assert their legitimacy in the field, reflected in the journey of street art from an illegal practice to celebrated artform. Cultural tourism is transformed through evolving relationships-in-practice, which contain the potential to develop new relationships (Huijbens and Jóhannesson, 2019). Evolving relationships are fed by global pipelines that link areas of local buzz, giving certain places a distinctive atmosphere at certain moments in time. This helps to position places on global lists and agendas, giving them (albeit often temporarily) a competitive edge in cultural markets.

However, simply having cultural resources is not enough. These resources need to be given meaning for different audiences and publics, which requires creativity on the part of the actors involved (Richards and Duif, 2019). The creative application of design, storytelling and curation has generated a flow of new cultural tourism experiences, based on popular and everyday culture, as well as high culture. The contexts of cultural tourism relate therefore not just to physical space, but also the making of places and the use of time, relationships and power, which bring together different groups of actors and create new relationships between them. Researching cultural tourism requires an ecosystem approach that links actors and contexts, focussing on the processes that connect the different elements of the system. In cities we see negotiations between the cultural Upperground, Middleground and Underground, producing distinctive atmospheres that mark them as 'the place to be' at a certain time. The combination of spatial and temporal resources stimulates the eventification of places for cultural tourism, heightening the Fear of Missing Out and producing a wider range of interchangeable experiences. The challenge for cultural tourism destinations, therefore, is to emphasize their unique combination of experiences, which are both embedded in local culture as well as being accessible to global audiences. The changing combinations of actors, resources and structures have important consequences for cultural tourism practices, as considered in the following chapter.

REFERENCES

Andron, S. (2018). Selling streetness as experience: the role of street art tours in branding the creative city. *The Sociological Review, 66*(5), 1036–57.
Aquino, J.F. and Burns, G.L. (2020). Creative tourism: the path to a resilient rural Icelandic community. In K. Scherf (ed.), *Creative Tourism and Sustainable Development in Smaller Communities* (pp. 165–99). Calgary: University of Calgary Press.

Bærenholdt, J.O. (2017). Moving to meet and make: rethinking creativity in making things take place. In J. Hannigan and G. Richards (eds), *The Sage Handbook of New Urban Studies* (pp. 330–42). London: Sage.

Barrera-Fernández, D. and Hernández-Escampa, M. (2017). From cultural to creative tourism: urban and social perspectives from Oaxaca, México. *Revista de Turismo Contemporâneo*, 5, 3–20.

Bathelt, H. and Schuldt, N. (2010). International trade fairs and global buzz, part I: ecology of global buzz. *European Planning Studies*, *18*(12), 1957–74.

Bathelt, H., Malmberg, A., and Maskell, P. (2004). Clusters and knowledge: local buzz, global pipelines and the process of knowledge creation. *Progress in Human Geography*, *28*(1), 31–56.

Berryman, J. (2013). Art and national interest: the diplomatic origins of the 'blockbuster exhibition' in Australia. *Journal of Australian Studies*, *37*(2), 159–73.

Bertacchini, E.E. and Re, A. (2017). *Investing in the City's Cultural Assets: The Local Economic Development Plan for Port Louis in Mauritius*. Milan: Fondazione Santagata.

Bessière J. (2012). *Innovation et Patrimoine Alimentaire en Espace Rural*. Paris: Editions Quae.

Bourdieu, P. (1984). *Distinction: A Social Critique of the Judgement of Taste*. London: Routledge.

Bragaglia, F. and Krähmer, K. (2018). 'Art barricades' and 'poetic legitimation' for squatted spaces: Metropoliz, Rome and Cavallerizza Reale, Turin. *Tracce Urbane. Rivista Italiana Transdisciplinare di Studi Urbani*, *2*(4), 106–25.

Briedenhann, J. and Wickens, E. (2004). Tourism routes as a tool for the economic development of rural areas – vibrant hope or impossible dream? *Tourism Management*, *25*(1), 71–9.

Brooks, A.C. and Kushner, R.J. (2001). Cultural districts and urban development. *International Journal of Arts Management*, *3*(2), 4–15.

Brouder, P. (2012). Creative outposts: tourism's place in rural innovation. *Tourism Planning & Development*, *9*(4), 383–96.

Brouder, P. (2019). Creative tourism in creative outposts. In N. Duxbury and G. Richards (eds), *A Research Agenda for Creative Tourism* (pp. 57–68). Cheltenham, UK and Northampton, MA, USA: Edward Elgar Publishing.

Campos, R. and Sequeira, Á. (2019). Entre VHILS e os Jerónimos: arte urbana de Lisboa enquanto objeto turístico. *Horizontes Antropológicos*, 55. http://journals .openedition.org/horizontes/3734 (accessed 18 December 2020).

CBS (2016). *Musea in Nederland 2016*. Den Haag: Centraal Bureau voor de Statistiek.

Chatzinakos, G. (2020). Places in the shadows of the city: the role of culture in the production and consumption of suburbia. PhD thesis, Manchester Metropolitan University.

Cohendet, P., Grandadam, D., and Simon, L. (2010). The anatomy of the creative city. *Industry and Innovation*, *17*(1), 91–111.

Colomb, C. (2012). Pushing the urban frontier: temporary uses of space, city marketing, and the creative city discourse in 2000s Berlin. *Journal of Urban Affairs*, *34*(2), 131–52.

Contemporary Art Market Report (2017). Popularity of Street Art. https://www.artprice .com/artprice-reports/the-contemporary-art-market-report-2017/popularity-of-street -art (accessed 18 December 2020).

de Andrade, P. (2018). Mobile cultural tourism. Art spaces, times and logos. *Lusophone Journal of Cultural Studies*, *5*(2), 365–78.

de Cauter, L. (1995). *Archeologie van de kick: verhalen over moderniteit en ervaring.* Leuven: Van Halewijck.

de Haan, J. (1997). *Het Gedeelde Erfgoed.* Den Haag: Sociaal en Cultureel Planbureau.

de Miguel Molina, M., de Miguel Molina, B., and Santamarina Campos, V. (2020). Visiting African American murals: a content analysis of Los Angeles, California. *Journal of Tourism and Cultural Change, 18*(2), 201–17.

de Pádua Carrieri, A., Luz, T.R., and Pereira, M.C. (2014). O Projeto Estrada Real. *Revista Anais Brasileiros de Estudos Turísticos – ABET, 4,* 54–63.

Den Dekker, T. and Tabbers, M. (2012). From creative crowds to creative tourism. *Journal of Tourism Consumption and Practice, 4*(2), 129–41.

Dias da Silva, R. (2019). What to do in Arroios, Lisbon's coolest neighbourhood. *Time Out,* 15 September. http://www.timeout.com/lisbon/arroios-lisbon-neighbourhood -guide (accessed 18 December 2020).

Diekmann, A. and Smith, M.K. (2015). *Ethnic and Minority Cultures as Tourist Attractions.* Bristol: Channel View.

Dimitrovski, D. and Crespi Vallbona, M. (2018). Urban food markets in the context of a tourist attraction – La Boqueria market in Barcelona, Spain. *Tourism Geographies, 20*(3), 397–417.

Dixon, R. (2011). Urban splash: street art in Lisbon. *Guardian,* 29 January. https://www .theguardian.com/travel/2011/jan/29/graffiti-street-art-lisbon-portugal (accessed 18 December 2020).

Duxbury, N. and Richards, G. (2019). *A Research Agenda for Creative Tourism.* Cheltenham, UK and Northampton, MA, USA: Edward Elgar Publishing.

ECTARC (1989). *Contribution to the Drafting of a Charter for Cultural Tourism.* Llangollen: European Centre for Traditional and Regional Cultures.

Fahmy, D. (2015). Berlin spending billions on arts and culture to draw tourists. *Skift,* 12 June. https://skift.com/2015/06/12/berlin-spending-billions-on-arts-and-culture -to-draw-tourists/ (accessed 18 December 2020).

Farole, T., Rodríguez-Pose, A., and Storper, M. (2011). Cohesion policy in the European Union: growth, geography, institutions. *Journal of Common Market Studies, 49*(5), 1089–111.

Florida, R. (2002). *The Rise of the Creative Class.* New York: Basic Books.

Franklin, A. (2017). Creative exchanges between public and private: the case of MONA (the Museum of Old and New Art) and the city of Hobart. In L.M. Alves, P. Alves, and F. García García (eds), *Libro de Actas V Congresso Internacional Cidades Criativas* (pp. 995–1005). Lisbon: CITCEM.

Galdini, R. (2020). Temporary uses in contemporary spaces. A European project in Rome. *Cities, 96,* 102445.

Gibson, C. and Connell, J. (2003). 'Bongo fury': tourism, music and cultural economy at Byron Bay, Australia. *Tijdschrift voor economische en sociale geografie, 94*(2), 164–87.

Gómez, M.V. and González, S. (2001). A reply to Beatriz Plaza's 'The Guggenheim-Bilbao Museum Effect'. *International Journal of Urban and Regional Research, 25*(4), 898–900.

González, R. and Medina, J. (2003). Cultural tourism and urban management in northwestern Spain: the pilgrimage to Santiago de Compostela. *Tourism Geographies, 5*(4), 446–60.

González, S. (2011). Bilbao and Barcelona 'in motion'. How urban regeneration 'models' travel and mutate in the global flows of policy tourism. *Urban Studies, 48*(7), 1397–418.

Gorchakova, V. (2017). Touring blockbuster exhibitions: their contribution to the marketing of a city to tourists. PhD thesis, Auckland University of Technology.

Gravari-Barbas, M. (2018). Tourism as a heritage producing machine. *Tourism Management Perspectives*, 25, 173–6.

Hanquinet, L., Savage, M., and Callier, L. (2012). Elaborating Bourdieu's field analysis in urban studies: cultural dynamics in Brussels. *Urban Geography, 33*(4), 508–29.

Häussermann, H. and Siebel, W. (1993). *Festivalisierung Der Stadtpolitik: Stadtentwicklung Durch Große Projekte*. Opladen: Westdeutscher Verlag.

Hayllar, B., Griffin, T., and Edwards, D. (2010). *City Spaces – Tourist Places*. London: Routledge.

Hesmondhalgh, D. (2002). *The Cultural Industries*. London: Sage.

Hewison, R. (1987). *The Heritage Industry: Britain in a Climate of Decline*. London: Methuen.

Hitters, E. and Richards, G. (2002). The creation and management of cultural clusters. *Creativity and Innovation Management, 11*(4), 234–47.

Hohn, U. (1994). The Bomber's Baedeker – target book for strategic bombing in the Economic Warfare against German Towns 1943–45. *GeoJournal, 34*(2), 213–30.

Hsieh, A.T. and Chang, J. (2006). Shopping and tourist night markets in Taiwan. *Tourism Management, 27*(1), 138–45.

Huang, C.H., Tsaur, J.R., and Yang, C.H. (2012). Does World Heritage List really induce more tourists? Evidence from Macau. *Tourism Management, 33*(6), 1457.

Huijbens, E.H. and Jóhannesson, G.T. (2019). Tending to destinations: conceptualising tourism's transformative capacities. *Tourist Studies, 19*(3), 279–94.

Huysmans, F., Van den Broek, A., and De Haan, J. (2005). *Culture-lovers and Culture-leavers: Trends in Interest in the Arts and Cultural Heritage in the Netherlands*. The Hague: Social and Cultural Planning Office.

Iribas, J.M. (2004). Evolución de las rutinas del espacio; las diferentes tipologías turísticas. In C. Jordá Such, N. Portas, and J.A. Sosa Díaz-Saavedra (eds), *Arquitectura moderna y turismo: 1925–1965: Actas IV Congreso Fundación DOCOMOMO Ibérico* (pp. 141–53). Valencia: Fundación DOCOMOMO Ibérico.

Jóhannesson, G.T. and Lund, K.A. (2018). Creative connections? Tourists, entrepreneurs and destination dynamics. *Scandinavian Journal of Hospitality and Tourism, 18*, 60–74.

Kikuchi, A. and Ryan, C. (2007). Street markets as tourist attractions – Victoria Market, Auckland, New Zealand. *International Journal of Tourism Research, 9*(4), 297–300.

Kühn, J.M. (2015a). The subcultural scene economy of the Berlin techno scene. In P. Guerra and T. Moreira (eds), *Keep It Simple, Make It Fast! An Approach to Underground Music Scenes* (pp. 281–6). Porto: Universidade do Porto.

Kühn, J.M. (2015b). The sources of 'Underground' in the Berlin House/Techno Scene economy. In F. Martínez and P. Runnel (eds), *HOPELESS YOUTH!* (pp. 64–7). Tartu: Estonian National Museum.

Landry, C. (2014). The City 1.0, The City 2.0 & The City 3.0. https://charleslandry.com/blog/the-city-1-0/ (accessed 18 December 2020).

Lash, S.M. and Urry, J. (1994). *Economies of Signs and Space*. London: Sage.

Liu, S. (2020). Cultural tourism policies and digital transition of ancient village heritage conservation in China. In V. Katsoni and T. Spyriadis (eds), *Cultural and Tourism Innovation in the Digital Era* (pp. 37–51). Cham: Springer.

Lourens, M. (2007). Route tourism: a roadmap for successful destinations and local economic development. *Development Southern Africa, 24*(3), 475–90.

Ludwig, C., Wang, Y., and Walton, L. (2020). *The Heritage Turn in China: The Reinvention, Dissemination and Consumption of Heritage*. Amsterdam: Amsterdam University Press.

MacCannell, D. (1976). *The Tourist: A New Theory of the Leisure Class*. Davis, CA: University of California Press.

Maitland, R. (2007). Tourists, the creative class and distinctive areas in major cities: the roles of visitors and residents in developing new tourism areas. In G. Richards and J. Wilson (eds), *Tourism, Creativity and Development* (pp. 95–108). London: Routledge.

Maitland, R. (2017). Cool suburbs: a strategy for sustainable tourism? In S.L. Slocum and C. Kline (eds), *Linking Urban and Rural Tourism: Strategies in Sustainability* (pp. 67–81). Wallingford: CABI.

Manning, J. (2019). The 50 coolest neighbourhoods in the world. *Time Out*, 17 September. https://www.timeout.com/coolest-neighbourhoods-in-the-world (accessed 18 December 2020).

Markwick, M. (2018). Valletta ECoC 2018 and cultural tourism development, *Journal of Tourism and Cultural Change, 16*(3), 286–308.

Marques, L. and Richards, G. (2014). *Creative Districts Around the World*. http://creativedistricts.imem.nl/ (accessed 18 December 2020).

Marshall, A. (1919). *Industry and Trade*. London: Macmillan.

Mayor of London (2017). *Take a Closer Look: Cultural Tourism in London*. London: Mayor of London.

McCarthy, J. and Wang, Y. (2016). Culture, creativity and commerce: trajectories and tensions in the case of Beijing's 798 Art Zone. *International Planning Studies, 21*(1), 1–15.

McHone, W.W. and Rungeling, B. (1999). Special cultural events: do they attract leisure tourists. *International Journal of Hospitality Management, 18*(2), 215–19.

McKercher, B., Ho, P.S., and Du Cros, H. (2004). Attributes of popular cultural attractions in Hong Kong. *Annals of Tourism Research, 31*(2), 393–407.

Michelson, A. and Paadam, K. (2016). Destination branding and reconstructing symbolic capital of urban heritage: a spatially informed observational analysis in medieval towns. *Journal of Destination Marketing & Management, 5*(2), 141–53.

Minton, A. (2006). *The Privatisation of Public Space*. London: RICS.

Munsters, W. (1994). *Cultuurtoerisme*. Leuven: Garant.

Munsters, W. (2011). Malta's candidature for the title of European Capital of Culture 2018: the cultural tourism perspective. https://surfsharekit.nl/publiek/zuyd/bfc1e641 -877c-4996-848c-6a9d0ec34990 (accessed 18 December 2020).

Novy, J. and Colomb, C. (2013). Struggling for the right to the (creative) city in Berlin and Hamburg: new urban social movements, new 'spaces of hope'? *International Journal of Urban and Regional Research, 37*(5), 1816–38.

O'Connor, J. and Gu, X. (2014). Creative industry clusters in Shanghai: a success story? *International Journal of Cultural Policy, 20*(1), 1–20.

OECD (2009). *The Impact of Culture on Tourism*. Paris: OECD.

OECD (2014). *Tourism and the Creative Economy*. Paris: OECD.

Oliveira, N. (2019). A Lisboa cosmopolita e o fascínio da diversidade. *Cidades. Comunidades e Territórios, 39*, 115–28.

Ooi, C.S. (2002). *Cultural Tourism and Tourism Cultures: The Business of Mediating Experiences in Copenhagen and Singapore*. Copenhagen: Copenhagen Business School Press.

Packer, J. and Ballantyne, R. (2016). Conceptualizing the visitor experience: a review of literature and development of a multifaceted model. *Visitor Studies, 19*(2), 128–43.

Palomares Alarcón, S. (2017). Los mercados como ejes vertebradores de la ciudad de Florencia desde el siglo XIX. In L.M. Alves, P. Alves, and F. García García (eds), *Libro de Actas V Congresso Internacional Cidades Criativas* (pp. 723–35). Lisbon: CITCEM.

Pappalepore, I. (2010). Tourism and the development of 'creative' urban areas: evidence from four non-central areas in London. PhD thesis, University of Westminster.

Pasquinelli, C. (2015). Urban tourism(s): is there a case for a paradigm shift? *Cities Research Unit Working Papers* no. 14, L'Aquila, Gran Sasso Science Institute.

Patuelli, R., Mussoni, M., and Candela, G. (2013). The effects of World Heritage Sites on domestic tourism: a spatial interaction model for Italy. *Journal of Geographical Systems, 15*(3), 369–402.

Philips, D. (2011). Mapping literary Britain: tourist guides to literary landscapes 1951–2007. *Tourist Studies, 11*(1), 21–35.

Picaud, M. (2019). Putting Paris and Berlin on show: nightlife in the struggles to define cities' international position. In G. Stahl and G. Bottà (eds), *Nocturnes: Popular Music and the Night* (pp. 35–48). Cham: Palgrave Macmillan.

Plaza, B. (2000). Evaluating the influence of a large cultural artifact in the attraction of tourism. The Guggenheim Museum Bilbao case. *Urban Affairs Review, 36*, 264–74.

Plaza, B. and Haarich, S.N. (2015). The Guggenheim Museum Bilbao: between regional embeddedness and global networking. *European Planning Studies, 23*(8), 1456–75.

Puczkó, L. and Ratz, T. (2007). Trailing Goethe, Humbert, and Ulysses: cultural routes in tourism. In G. Richards (ed.), *Cultural Tourism: Global and Local Perspectives* (pp. 131–48). New York: Haworth.

Rapp, T. (2009). *Lost and Sound: Berlin, Techno, und der Easyjetset.* Frankfurt am Main: Suhrkamp.

Richards, G. (1996). Production and consumption of European cultural tourism. *Annals of Tourism Research, 23*(2), 261–83.

Richards, G. (2000). World culture and heritage and tourism. *Tourism Recreation Research, 25*(1), 9–18.

Richards, G. (2001). *Cultural Attractions and European Tourism.* Wallingford: CABI.

Richards, G. (2011). Creativity and tourism: the state of the art. *Annals of Tourism Research, 38*(4), 1225–53.

Richards, G. (2014a). Cultural Tourism 3.0. The future of urban tourism in Europe? In R. Garibaldi (ed.), *Il turismo culturale europeo. Città ri-visitate. Nuove idee e forme del turismo culturale* (pp. 25–38). Milan: FrancoAngeli.

Richards, G. (2014b). Tourism and creativity in the city. *Current Issues in Tourism, 17*, 119–44.

Richards, G. (2017). Tourists in their own city – considering the growth of a phenomenon. *Tourism Today, 16*, 8–16.

Richards, G. (2020a). The value of event networks and platforms: evidence from a multi-annual cultural programme. *Event Management.* https://doi.org/10.3727/152599520X15894679115501.

Richards, G. (2020b). Cities, events and the eventful city. In S.J. Page and J. Connell (eds), *The Routledge Handbook of Events* (pp. 273–86). London: Routledge.

Richards, G. and Duif, L. (2019). *Small Cities with Big Dreams: Creative Placemaking and Branding Strategies.* New York: Routledge.

Richards, G. and Marques, L. (2018). *Creating Synergies between Cultural Policy and Tourism for Permanent and Temporary Citizens*. Barcelona: UCLG/ICUB.

Richards, G. and Palmer, R. (2010). *Eventful Cities: Cultural Management and Urban Revitalisation*. London: Routledge.

Richards, G. and Tomor, Z. (2012). *Leisure Clusters: From Theory to Practice*. Tilburg: Tilburg University. https://www.academia.edu/1235396/Leisure_Clusters _From_theory_to_practice (accessed 18 December 2020).

Richards, G., Hitters, E., and Fernandes, C. (2002). *Rotterdam and Porto, Cultural Capitals 2001: Visitor Research*. Arnhem: Atlas.

Ritchie, J.B. and Zins, M. (1978). Culture as determinant of the attractiveness of a tourism region. *Annals of Tourism Research, 5*(2), 252–67.

Rodríguez, L., Vecslir, L., Rubio Vaca, J.F., and Molina Restrepo, J.J. (2020). De barrios tradicionales a nuevos productos turísticos. Dinámicas urbanas recientes en Palermo Viejo (Buenos Aires) y Usaquén (Bogotá). *Anales de Investigación en Arquitectura, 10*(1), 65–87.

Rothnie, N. (1992). *The Baedeker Blitz: Hitler's Attack on Britain's Historic Cities*. Staines: Ian Allan.

Russo, A.P. and Richards, G. (2016). Introduction. In A.P. Russo and G. Richards (eds), *Reinventing the Local in Tourism* (pp. 1–12). Bristol: Channel View.

Sacco, P.L. (2011). Culture 3.0: a new perspective for the EU 2014–2020 structural funds programming. Paper produced for the OMC Working Group on Cultural and Creative Industries. http://www.gepac.gov.pt/gepac-dsepac/estudos-e -estatisticas/estudos/0408-culture-30-a-new-perspective-for-the-eu-2014-2020-pdf .aspx (accessed 18 December 2020).

Sacco, P.L. and Blessi, G.T. (2007). European culture capitals and local development strategies: comparing the Genoa 2004 and Lille 2004 cases. *Homo oeconomicus, 24*(1), 111–41.

Šebová, M., Peter Džupka, O.H., and Urbancíková, N. (2014). Promoting and financing cultural tourism in Europe through European capitals of culture: a case study of Košice, European capital of culture 2013. *Amfiteatru Economic Journal, 16*(36), 655–71.

Shaw, S.J. (2007). Ethnic quarters in the cosmopolitan-creative city. In G. Richards and J. Wilson (eds), *Tourism, Creativity and Development* (pp. 189–200). London: Routledge.

Simons, I. (2020). Changing identities through collective performance at events: the case of the Redhead Days. *Leisure Studies*, 1–17.

Skinner, J. and Jolliffe, L. (2017). *Murals and Tourism: Heritage, Politics and Identity*. London: Routledge.

Smith, M.K. (2015). *Issues in Cultural Tourism Studies* (3rd edn). London: Routledge.

Soares Neves, P. and de Freitas Simões, D.V. (2015). Methodologies for research. *Street Art & Urban Creativity Scientific Journal, 1*(1), 4.

Sontag, S. (2001). *On Photography*. London: Macmillan.

Steiner, L. and Frey, B.S. (2012). Correcting the imbalance of the World Heritage List: did the UNESCO strategy work? *Journal of International Organizations Studies, 3*(1), 25–40.

Sun, Y. (2014). Business composition change in the 798 Art District of Beijing, and reasons behind it. PhD thesis, Columbia University.

Tan, S.K., Luh, D.B., and Kung, S.F. (2014). A taxonomy of creative tourists in creative tourism. *Tourism Management, 42*, 248–59.

Throsby, D. (2001). *Economics and Culture*. Cambridge: Cambridge University Press.

Throsby, D. (2008). The concentric circles model of the cultural industries. *Cultural Trends*, *17*(3), 147–64.

Timothy, D.J. (2018). Cultural routes: tourist destinations and tools for development. In D.H. Olsen and A. Trono (eds), *Religious Pilgrimage Routes and Trails: Sustainable Development and Management* (pp. 27–37). Wallingford: CABI.

Truman, D.R. (2010). *Mods, Minis, and Madmen: A True Tale of Swinging London Culture in the 1960s*. Bloomington: iUniverse.

Turgeon, L. (2014). The politics and the practices of intangible cultural heritage. *Ethnologies*, *36*(1–2), 5–25.

UNESCO (1972). *Convention Concerning the Protection of the World Cultural and Natural Heritage* adopted by the General Conference at its seventeenth session in Paris, 16 November. Paris: UNESCO.

UNESCO (1994). *Global Strategy for a Representative, Balanced and Credible World Heritage List*. Paris: UNESCO. https://whc.unesco.org/en/globalstrategy/ (accessed 18 December 2020).

UNESCO (2020). *Museums around the World in the Face of COVID-19*. Paris: UNESCO. https://unesdoc.unesco.org/ark:/48223/pf0000373530 (accessed 18 December 2020).

UNWTO (2018). *Report on Tourism and Culture Synergies*. Madrid: UNWTO.

Van der Duim, R. (2007). Tourismscapes: an actor-network perspective. *Annals of Tourism Research*, *34*(4), 961–76.

Vanolo, A. (2008). The image of the creative city: some reflections on urban branding in Turin. *Cities*, *25*(6), 370–82.

Visit Berlin (2017). Number of international visitors to Berlin exceeds five million for the first time. https://about.visitberlin.de/en/press/press-releases/number -international-visitors-berlin-exceeds-five-million-first-time (accessed 18 December 2020).

Wang, X. and Liu, Y. (2019). Operation pilot of Chinese museum night exhibition and its significance. *Advances in Social Science, Education and Humanities Research*, *356*, 975–9.

Warde, A. (2004). Practice and field: revising Bourdieusian concepts. Centre for Research on Innovation & Competition: University of Manchester, Working Paper 65.

Wilkinson, R. (2015). *Lisbon Street Art*. London: Blurb.

Williams, K.R. (2018). Making space, making history: cultural work, heritage and the production of space at Southbank Centre. PhD thesis, City, University of London.

Wirth, R. and Freestone, R. (2003). Tourism, heritage and authenticity: state-assisted cultural commodification in suburban Sydney, Australia. *Perspectivas Urbanas/ Urban Perspectives*, *3*, 1–10.

Wynn, J.R. (2016). *Music/City: American Festivals and Placemaking in Austin, Nashville, and Newport*. Chicago, IL: University of Chicago Press.

Xue, C.Q., Sun, C., and Zhang, L. (2020). Producing cultural space in the Chinese cities: a case study of grand theaters in Shanghai. *Journal of Architecture and Urbanism*, *44*(1), 32–43.

Yang, C.H., Lin, H.L., and Han, C.C. (2010). Analysis of international tourist arrivals in China: the role of World Heritage Sites. *Tourism Management*, *31*(6), 827–37.

Young, A. (2013). *Street Art, Public City: Law, Crime and the Urban Imagination*. London: Routledge.

Yuan Yuan, V. (2020). *The Economic Logic of Chinese Cultural-Creative Industries Parks – Shenzhen and Guangzhou*. London: Palgrave Macmillan.

Zeppel, H. (2002). Cultural tourism at the Cowichan native village, British Columbia. *Journal of Travel Research*, *41*(1), 92–100.

Zhou, L., Tang, J., and Zou, R. (2019). Creative tourism, social capital, and the transformation of urban villages. *Travel and Tourism Research Association: Advancing Tourism Research Globally*, 39. https://scholarworks.umass.edu/ttra/2019/research _papers/39 (accessed 18 December 2020).

Zukin, S. (2010). *Naked City: The Death and Life of Authentic Urban Places*. Oxford: Oxford University Press.

4. The consequences of cultural tourism practices

INTRODUCTION

Every practice has certain consequences for the actor and/or context which can be intended and/or unintended (Giddens, 1979, 1984). Intended consequences are expectations or purposes of actors about their actions, such as the happiness stimulated by a successful holiday, learning new things or group cohesion (Bargeman and Richards, 2020). The unintended consequences of tourism practices may include environmental damage, commodification of culture or increasing hostility to tourists among residents.

Cultural tourism has many consequences – personal, experiential, social, cultural and economic, for example. Even within a single journey, many different consequences may emerge for the tourist, for the places they visit, for the local community or for those who manage tourist destinations. Cultural tourism practices are extremely varied in terms of participants and their motivations, the places and events they visit and the experiences that are co-created together with others in the destination. The range of consequences or effects is therefore also varied, from positive effects on cultural development, strengthening of local traditions and identity and more appreciation for local culture, to negative effects such as environmental damage or overcrowding (Csapo, 2012).

Analysing the cultural consequences of tourism is challenging, however, because of the complexity of culture itself, and the fact that cultural change is a long-term process. Much research on the consequences of cultural tourism relates to impacts – the immediate consequence of cultural tourism experiences or encounters, such as expenditure by cultural tourists (for example, Pulido-Fernández, Cárdenas-García and Carrillo-Hidalgo, 2016) or culture shock (Pearce, 1995). But the more important consequences of cultural tourism relate to longer-term effects, such as the degradation of local culture, changing values, changes in the position of women, increased quality of life and well-being.

This chapter argues for a radical shift in how we view the effects of cultural tourism. Most previous studies of cultural tourism consequences have centred on the short-term impacts of cultural tourism, without considering the broader forces that produce these impacts, or discriminating between different types of consequences. Here, we present an argument based on practice theory, for a distinction between the internal and external consequences of cultural tourism practices. Firstly, we describe a model of cultural tourism practices that conceptualizes them as a form of interaction ritual, driven by a search for emotional energy, and then we consider the consequences that these rituals produce.

PRACTICES AND THEIR CONSEQUENCES

Cultural tourism is a social practice, or, more accurately, a series of related social practices. Schatzki (1996, p. 98) refers to 'integrative practices', which are 'the more complex practices found in and constitutive of particular domains of social life'. Examples he cites include farming practices, cooking practices and business practices. Cultural tourism can also be viewed as an integrative practice, and the domain of cultural tourism can be conceptualized as a coordinated entity which requires performance for its existence (Schatzki, 1996).

The doings and sayings of cultural tourism actors are the performances that sustain the practice, including activities in a range of different contexts, such as visiting museums and monuments, taking photos, buying souvenirs, and recounting our experiences to others in person or on social media. Cultural tourism is, like any established practice, a collective and historic achievement, developed over time by a group of practitioners (McNamee, 1994). Originally, the practitioners constituted a small and privileged group following the Grand Tour, but as others assumed elements of the practice, the cultural tourism market expanded. As the practice became more widespread, it also became more widely recognized, and 'cultural tourists' became an identifiable social group. The field has also been structured through institutionalization, with the growth of destinations, specific attractions and facilities, itineraries and intermediaries.

One of the major consequences of the performance of a social practice is the continuation of the practice itself, which requires the production of goods. MacIntyre (1981) recognizes two types of goods generated by social practices. Internal goods are intrinsic qualities specific to the practice – rewards that can only be attained through subordination to, and immersion in, the practice itself. This requires practitioners to acquire competences that facilitate appreciation of the internal qualities of the practice and its demands, rhythms and standards (Banks, 2012). These internal goods are contrasted with the external goods obtained from a practice, such as money or prestige. Whereas internal goods tend to be specific to a practice, external goods can be obtained from many kinds of practices. MacIntyre (1981) links the development of internal goods to the ongoing achievement of standards of excellence, a shared commitment to the practice. The notion of practice therefore relates not to the performance of individual actors, but to the collective commitment to the standards of worth that are internal to the practice. Without this commitment, the practice will wither and die through lack of internal goods. Practices also need to develop institutions that provide external goods, such as economic resources, to maintain themselves.

Bargeman and Richards (2020) proposed a model accounting for the development and maintenance of social practices in terms of their ability to generate internal and external goods for groups of practitioners, largely based on the ideas of Randall Collins (2004). Collins (2004) argues that much social behaviour is organized around Interaction Ritual Chains (IRCs), which Collins sees as 'a theory of individuals' motivation based on where they are located at any moment in time ... in their market of possible social relationships' (p. xiv). Participation in IRCs generates what Collins calls 'Emotional Energy', or 'the master motive across all institutional arenas'. People are attracted to particular rituals or practices because of the Emotional Energy (EE) they can gain from them. Collins identifies some key features of such practices:

1. Two or more people in co-presence: bodily assembled and, through neurological feedback loops, able to charge a situation with excitement and significance.
2. A boundary that demarcates insiders from outsiders, giving participants a privileged sense of inclusiveness.
3. All parties to the encounter have a common focus of attention.
4. Participants share 'a common mood or emotional experience'.

When the interaction ritual is performed successfully, this produces a number of outcomes:

1. Individuals feel solidarity with one another; they imagine themselves to be members of a common undertaking.
2. They are infused with EE, a feeling of exhilaration, achievement and enthusiasm which induces action.
3. Interaction ritual membership generates collective symbols that are defended and reinforced.
4. Violations of these symbols provoke righteous indignation towards, and sanctions against, those guilty of transgression.

From this perspective, cultural tourism represents a set of social practices, or a ritual form of behaviour, which also conforms to the conditions outlined by Collins (2004). It has barriers to outsiders (based on ideas about legitimate forms of tourist behaviour), a shared focus of attention on cultural objects and manifestations, a shared mood or experience (such as a desire to learn) and a high degree of physical co-presence (most obvious at overcrowded must-see attractions).

The interaction ritual of cultural tourism also produces a series of outcomes, or consequences. Solidarity is produced by collective consumption, giving people a sense of engaging in the continuity of culture. Emotional energy is generated by the strong affective experience of cultural sites, which leads to repeat visitation and continuance of the practice. The importance of collective symbols of different cultures, such as national identity or symbolic heritage sites, are reconfirmed by tourist visitation. Punishment of transgressions of the ritual is evident in examples such as fines for tourists bathing in the Trevi Fountain in Rome or the jailing of tourists behaving disrespectfully at monuments in Indonesia.

Collins' (2004) model provides a particularly useful means of understanding the dynamics of cultural tourism at a meso level, analysing the factors that stimulate groups of people to consume culture. Bargeman and Richards (2020) argue that this meso-scale perspective should be linked to an understanding of the motivations and behaviour of different actors (micro-level), as well as the contexts that condition the behaviour of actors and the development of specific forms of ritual behaviour (macro-level). This social practice approach to tourism and leisure builds on foundational modes of practice theory. These include the first generation of practice theorists (Giddens, Bourdieu) who analysed the social practice as an isolated phenomenon, and the second generation of practice theorists (for example, Shove, Schatzki, Reckwitz and Spaargaren) who paid more attention to the dynamics and interrelatedness of practices. Bargeman and Richards (2020) argue that while the first generation practice theorists help us deal with the actor-structure divide, and the second generation theorists enable us to distinguish different types of practices and their dynamics, the performance turn in tourism requires a further conceptualization of practices-as-performances in which different actors meet and interact. This is where the work of Collins (2004) is particularly valuable, as he provides a model for analysing group interactions and their consequences, and the interactions and performances that construct experiences, meanings and emotions (Weenink and Spaargaren, 2016). Another important aspect of Collins' work is the idea that individual participants develop IRCs as they move from one practice to another in search of increased levels of EE. This provides a dynamic feedback loop that can explain the development of a 'tourism practice career' among participants (Bargeman and Richards, 2020).

Figure 4.1 illustrates the main principles of the model applied to cultural tourism practices. The centre of the diagram focusses on the four main elements of Collins' IRC, which combine to generate collective effervescence. Physical co-presence is an important element of Collins' model of IRC because the physical signals given off by people engaged in the ritual cause entrainment. This also happens at cultural tourism sites and events, where the experience of being in the shared presence of others consuming culture can induce hushed reverence (as in the case of a monumental building) or emotional excitement (at a packed music festival). For the collective atmosphere to build, the limits of the experience need to be defined, and as MacCannell (1976) suggests, cultural tourists are filtered and pointed to sites of significance by a series of markers. The markers help to focus attention on specific things worthy of note, such as a historic building or the site of a dramatic event, marking out 'must-see sights'. The specific atmosphere created by these elements of the cultural tourism practice creates a shared mood, which can engender emotional connections between people and the places they visit, stimulate contemplation and generate feelings of pleasure. The combined product of these ritual elements is collective effervescence, which has consequences for both actor and context.

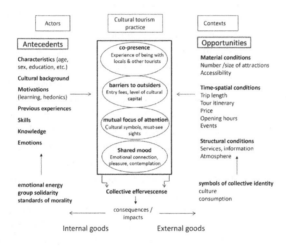

Source: Developed after Bargeman and Richards (2020).

Figure 4.1   A model of ritual behaviour in cultural tourism

Figure 4.1 shows two feedback loops: one that circles through emotional energy to feed the antecedents of the practice with internal goods, and another that provides opportunities essential to support the collective practice through external goods, feeding collective identity and securing resources. For the individual actor, the generation of EE helps to stimulate emotions, pleasure, knowledge and skills, as suggested by Scitovsky (1976), leading to a search for new experiences. These can be gained through further engagement with the cultural tourism practice, leading to the linkage of interaction rituals into chains, as suggested by Collins (2004). The consequences of the practice for the context include a strengthening of symbols of collective identity and the cultural ecosystem as a whole, stimulating the provision of cultural tourism resources and the development of new institutions and contexts that support the continuation of the practice.

In the development of the context, the standards of morality provide a filter of what to present to cultural tourists, and how it should be presented – the types of attractions, events and experiences that will be encountered in the destination. This selection process raises issues of power: which elements of culture and creativity should be highlighted as appropriate for tourism consumption?

In the past, studies of ritual tended to emphasize continuity and embeddedness, studying rituals in a single, unchanging context. An important contribution of Collins (2004) was to develop the idea of ritual chains, through which the individual can seek renewed EE, not only through repetition of the same ritual, but by moving from one ritual to another. What is important is not the ritual per se, but the outcomes of the ritual. This produces a dynamism, which is particularly strong in the case of tourism: the actors involved in the ritual, particularly the tourists, are constantly changing, participating in cultural tourism rituals in new contexts, in search of new sources of EE. The producers, as we saw in Chapter 2, are also changing: searching for new ways of delivering EE by looking for new concepts, or copying ideas they have encountered elsewhere. In our model, therefore, EE becomes the driver of a search for and the development of new cultural tourism experiences.

This provides an interesting new dimension to the study of skilled consumption (see Chapter 2). Scitovsky (1976) sees the search for novelty and excitement as the main driver for consumption, and this can stimulate a search for new experiences, constantly seeking out new ways of developing consumption skills. However, EE and skill development can also be achieved by transferring the same cultural tourism practice to new locations. This may be an important explanation for the growing popularity of city trips, for example. As people engage more with urban cultural tourism, they learn to 'read' cities better and to discover and appreciate new aspects of urban culture (Wolfram and Burnill-Maier, 2013), generating higher consumption skills and levels of EE. As Scitovsky (1976) observes, cities represent rich storehouses of past novelty accumulated over time. Engaging in the cultural tourism ritual provides the consumption skills to access the stock of past novelty embedded in cultural heritage. Producers also seek to enhance this stimulation by developing new means to access past novelty, for example through new technologies (see Chapter 6).

Scitovsky's (1976) approach to skilled consumption (which can also be applied to skilled production) is largely viewed through the lens of the individual, which may seem at odds with the collective approach of Collins. However, as McNamee (1994) emphasizes, the history of the practice is also important. We may travel as individuals, but we are inspired by the cultural tourists that have gone before us, their travels described in travel books, novels and travel blogs. The Grand Tour is not just a historical artefact, but a model of 'doing tourism' that also helps to inspire many contemporary travellers. Over the centuries, new models have also emerged. Cultural travellers not only follow in the footsteps of Odysseus or Homer, or the Romantics, but also Bruce Chatwin, Nicolas Bouvier, Freya Stark and Anthony Bourdain. Their ways of travelling to encounter culture are transmitted by countless travel guides, and the blogs and websites of travel influencers (for example, www.experimentaltraveler.com, inspired by Chatwin). These highlight important aspects of the cultural tourism practice individual travellers can follow to maintain the collective ethos of cultural tourism. An IRC can therefore also be an individual activity, suffused by the communion of historical and collective practice, or the EE facilitated by virtual co-presence.

The focus on EE in practices also places emotions more centrally in the study of cultural tourism. This parallels the emotional turn, and increased attention for affect in the social sciences generally and in tourism research (for example, Buda, d'Hauteserre and Johnston, 2014). This also generates different research questions – how do cultural attractions make people feel, about the places they visit, about the local community, about themselves? The model also provides a potential new view of the behavioural economics of cultural tourism. If we replace economic utility with emotional energy as the driving force for decision-making, a new perspective on cultural tourism behaviour emerges, centred on the social group rather than just the individual. Arguably, this model can be applied to a wide range of different practices, such as the street art practice described in Chapter 3 (Figure 4.2).

Our new model of the cultural tourism ritual is also a tool for rethinking the consequences of cultural tourism practices and shifting from an impact to an effect focus. In the remainder of this chapter, we consider some of the many cultural, economic and social consequences of cultural tourism practices, concentrating on how these are generated and shaped by both the actors and the contexts of practices.

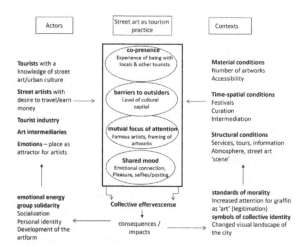

Figure 4.2   Street art as cultural tourism ritual

CULTURAL EFFECTS OF CULTURAL TOURISM PRACTICES

The cultural tourism practice has effects on culture both in terms of individual actors, because it co-creates cultural experiences, and the context, because it affects the cultural ecology of the destination. In many previous studies, the individual experience of culture has been treated as independent of the consumption and production context. However, recent research has underlined the fact that the cultural tourism experience will vary significantly according to the setting. The visitor experience is an outcome of the background and previous experiences of the visitor, as well as the context provided by the cultural site producer or manager.

Zatori, Smith and Puczkó (2018) measured the impact of service providers on tourist experiences in the case of guided sightseeing tours in Budapest, and found four experience dimensions; emotional, mental, flow-like and social experience-involvement. Levels of interaction influenced levels of experience-involvement the most, with higher quality experiences linked to tourists having more control over their own experiences. An interactive experience environment and customizable service can thus lead to deeper on-site experiences (greater experience-involvement), which increases perceived authenticity and memorability of the experience. As Packer and Ballantyne (2016) suggest, experiences are influenced by visitor background and previous experience, as well as the setting provided by the producer.

Richards, King and Yeung (2020) extended these findings by studying the experiences of cultural tourists in Hong Kong visiting attractions, events and tours. Utilizing an experience scale based on the work of de Geus, Richards and Toepoel (2016) originally applied to events, they also found four dimensions of experience: cognitive, conative, affective and novelty. The balance of these different dimensions varied according to the profile and cultural background of visitors and the context provided by the cultural setting. Overall experience was most strongly related to the conative experience dimension, followed by affective, cognitive, and finally novelty experiences. This supports the contention of Zatori et al. (2018) that involvement is important in the cultural tourism experience, but challenges the assumption that learning is the most important determinant of cultural tourism experience (Richards, 1996). The importance of involvement was also confirmed by the highest overall experience scores being generated by events, followed by tours and attractions. This suggests a continuum from more active to more passive types of experiences. In line with the shift towards postmodern ordering of cultural sights, the strongest experiences were generated by smaller and more intimate attractions rather than major, iconic sites. Visitors who had been to a number of different sights during their stay also had stronger experience reactions than visitors to fewer sights. This suggests the development of a 'visitor destination journey', in which the combination of different experiences influences satisfaction and behavioural intentions. Positive consequences of the cultural experience had significant impacts on behavioural outcomes, as interaction ritual theory suggests. Stronger experiences stimulated higher levels of satisfaction, intention to return and intention to recommend. These behavioural outcomes were most strongly correlated with the conative dimension of experience, again underlining the importance of engaging experiences.

In Italy, Conti, Forlani and Pencarelli (2020) found that the city of Urbino provided experiences with an emotional dimension linked to beauty, the historic landscape, and to aesthetics in general. Visitors appreciated the art, history and culture embodied in the Ducal Palace and enjoyed the general atmosphere, the architecture of the city and the surrounding landscape. Conti et al. argue that the aesthetics dimension of experience dominated, irrespective of visitor characteristics. This is consistent with 'a modern vision of tourism, in which the tourist takes a rich and multidimensional approach. S/he is not relegated to being a flodern who simply walks and observes the city, but acts more like a chorister who experiences the journey deeply and feels and identifies with the local community' (p. 417).

Richards and van der Ark (2013) found that holiday type and attraction setting had a strong influence on the type of culture consumed by tourists. Using multiple correspondence analysis (MCA) they mapped the social space of cultural tourism in terms of holiday type and attraction type. Using data from the ATLAS Cultural Tourism Research Project (Richards, 2010), they found a two-dimensional MCA solution, with a horizontal static to dynamic axis (ranging from monuments and museums to performances and events) and a vertical axis ranging from low-brow to high-brow culture settings. The data show that as age, income and education levels increase, the general cultural consumption pattern becomes more static and more high-brow, suggesting the development of a cultural tourism 'travel career' being built up over time, with more 'classic' forms of culture being consumed in later life. This also seems to support the idea that participants shift between IRCs in search of different sources of EE. These analyses indicate a complex pattern of experiences influenced by the background of the participants and the context in which consumption occurs.

As du Cros and Jolliffe (2011) show in the case of Macau, art experiences in cities consist of complex bundles of practice elements – artists, galleries, tours, events, cultural intermediaries, tour companies, etc. Art events are in constant flux, relying on ad hoc groupings of galleries and artists for their organization and management while seeking new ways to survive financially. This complexity makes it difficult to analyse the emerging practices, but du Cros and Joliffe argue that this complexity is a necessary part of the creativity that distinguishes art events from institutionally planned events. In Macau, it seems a critical mass of galleries and/or studios is needed to support a significant bundle of events. In other words, cultural tourism practices (and local arts consumption practices) need to be supported by an ecology, or system, of culture (internal goods), and the cultural system needs the external goods provided by tourism to prosper.

The search for external goods means cultural tourism may be used for audience development in places which have small local audiences and need to expand their geographic catchment by attracting tourists. Cultural tourism development thus becomes a policy of supporting the cultural sector and maintaining cultural facilities (Richards and Marques, 2018). This logic seems to enjoy widespread support from the citizens of Barcelona, despite the continuing debate about the tourism model of the city. The option of promoting cultural tourism was consistently supported by over 90 per cent of residents between 2005 and 2014, and levels of support rose slightly over this period. Over three-quarters of residents also agreed that tourism contributed to maintaining cultural institutions in the city, and that the presence of tourists was compatible with the cultural identity of Barcelona (Ajuntament de Barcelona, 2017).

There is also increasing attention being paid to the effects of tourism on informal arts and crafts. In Portugal, Bakas, Duxbury and Vinagre de Castro (2019) found that the development of creative tourism in rural areas depended on the functioning of the cultural system, with artisan entrepreneur–mediators acting as networking agents who link artisans and tourists. These mediators are not always local people, but they become embedded in the place through their interest in art and culture. Jenkins and Romanos (2014) analysed the relationship between tourism and the economic and artistic well-being of artists in Bali. They interviewed artists, gallery owners, tourist guides, artist cooperatives and local government officials in Ubud, and concluded that arts-related tourist experiences decreased economic uncertainty for artists by encouraging longer stays and making the destination artistically unique. 'Slow' and purposeful arts tourism seems to offer the greatest artistic and economic benefits to local artists, and Jenkins and Romanos (2014) suggest that instead of trying to recapture or preserve the past, artists should adopt future-orientated, hybrid production models. This arguably will appeal particularly to culturally motivated visitors who want to experience art and interact with local communities.

These discussions highlight the question of what type of outputs should be generated by cultural tourism practices, and who should benefit from these outputs. In many cases, discussions around the consequences of cultural tourism revolve around the 'authenticity' that is created.

AUTHENTICITY

Authenticity is a problematic concept, because it can be interpreted in many ways. Unless researchers specify what they mean by 'authenticity', the concept is essentially meaningless. But the idea that cultural tourists seek authentic cultural experiences, and are constantly denied it by the staging of experiences, is widespread in the literature (Schouten, 2007). For example, Re (2018) argues that 'The authentic and genuine values of a heritage may in fact be compromised by the process of making it more amenable to the tastes of consumers.' Such ideas often hinge on an objective concept of authenticity – that something can be judged to be authentic because of its historical context, or because of validation by some authority or expert (Munsters and Melkert, 2010). But as the museum has declined as an authoritative arbiter of meaning, and the position of the expert has been undermined by the multiple voices of postmodernity, so has the objective view of authenticity. Gkoumas and D'Orazio (2019) argue that etic notions of objectivism and constructivism tend to present a relatively uncomplicated view of authenticity. In contrast, they advocate an interpretive, etic approach to provide an existential view of authenticity. The challenge to the objective approach to authenticity has grown to such an extent that Munsters and Melkert (2010) presented this view as 'thinking the unthinkable'.

Actors vary in their needs for authenticity, as Erik Cohen (1979, 1988) has long argued. Even museum curators differ in terms of their concepts of authenticity, as Chhabra (2008) found in his research on US museums. He out-

lined a continuum of positions on authenticity from pure essentialism through
negotiation (essentialism/constructivism) as a middle position, and pure
constructivism at the other extreme. He found that museum staff's approach
to authenticity reflected their context, in terms of stakeholders, power positions and funding sources. Curators at institutions with members as important
stakeholders tended to internalize the dichotomy between essentialism and
constructivism, with their own essentialist views tempered by the need to
pursue a postmodern approach favoured by members. Such negotiations about
the nature of authenticity can, according to Chhabra (2008), foster 'hybrid
authenticity'. Munsters (2001) also identifies a 'cultural tourism field of
tension' developing between cultural and commercial objectives in museums
in the Netherlands. European museums are often less responsive to publics
(including tourists) than their North American counterparts, because of the
large element of public funding many European institutions enjoy. Instead,
they need to respond more to public policy measures, because museum
funding is often dependent on specific indicators, such as increasing audience
diversity (Sandell, 2003).

Over time, notions of authenticity have been placed in a more relational
and constructivist context (Therkelsen, Jensen and Lange, 2019). In a specific
place, more emphasis falls on the affective dimension of experience. The fight
to define something as authentic is part of the struggle over space and identity.
Place myths are linked to subjective, affective experiences and are increasingly
important to the marketing of cultural destinations. Therkelsen et al. (2019)
analyse this link in the case of a fire-ravaged historic hotel on the Danish coast,
the ruins of which became an important signifier of the authenticity of the new
hotel rising from the ashes. In cities this can involve the search for 'authentic'
urban life, which Zukin (2010) links to small, family-owned businesses and
restaurants, non-chain boutiques and independent art galleries, which are being
driven out of the city.

Russo and Richards (2016) link to Zukin's argument in their conception
of the 'local' as assemblage of elements that confers authenticity, which is
being constantly performed as a ritual by a shifting set of actors. They see the
local as the 'new touchstone of authenticity': in many settings more important
than concepts such as originality or age. In consuming the local, tourists are
willing to overlook apparent incongruities in the origin and location of cultural
elements, thanks to the patina of authenticity derived from the local setting.
The fetish of the local has also shifted the focus of cultural tourism consumption from authentic places to authentic people. Tour guides no longer base
their claims to authority solely on the age or importance of the phenomena
being displayed, but also on their own relationship to them. As we saw in the
examples of street art guides in Chapter 3, knowing the artists and the 'scene'
confers an air of authenticity. This relationality also directly impacts tourist

experiences, as in Macau, where Suntikul and Jachna (2016) found that visitors who had interacted with local people had a higher intention to return.

The authenticity generated by cultural tourism practices is a malleable, negotiated concept. The following section considers the consequences of this negotiation in the practice of flamenco tourism.

Flamenco Tourism and the Production of Authenticity

Different forms of dance, because of their popularity as tourist entertainment and their scope for adaptation and interpretation, have been analysed as objects of cultural tourism. Dances which are seen as emblematic of certain places, or the basis of place myths, are particularly prominent. Flamenco in Spain has been widely researched as a spectacle offered to tourists and as a basis for cultural and, more recently, creative tourism.

Once claimed by Franco as a national symbol and tourist attraction (Thimm, 2014), in democratic Spain it has become much more contested, with regions trying to develop their own cultural images. Millán Vázquez de la Torre, Millán Lara and Arjona-Fuentes (2019, p. 3) analyse the position of flamenco in the autonomous community of Andalucía, where it originated. The debate on the authenticity of flamenco and other dance performances becomes more complex in the context of tourism. As 'idiosyncratic historical, religious, and social elements of the culture are arcane to foreigners', they argue, 'Tourists will, therefore, hardly be able to feel emotions when partaking something for which they are not prepared. This leads to suspicion as to the product's authenticity, and to what degree the performance is adulterated and geared toward tourism.'

Millán Vázquez de la Torre et al. (2019) trace the development of flamenco from its roots as a popular artform to national symbol and designation as Intangible World Heritage. Flamenco is important to Andalucía culturally and economically, with 625,000 flamenco tourists spending €543 million in the region in 2004. Perhaps for this reason *Flamenco in Andalusia* was institutionalized in the region's statutes, which claim 'the exclusive competence in the field of knowledge, conservation, research, instruction, promotion and diffusion of flamenco as a singular element of the Andalusian cultural heritage'. The claiming and framing role of the public authority was extended when flamenco was recognized as Intangible World Heritage in 2010. But there is debate regarding the authenticity of the flamenco venues offered to tourists, and the possible 'adulteration' of the artform for their needs.

Matteucci (2014) explores cultural tourists' experiences of flamenco in the city of Seville. He found that tourists use flamenco to differentiate themselves from other social groups, and through creative practices they seek to increase their self-esteem and to use their bodies for self-expression and self-exploration. But as Aoyama (2009) argues in her analysis of the geography of flamenco tourism in Seville, cultural tourists wishing to penetrate the cultural roots of flamenco must also explore the city. Flamenco performances for mass tourists are staged in *tablaos* (locations offering shows, often combined with dinner) close to hotels and restaurants, whereas the flamenco schools are linked to flamenco clubs (*peñas*) further from the centre (see also Thimm, 2014). Creative tourists wishing to learn flamenco must penetrate the everyday fabric of the city to build their skills, while the performances in the city centre generate revenue from mass cultural tourists to keep the artform alive. Aoyama characterizes this as 'multiple and overlapping attempts to develop a site of staged authenticity', and that the survival of flamenco depends on successfully staging this authenticity (2009, p. 100). The overlapping flamenco practices in Seville show that practices do not exist in isolation, but they are connected to other practices in bundles and complexes (Shove, Pantzar and Watson, 2012). The flamenco clusters in Seville represent the physical locations at which these practice bundles become visible, and create local buzz, enabling the city to use flamenco to differentiate itself from other Spanish cities (Thimm, 2014). This is important in view of the competition from other cities, such as Córdoba, which is developing flamenco tourism as part of a wider cultural product (García García, 2020). Unlike Seville, flamenco is not a primary visit motivation for tourists in Córdoba, because of the weaker offer.

Flamenco tourism is a complex bundle of cultural practices integrating a range of different actors, who collaborate to transform flamenco from an artform to a consumable tourism product. These actors derive external goods from tourism and the creative industries linked to flamenco, but supporting this industry also requires the development of an image emotionally linked to flamenco attributes such as passion, eroticism and idiosyncrasy, which are supported by the internal goods of the practice. Supporting cultural tourism therefore requires a keen understanding of the entire creative ecology of flamenco in Seville and Andalusia (Thimm, 2014).

ECONOMIC CONSEQUENCES

The economic impacts of cultural tourism are important for policy makers and producers. Much early research interest was devoted to identifying the economic impacts of tourism for cultural institutions, such as museums and heritage sites (Silberberg, 1995). In their review, Gratton and Richards (1996) pointed to falling national cultural budgets in Europe stimulating cultural institutions to pay more attention to tourism as a source of revenue.

The increased economic emphasis of cultural tourism became evident in the European Capital of Culture (ECOC) programme. Originally launched by the European Union (EU) to showcase European culture and diversity (Richards,

1996), the aims of cities gradually became more focussed on economic outputs. Glasgow in 1990 was the first ECOC to have explicit economic development goals, including improving the image of the city to attract cultural tourism (Richards and Wilson, 2004). This formula was subsequently emulated by other cities, most notably Antwerp (1993), Lille (2004) and Liverpool (2008).

The increasing combination of cultural and economic development goals created more attention for the 'cultural industries'. Myerscough's (1988) work on the impact of the cultural industries in the UK indicated that tourists were an important source of income, with tourists to art attractions spending an average 50 per cent per day more than day visitors. In Amsterdam, van Puffelen (1987) estimated foreign tourists accounted for 77 per cent of total art tourism spend. In the USA, Tighe (1985) argued that cultural tourists tended to be 'up-scale', drawn from better paid, professional occupations with higher education levels. This high-spending group was the focus of increasing interest from cities and rural regions in developing cultural tourism.

The 1990s, as Bendixen (1997) reported, was a boom period for cultural tourism, seen as important economically because it attracted high-spending tourists. Kneafsey (1994) even dubbed the cultural tourist the 'patron saint of Ireland' in reference to that country's pursuit of culturally motivated visitors. Studies emerged that charted patterns of cultural tourism expenditure, primarily for visitors to cities and attractions. In the Netherlands, Dietvorst (1994, p. 71) reported that 'Interest in the city and in certain cultural manifestations has grown since the early 1980s because cultural tourism has had a significant influence on the development of tourism and recreation as a whole. Better still, culture has become a significant economic factor.'

This was a message that quickly spread, propelled by studies by international organisations, including the UNWTO and UNESCO. Nurse (2001) analysed the impacts of cultural events, including Reggae Sunsplash in Jamaica, Trinidad Carnival and the St Lucia Jazz Festival. These attracted music tourists and generated spend in the low season in the Caribbean. He found that events had a significant impact on the tourism sector in terms of creating a new tourism season, generating new tourism demand, generating significant tourism spend, boosting exports and attracting knowledgeable, upmarket tourists. The Trinidad Carnival and the St Lucia Jazz Festival were both estimated to have generated US$14 million in visitor spending, which in the case of Trinidad accounted for 7 per cent of total annual visitor spend.

In South Africa, Saayman and Saayman (2006) also argued that cultural events can provide economic impacts in the low season. They compared the impacts of three arts festivals in South Africa: Klein Karoo Nasionale Kunstefees, the Grahamstown National Arts Festival and the Aardklop Arts Festival, finding that festival location to a large extent determines the origin of attendees, who have different levels of spending. The context of the location in terms of infrastructure and facilities also helps in attracting a wider audience. Saayman and Saayman suggest that regional governments should focus on developing new events in small towns, since this contributes significantly towards income generation.

Beyond generating income, cultural events also stimulate regeneration. Parlett, Fletcher and Cooper (1995) described the role of cultural tourism as a basis for economic and physical regeneration in Edinburgh where the Old Town Renewal Trust was formed to help harness tourism as a regeneration tool. Law (1992) also charted the growing use of cultural tourism in former industrial cities as a means of stimulating development and expenditure. Cultural attractions were also used as anchors for urban redevelopment, as Page (1993) describes in the case of the National Museum of New Zealand in Wellington.

In Spain, Herrero, Sanz, González and Sanz (1998) examined the cultural economy of the Castilla y León region, and found that between 1970 and 1997 the number of museums more than doubled, while the number of visitors increased almost tenfold. The economic effects of cultural tourism were also analysed in a Brazilian context by Lage and Milone (1995) who argued that growth in cultural tourism could not only grow the economy, but also increase cultural understanding between visitors and residents.

Studies of visitor expenditure gave way to more sophisticated analyses, including data mining and econometric modelling of cultural tourism impacts. Growing interest in the economic consequences of cultural tourism was marked by a special issue of the *Journal of Cultural Economics* on 'The Economics of Cultural Tourism' in 2017. This includes papers analysing the spending habits of cultural tourists in Amsterdam (van Loon and Rouwendal, 2017) and the impact of cultural participation in attracting cultural tourists (Guccio, Lisi, Martorana and Mignosa, 2017). In their introduction to the special issue, Noonan and Rizzo (2017) admit that little theoretical advancement has been made. The editors identify new areas of application, such as drug tourism, language tourism and film festivals, as well as the potential for work in new areas – such as online 'crowdsourcing' and cultural conventions: 'At its heart, the distinction between cultural tourism and tourism generally may be a false distinction … Moving in the direction of developing more distinctly cultural economic theories of tourism presents an important challenge to the field' (Noonan and Rizzo, 2017, p. 104). From a practice perspective, however, this lack of distinction may simply reflect a bundling of cultural tourism practices.

The availability of time-series data now makes it easier to study economic effects of cultural tourism over time. For example, Spain has longitudinal surveys of domestic and international tourists that provide a wealth of data to be mined. Artal-Tur, Briones-Peñalver and Villena-Navarro (2018) show the leading role cultural activities play in attracting long-haul and first-time visitors to Spain. Cisneros-Martínez and Fernández-Morales (2015) also demonstrate the role of cultural tourism in reducing seasonality in Andalucía.

In Italy, Guccio et al. (2017) assessed the impact of the monetary value of cultural heritage on tourism. They found that €1 million worth of cultural heritage generated about 1000 more cultural visitors, which underlines the strong relationship between the regional performance of the tourism sector and cultural visitors. Di Lascio, Giannerini, Scorcu and Candela (2011) also looked at the attractiveness of art exhibitions for tourists in Italy. They found a positive one-year lagged effect of modern art exhibitions on tourism and a positive mild effect of contemporary art exhibitions on tourist flows. They conclude that art exhibitions increase tourist flows if they are soundly embedded in the destination.

Frey (2009) argues that such impact studies only capture a limited range of the economic effects of cultural tourism. He advocates the willingness-to-pay approach, which focusses on the net utility created by a cultural site, capturing its value above and beyond market effects. Visitors are asked how much they would be willing to spend to visit a cultural site, and their answer considers both benefits and costs of a visit. These studies can also extend to residents, enabling negative external effects to be evaluated. In the case of crowded city centre cultural sites, it may also be possible to value 'willingness-to-wait' to see major attractions (Riganti and Nijkamp, 2008). However, Plaza (2010) suggests there may be better options for measuring the impact of iconic museums, since their value far overshadows the willingness of individual visitors to pay, or to wait.

Despite growing interest from economists, much economic research still relates to the short-term impacts of cultural tourism practices, rather than their long-term effects.

SOCIAL CONSEQUENCES

Cultural tourism can arguably increase social cohesion, develop social capital and enhance local pride. There is relatively little empirical work on these issues, however, because they are difficult concepts to measure. In terms of social cohesion, cultural tourism can bring together divided communities around a shared heritage, as Viljoen and Henama (2017) indicate in the case of South Africa. They argue that in the post-Apartheid era, heritage tourism has been a way of strengthening community identity and social cohesion. In Spain, Sanagustín-Fons, Tobar-Pesántez and Ravina-Ripoll (2020) show that the European Holy Grail Route to Valencia generates social cohesion for the communities along the route. The route helps to support social networks and cultural associations, and fosters a sense of local belonging.

Putnam (2000) views social capital as the collective value of the social networks in a community, which can be measured in terms of trust and reciprocity at individual and community levels. He identifies two main elements of social capital: bonding capital, which is based on close, frequent social ties, and bridging social capital, which generates links to other groups. The former can be seen as crucial to generating internal goods, and the latter as a source of external goods. Martínez-Pérez, García-Villaverde and Elche (2016) analysed firms located in World Heritage Cities in Spain, and found that combining bonding and bridging capital through 'ambidextrous knowledge strategies' can help cultural tourism firms to become more innovative. Building social capital is particularly important as the focus of cultural tourism shifts towards creativity and intangible culture (D'Auria, 2009). When the resources involved in cultural tourism are intangible, they tend to rely more on social networks, and the bonding and bridging capital in the local community. In Catalunya, Richards and Wilson (2005) found high levels of social capital among local residents, particularly in terms of cultural association membership. Active involvement in local associations supported participation in cultural events and activities, which are also linked with more positive attitudes towards cultural change and tourism. The research underlines, however, that levels of social capital are not uniform across regions or local communities, and that more attention needs to be paid to the distribution of bonding and bridging capital in understanding the social consequences of cultural tourism.

The context of cultural tourism resources plays an important role in generating local pride, as Davis (2004) shows in the case of ecomuseums in France, Canada and Japan. Ecomuseums curate the material and intangible cultural resources in a specific region, providing a link between environment, culture and place, which can generate high levels of local pride. These facilities are often located in areas where local culture is under threat, such as peripheral rural regions. Because of their place-bound focus, ecomuseums feature elements of cultural heritage that are important to local people. Davis (2004, p. 45) argues this is not 'high culture, but the material culture and intangible heritage that signify the special nature of places, cultural touchstones defined and selected by local people'. In the USA, Besculides, Lee and McCormick (2002) measured the perceptions of cultural tourism of people living along the Los Caminos Antiguos Scenic and Historic byway in Colorado, and found that an increase in local pride was seen as a positive benefit, particularly by Hispanic residents.

MASS CULTURAL TOURISM EFFECTS

Overcrowding is an unintended, but highly visible consequence of a growing cultural tourism practice. Cultural tourism resources are often concentrated in the centre of major cities (Richards, 2001), and this has led to a 'vicious cycle' of cultural tourism (Russo, 2002), in which central sites become ever more popular, leading to declining quality of experience.

Capocchi, Vallone, Pierotti and Amaduzzi (2019) claim that the term 'overtourism' emerged in 2016, but it seems that the Dutch concept of *overtoeristisering* (or overtouristification) was first mentioned by Myriam Jansen-Verbeke in the Belgian city of Brugge (Bruges) in 1990, and specifically linked to cultural tourism by Wil Munsters in 1994. In this period, descriptions of overcrowded heritage sites appeared in other places. For example, in Malta, Boissevain (1996) describes Mdina as an extreme example of the impact of cultural tourism, as a small walled city with a population of only 200 residents, inundated by hundreds of thousands of visitors every year. This highlights an undesirable consequence of the cultural tourism practice, concentrating tourists at 'must see sights' (MacCannell, 1976).

In the digital era, concentration around sites that rank highest on social media produces similar consequences. For example, van der Zee, Bertocchi and Vanneste (2020) analysed TripAdvisor data to identify 'hotspots' of tourism activity in Antwerp. They found that visitors who reviewed one location tended to post several more reviews, often concentrated on locations with many other reviews. These hotspots generally occur in the historic city centre, particularly close to cultural attractions such as the cathedral, the market square and Rubens House. The city centre hotspots were also linked to terms such as 'medieval' and 'baroque' in reviews. Long-haul visitors tended to focus on the 'must-see sights' around the cathedral, whereas residents and domestic tourists reviewed more museums, heritage attractions and the zoo. Slightly different patterns were found for the new cultural cluster around the Museum aan de Stroom (MAS) and the Red Star Line Museum, which are within walking distance of each other on the northern fringe of the city centre. International tourists visit the MAS museum, but they do not stay long in the area. Van der Zee et al. (2020) find there is an 'information cascade' in the city, with social media data focussed on the city centre guiding even more visitors there. This presents a challenge in spreading cultural tourists to new locations. In Barcelona, similar issues have been noted, with major sites accounting for a large proportion of cultural tourism activity (Richards, 2016). The Sagrada Familia is the most visited cultural site in Barcelona, with more than 4.5 million paying visitors in 2019. But there are also a further million plus visitors who walk around the Basilica without entering.

The growth of budget airlines, budget hotels and short break holidays have also strengthened mass urban tourism (Pasquinelli, 2015). This is often focussed on specific cultural attractions and events, particularly in the centre of larger cities, giving rise to increased tourism pressure, physical problems of overcrowding, a reduction in social well-being, the quality of urban space and cultural experience, and a number of economic consequences, such as gentrification, increased prices and loss of local amenity and identity (Kim, Kim and Woo, 2020; Sequera and Nofre, 2018).

Care must be taken not to confuse the effects of gentrification, which is a general process of urban change, and touristification, which is a specific effect of tourism (Ollero, Capellán and Pozo, 2019). Studies are now emerging that attempt to unravel these different effects. As Romão, Kourtit, Neuts and Nijkamp (2018) show, both tourists and residents are attracted to places that have cultural and tourism resources. López-Gay, Cocola-Gant and Russo (2020) also note that in the centre of Barcelona, tourist attractiveness and the attraction of transnational residents are mutually reinforcing processes, resulting in more wealthy, 'footloose' groups gaining control of space relative to less mobile populations. The coincidence of residential and tourist amenity in city centres is often a source of conflict. In the Spanish city of Málaga, for example, 80 per cent of housing in the city centre had listings on Airbnb in 2017 (Sánchez, Urrestarazu and Garcia, 2019). Alemida-García, Cortés-Macías and Balbuena-Vázquez (2019) identified two groups of historic centre residents with opposing attitudes towards tourism. On the one hand, there is a 'tourism-philic' group in the traditional resident population, generally older people who are more concerned with gentrification than the presence of tourists. On the other hand, tourism-phobia is expressed by highly educated liberal professionals, the 'new cultural intermediaries' who live in the historic centre because of its cultural value. They see tourism growth as a negative change that has devalued their cultural amenity. In other words, cultural tourism-phobia is a consequence of different practices of cultural consumption.

PLACE IMAGE EFFECTS

Cultural events, such as the ECOC, have been shown to have significant image impacts in the cultural year itself (Guerreiro, Mendes, Fortuna and Pinto, 2020; Luxemburg and Greater Region, 2008) and other studies indicate there can also be longer-term image effects.

In the case of Rotterdam, Richards and Wilson (2004) found that the ECOC significantly improved the image of Rotterdam as a cultural city, transforming its previous positioning as an industrial port city. The wave of new cultural events staged in the ECOC year of 2001 also helped to boost the image of Rotterdam as a lively and attractive city. Longer-term image effects were strengthened by the establishment of Rotterdam Festivals after the ECOC, which has worked to position Rotterdam as a 'festival city' (Richards, 2017a).

Longer-term monitoring of cultural tourism development was undertaken in the Romanian city of Sibiu, which staged the ECOC in 2007. Sibiu organized many cultural events in 2007, and redeveloped the city centre, renovating many historic buildings in the Old Town area and upgrading cultural attractions such as the Bruckenthal Fine Arts Museum. The aims for the ECOC included raising the international profile of the city and attracting international cultural tourists. The event generated significant tourism impacts, with a 19 per cent growth in arrivals in 2007. Richards and Rotariu (2015) also found that the proportion of cultural tourists was particularly high in 2007, and in subsequent years tourists frequented a wider range of attractions, including the renovated Lower Town area. The perceived visit quality also increased, along with the appreciation of the atmosphere, linked to a significant improvement in cultural events and attractions (Nicula and Chindriş, 2017; Rotariu and Stela, 2017). The event also stimulated long-term growth in cultural tourism demand, which in turn stimulated the development of more accommodation and attractions. Between 2007 and 2015, total tourist arrivals grew by 107 per cent. The proportion of foreign cultural tourists rose from 30 per cent in 2010 to 40 per cent in 2015, which was linked to a steep growth in tourism revenues as well. Perhaps most importantly, Sibiu was put on the map. The improved image of the city was most noticeable in 2007, with widespread media coverage, but there was also a considerable longer-term effect. The rejuvenation of the city continued to be promulgated through the national and international media, and over 90 per cent of tourists and residents agreed that the image of the city had improved. Sibiu was listed among 'Europe's Most Idyllic Places to Live' by *Forbes Magazine* and in 2011 it was the only Romanian city to be awarded three stars in the *Michelin Green Guide*, indicating that it had become a must-see destination (Richards and Rotariu, 2015).

PUBLIC POLICY CONSEQUENCES

One outcome of growing cultural tourism is increased public policy attention for this practice, and most of these policies are designed to increase levels of cultural tourism. When asked by the UNWTO (2018) if their tourism policy included cultural tourism, 90 per cent of countries consulted indicated that it did, and almost 70 per cent saw cultural tourism as a 'very important' element of policy. Cultural tourism policy is usually justified by the importance of this practice both for culture and the economy. For example, Maltese tourism policy indicates that over three-quarters of international tourists undertook at least one cultural visit and that 8 per cent of total tourist expenditure went to the cultural and creative industries, twice the proportion of resident cultural expenditure (UNWTO, 2018). The general needs and priorities of many countries related to tourism and culture were reflected in the cultural tourism policy of Costa Rica, which listed its primary needs as:

1. Developing public policy on cultural tourism;

2. Coordination among state institutions in defining cultural tourism objectives;
3. Developing specific statistics to measure cultural tourism; and
4. Providing budget for the development of cultural tourism. (UNWTO, 2018)

At regional and local level, cultural tourism is also often linked to economic development agendas. For example, the cultural tourism vision for London (Mayor of London, 2017a) begins with the observation that 'cultural tourists spend £7.3 billion a year, generating £3.2 billion for our economy and supporting 80,000 jobs in the capital'. The policy also integrates the tension between must-see sights and 'off the beaten track' forms of cultural tourism:

> London's top 20 attractions account for 90 per cent of visits by tourists, but the success of events and attractions like Secret Cinema, which draws almost 50 per cent of its audience from outside the capital, and the weekend crowds heading to places like Brick Lane and Borough Market, indicates that tourists also have an appetite for more local and niche activities that will provide more 'authentic' cultural experiences.

A major city like London therefore embraces many different facets of cultural tourism policy, which include generating economic impacts, but also animating different parts of the city, supporting cultural diversity through visits to cultural clusters related to ethnic minorities (Diekmann and Smith, 2015) and providing 'authentic' experiences for tourists. One of the challenges that the London policy makes clear is the complexity of networks which the cultural and tourism sectors encompass. Cultural tourism policy covers traditional cultural institutions such as museums, and also intangible heritage and 'everyday culture' (Richards, 2011), which go far beyond the remit of standard cultural tourism policy.

A challenge in coordinating policy across culture and tourism is the fact that they are not equal partners. Not only do they tend to speak different languages, but culture has a more vested social position than tourism. The relationship between tourism and culture is therefore sown with issues of power, as Cousin (2008) indicates. The policy and linguistic gap between tourism and culture creates a space for public sector actors to fill, with a mixture of appeals to identity and market failure. In the case of a small town in France, Cousin argues that 'the symbolic efficacy of cultural tourism is not to be found in the reality of tourist practices, but in the role of identification and legitimation which tourism plays for the local authorities' (p. 193). Actors develop policies for their own ends rather than the benefit of either tourists or locals:

> Cultural tourism policy is imagined to involve attracting tourists for the benefit of local citizens. I argue that both tourists and citizens are quite absent from this equation. Heritage is first and foremost a place for the demonstration of power, from the

power of the ancient Courts to that of the contemporary authorities. (Cousin, 2008, p. 202).

The problem of location is diminished through the creation of new narratives of centrality, which influences the exercise of power:

> tourism policy creates a new territory (the 'pays'), with spatial boundaries that permit the town to be a capital. It also promotes three famous women as heroes laying claim to a special place in the history of France. Names of places, territory and food products are shaped to fit both national and local identification. (Cousin, 2008, p. 202)

Cousin provides two interpretations of these power struggles, sociological and anthropological:

1. The rhetoric of economic development through tourism becomes a pretext for urban, heritage and cultural policies principally directed at an influential elite and to part-time residents coming from the same social group. This may explain the overlapping consumption patterns of many cultural tourists and residents (see Chapter 5).
2. The framing of histories and territories with attractive tourism images aims to increase the symbolic, economic and political value of these spaces. Here, 'cultural tourism discourse has a role of identification and legitimization in this context. The activation of tourism is an activation of desire: the desire of a collectivity to see itself in the best light, by imagining an abstract desire for itself, into which it may dissolve' (Cousin, 2008, p. 207).

These analyses show that cultural tourism policy relates not just to what governments do or say, but also what they don't do or say (Richards, 1995). Because culture is so difficult to define and is in any case contested, this leaves plenty of room for governments to include or exclude particular activities, features or groups in cultural tourism policy, and to shape others to fit broader political agendas.

The use of cultural tourism as a field for wider political debates is also discussed by Vargas (2015) in the Catalunya region of Spain. He argues that cultural tourism 'helped to sharpen the Catalans' zeal in managing and promoting their distinctiveness' (p. 37) from the rest of Spain, becoming a tool for the separatist movement. In addition to the familiar 'Catalonia is not Spain' placards at FC Barcelona football matches, cultural tourism has been deliberately politicized by nationalist actors:

> Modernist architects and modern artists, leaders of the excursionist movement, and also managers of the tourism sector – promulgated the myths, created the folklore

and tradition, and rebuilt the infrastructure that gave weight and substance to assertions of Catalan distinctiveness. (p. 44)

Catalan cultural symbols, such as the building of human castles, or *castells*,
often refer to a medieval past in which Catalunya was an independent state.
This image has been carefully crafted over the years, especially in Barcelona.
The façade of Barcelona Cathedral, which dates from around 1900, is an 'early
appearance of efforts to manufacture tourist experience in Barcelona'. Since
then, the spatial extension of the medieval imagining of Catalunya has grown
through the development of new tourist spaces and events (Richards, 2007).

In Thailand, Singh and Hart (2007) examine the links between globalization and sex work from the perspective of national and international cultural
policies impacting tourism. They argue that many issues lie at the margins of
cultural tourism policy, and in Thailand sex work is one of these: 'a deeply
controversial side of cultural policies and tourism' (p. 156). Taking a cultural
economics perspective, they argue that the valuation of sex work is difficult,
involving mapping economic and human rights issues. The conflation of
cultural tourism and sex tourism is not as strange as it may at first seem: 'The
tourist in Bangkok who transacts for sex may also visit Bangkok's many cultural heritage sites, attend a performance of the Thai dance *Khon*, and go for
a dinner cruise on the Chao Phraya River' (p. 157). By placing the sex industry
in the context of cultural industries and tourism policies, Singh and Hart (2007)
draw attention to 'an industry that dare not speak its name ... which is also
part of "cultural tourism"' (p. 170). Part of the policy discourse on this intersection is precisely the official refusal to name it – a power that itself renders
sex workers powerless. And Singh and Hart (2007) conclude that 'whatever
definition may be used to examine cultural industries, sex work cannot be
excluded' (p. 170), which by implication suggests that cultural tourism also
includes sex tourism.

Singh and Hart's discussion of the boundaries of the cultural and creative
industries also touches on the recent reframing in policy terms of cultural
tourism into creative tourism. As O'Connor (2009) argues, the creative industries label became more politically attractive in the 1990s, as governments
developed instrumental policies related to new and dynamic areas of the
economy unhindered by their associations with the traditional order and 'high
culture'. The avoidance of the word 'culture' by Thatcher's government in the
UK led to the creation of the Department of National Heritage, which coinci-
dentally brought together culture and tourism in a single government department for the first time (Richards, 1995). The creative industries covered many
growing areas of the new economy which were also closer to commercial
businesses rather than publicly funded culture. In this sense, the convergence
of creative industries and tourism policies represents a growth in the economic

justifications for cultural tourism. However, the reframing of cultural tourism policy in terms of creativity has also allowed new arenas for cultural tourism practices to emerge. As we have seen in Chapter 3, experiences related to intangible and contemporary culture, such as creative clusters, cultural theme parks and everyday life, are growing areas of cultural tourism activity.

One of the reasons for the growing emphasis on creativity in cultural tourism is also the shift towards new markets in Asia, Africa and Latin America. As Steiner and Frey (2012) have pointed out, these regions have less supply of major heritage sites than Europe and North America, as highlighted by UNESCO designations. Many countries and regions have therefore turned to new and emerging areas of culture and creativity to develop cultural tourism. Richards (2017b) describes the growth of creative experiences in Asia, including creative clusters in China, creative tourism programmes in Thailand and *Hallyu* tourism products in South Korea. Many of these programmes are characterized by a top-down approach, with government ministries directing and/or funding new developments. In China, there is now a joint ministry for culture and tourism, a structure also seen in many other countries (UNWTO, 2018). This is related not only to economic development agendas, but also a recognition that cultural tourism can be a tool for developing soft power and improving the international image of places.

LIES, DAMN LIES AND CULTURAL TOURISM: TOWARDS A NEW CONCEPTUAL DEFINITION

Power struggles in the cultural tourism practice are also evident in debates about the definition of cultural tourism. Definition is important not just as an academic exercise, but also because this establishes important premises, such as who is a cultural tourist, and how big the cultural tourism market is. Framing cultural tourism as a large and rapidly growing market gives power to existing actors in the field, as well as attracting new actors who in turn extend the boundaries of the field still further.

The idea that cultural tourism accounts for almost 40 per cent of international tourism is very deeply embedded, even though the evidence was thin for a long time. As the UNWTO *Report on Tourism and Culture Synergies* (2018, p. 74) revealed:

> One of the reasons for this belief was the widely-quoted statement by Bywater (1993) that the World Tourism Organization has estimated that 37% of all trips have a cultural element and that the growth rate in trips of this kind to the end of the century will be 15% annually.

Interestingly, the UNWTO themselves were unable to find the origin of this statement, which was probably an off-the-cuff remark to a journalist by a UNWTO staff member. There is nothing new about fake news.

Despite the lack of empirical evidence to back up the 37 per cent figure (an uneven number always sounds less made-up), the authority conferred on it by the UNWTO name ensured that it endured. A quarter of a century later, this mantra was repeated by the Mayor's Office in London: 'Cultural tourism now accounts for 37 per cent of world travel and is growing fast – at a rate of 15 per cent year on year' (Mayor of London, 2017b, p. 22). Interestingly, as the UNWTO (2018) later established, the 37 per cent figure is close to the actual level of cultural activities undertaken by international tourists, or in other words, a wide definition of cultural tourism.

But is 'cultural tourism' growing? The evidence is mixed. A UNWTO (2018) survey indicated an average global growth rate for international cultural tourism of 4.5 per cent per annum over the previous five years, slightly higher than international arrivals as a whole (4 per cent). Most countries surveyed also expect cultural tourism to grow relatively rapidly in future. A similar picture emerges from a survey of cultural institutions in Germany, where Burzinski, Buschmann and Pröbstle (2018) found that 50 per cent of cultural institutions had seen an increase in cultural tourist visits over the past five years.

Millán Vázquez de la Torre et al. (2019) argue that most growth in cultural tourism derives from new market niches, including architecture, gastronomy, literature, film, urbanism, shopping, language and flamenco. These are often treated as distinct markets once they attract the attention of policy makers and academics. Gastronomy is a good case in point, since growing attention for this field has spawned a flood of new tourism policies and development programmes in recent years, together with a raft of academic studies (Richards, 2015, see Chapter 5). While there has been much debate about whether to refer to the gastronomic experiences of tourists as gastronomy tourism, food tourism or culinary tourism (Stone, Migacz and Wolf, 2019), less attention is paid to the basic question of whether gastronomic experiences should also be considered 'cultural tourism'.

Such debates about the boundaries of cultural tourism make it difficult to measure the number of cultural tourists. In the UNWTO (2018) study, for example, 65 per cent of countries surveyed reported collecting specific data on cultural tourism, with most countries basing their estimates on the proportion of visitors undertaking cultural activities. This tends to generate large numbers of cultural tourists, whereas asking tourists about their motivations gives much lower results (UNWTO, 2018).

Where there are consistent measures of cultural tourism over time, doubt has been cast on the idea that cultural tourism is growing particularly rapidly. In Malta, longitudinal data were collected on the number of inbound tourists who indicated culture and history as one of their reasons for visiting the island. Taking this broad definition, the proportion of cultural tourists rose from 19 per cent in 1991 to 32 per cent in 1996 and over 50 per cent in 2018 (Attard, 2018; Ebejer, 2019; Malta Tourism Authority, 2020; Markwick, 1999; Munsters, 2011). This might be a vindication of Malta's attempts to reduce dependence on beach tourism by developing the cultural tourism market or 'quality tourism'. In contrast, a narrow definition based on tourists with culture as their main motivation indicates a decline from 13 per cent in 2007 to 10.8 per cent in 2019. Even the policy emphasis on developing cultural tourism related to the 2018 ECOC did little to stimulate the growth of cultural tourism in the narrow sense. Markwick (2018) estimates that the growth in the number of 'specific cultural tourists' in 2018 was around 70,000, out of a total tourism growth of 326,000 (or 21 per cent of the increase). The proportion of cultural tourists depends greatly on location. Tourists staying in Valletta exhibited higher interest in history and culture in 2015, with 33 per cent greatly motivated by culture, or about three times the level for visitors to Malta as a whole (Sultana and Attard, 2016).

The Maltese data indicate that the growth of general cultural tourism has been significant, whereas specific cultural tourism has declined. Defined in narrow terms, therefore, rather than being a large, fast-growing market, cultural tourism would be a small, declining market. These data suggest, at least in the case of Malta, that mass cultural tourism is growing at the expense of more specialized niches. They also highlight that the volume of cultural tourism is highly dependent on definition, which also brings us back to the question: what is cultural tourism?

What Is Cultural Tourism?

One of the first definitions of cultural tourism appeared in the Brussels Charter adopted by the International Council on Monuments and Sites (ICOMOS) in 1976, which saw it as a form of tourism aiming to discover and learn more about monuments and places of historical and artistic interest. This confirmed the close link between learning and cultural tourism, which has been a recurring theme ever since (Richards, 2018). The World Tourism Organization (1985) also produced two early definitions: one narrow and the other broad. The narrow definition included 'movements of persons for essentially cultural motivations such as study tours, performing arts and cultural tours, travel to festivals and other cultural events, visits to sites and monuments, travel to study nature, folklore or art, and pilgrimages'. The wide definition, in contrast, covered 'all movements of persons, ... because they satisfy the human need for diversity, tending to raise the cultural level of the individual and giving rise to new knowledge, experience and encounters' (Richards, 1996, p. 24).

These narrow and wide concepts also reflect a qualitative difference between conceptual and measurement-based definitions. We need conceptual definitions to try and understand what cultural tourism means, but we need more practical, technical definitions to be able to measure it. ATLAS adopted this two-track approach in developing its Cultural Tourism Research Project in 1991 (Richards, 1996, p. 24). The conceptual definition was: 'The movement of persons to cultural attractions away from their normal place of residence, with the intention to gather new information and experiences to satisfy their cultural needs.' The technical definition included: 'All movements of persons to specific cultural attractions, such as heritage sites, artistic and cultural manifestations, arts and drama outside their normal place of residence.'

The conceptual definition underlines the importance of establishing motivation as the basis for identifying cultural tourists, arguing that cultural tourists are basically differentiated by their desire to learn and to acquire cultural capital. The role of motivation was also underlined by other definitions emerging in the 1990s, such as Silberberg's (1995, p. 361): 'visits by persons from outside the host community motivated wholly or in part by interest in the historical, artistic, scientific or lifestyle/heritage offerings of a community, region or institution'. Bendixen (1997) also took a broad approach, defining cultural tourism as 'the organisation of tours to visit places or sites of cultural heritage, participation in cultural events or artistic performances'.

Cultural tourism is dependent on modes of production and consumption, and therefore also depends both on the actor and context (see Chapter 3). Prentice (2003, p. 13) argued that cultural tourism is 'constructed, proffered and/or consumed as an appreciation of culture'. For Stylianou-Lambert (2011), a 'cultural tourist' is defined as any individual who visits cultural institutions or places such as museums, archaeological and heritage sites, operas, theatres, festivals or architecture while away from home. More recently, the idea of 'engagement' has become more important in studies of cultural tourism, which Smith (2009, p. 17) defined as 'passive, active and interactive engagement with culture(s) and communities, whereby the visitor gains new experiences of an educational, creative and/or entertaining nature'. Motivation and engagement therefore become important means of distinguishing between two key groups of cultural tourists: tourists who consume culture because it is their main motivation, and those for whom culture is only a complement, secondary motivation or even accidental discovery (Jovicic, 2016).

The UNWTO (2018, p. 9) adopted a new definition of cultural tourism in 2017, taking a broad, conceptual approach:

> Cultural tourism is a type of tourism activity in which the visitor's essential motivation is to learn, discover, experience and consume the tangible and intangible cultural attractions/products in a tourism destination. These attractions/products

relate to a set of distinctive material, intellectual, spiritual and emotional features of a society that encompasses arts and architecture, historical and cultural heritage, culinary heritage, literature, music, creative industries and the living cultures with their lifestyles, value systems, beliefs and traditions.

In comparison to the UNWTO definition from 1982, this update reveals several elements. Firstly, there is continuity in terms of motivation (with a focus on learning), but also several differences:

1. A shift from tangible to intangible culture as the focus of cultural tourism.
2. A shift from folklore to lifestyles, value systems, beliefs and traditions.
3. The increasing centrality of experience.
4. An emphasis on distinctive elements of culture.
5. Emotional features of culture are included.
6. Specific niches, such as gastronomy, literature, music and creative tourism are identified.

Over time we can also see definitions of cultural tourism shifting from tourism motivated by learning (Richards, 1996; Silberberg, 1995), to co-creation and engagement in the construction of experiences (Prentice, 2003; Smith, 2009) and a broader concept of tangible and intangible culture and contemporary lifestyles (UNWTO, 2018).

This development relates both to the shifting nature of culture and to changes in tourism. Complexity has increased as views of culture have become broader, more inclusive and dynamic. The shift from high or elite culture as the target of cultural tourism towards everyday or popular culture is also linked with a broadening view of culture from product-based to process-based, and from cultural homogeneity to heterogeneity. In terms of tourism, we also see a reframing from meeting the needs of visitors (or consumption) at specific cultural sites or attractions, towards ideas of engagement and co-creation, also implicating a wider range of actors and contexts in creating cultural tourism experiences.

The evolution of definitions of cultural tourism indicates increasing complexity, which matches the development of the field, as well as a growing body of research and knowledge. In this increasingly complex environment, there is still a lack of attention for the reasons *why* we are defining cultural tourism. It is not a neutral idea, but a power-laden concept, with implications in the real world, as we see from the widespread adoption of cultural tourism policies. The definitions we use should be developed with particular purposes in mind. It is different, for example, to ask who is motivated by culture to travel to a destination, and who actually consumes what forms of culture in the destination. The ATLAS research showed, for example, that the proportion of tourists visiting some form of cultural attraction (or 'general cultural tourists') was around

40 per cent (Richards, 2001). This finding is important in terms of planning for cultural tourism, since it provides some estimate of the volume of tourists who might be expected to visit cultural sites while on holiday. On the other hand, those tourists specifically motivated by culture to travel (and who therefore might be directly influenced by marketing to visit a specific destination) are far fewer. The ATLAS research indicated only 5–10 per cent of all tourists are 'specific cultural tourists'. In other words, there is a big difference between the number of tourists who have a high level of engagement with culture and those who see culture as one more experience for the bucket list.

The definition of cultural tourism therefore becomes a key issue, both for understanding and measuring cultural tourism, as Richards (2018) discusses. From a conceptual point of view, one of the major challenges is that the scope of culture considered suitable for tourist consumption continues to expand. The concept of culture itself has been enlarged by the cultural and creative turns, and the acceptance of plural and diverse readings of culture. In the past, high culture was the basic target of cultural tourism, but the growing recognition of the value of popular and traditional culture has vastly expanded the legitimate objects of cultural tourism. Heritage has also expanded its temporal extent, as the 'heritage horizon' has increasingly approached the present (Richards, 2001). Whereas heritage was once considered a product of the distant past (Lowenthal, 1985), it is now being continually brought up to date, with UNESCO launching a programme to conserve the built heritage of the 20th century in 2001.

Redefining Cultural Tourism

Cultural tourism has shifted from a practice of visiting cultural highlights to emergent cultural experiences co-created between actors and contexts. The expansion of the cultural resources offered to and consumed by the cultural tourist means that cultural tourism is effectively everywhere, located not just in traditional cultural destinations or sites, but also in the everyday (Richards, 2011).

To address this complexity, we need a new definition of cultural tourism that is not predicated on the idea of tourism and culture as distinct realms separated from everyday life, and which recognizes the dynamic relationship between these fields. We therefore propose seeing cultural tourism as a social practice, helping overcome the duality of actor and structure. In moving through the ritual of cultural tourism, as Richards (2018) suggests, actors encounter and reassemble practice elements, linking competences, meanings and materials, threading through different contexts as they go (Shove et al., 2012). We can therefore see cultural tourism from a practice perspective as:

> A bundle of tourism practices and rituals that focus attention on tangible and intangible heritage, cultural manifestations and creative processes, enabling actors to develop competences which generate meaning, emotional energy and other internal and external goods.

This definition focusses not on tourists as consumers, of cultural resources as goals, but the consequences of the practice for actors, both consumers and producers. As explained earlier in this chapter, cultural tourism practices provide both the internal goods, or intrinsic motivations and morality, that drive the cultural tourist to seek out new experiences (Leiper, 1990) and the external goods that provide institutional support for the practice, such as money or prestige. The basis of the cultural tourism practice model in ritual also links with seminal formulations of tourism practice (Cohen, 1979; MacCannell, 1976).

The bundling of practices (for example, Lamers and Pashkevich, 2018) is important because cultural tourism is more than a single practice. This is evident from the fragmentation of the cultural tourism field into different niches, where each cultural tourism niche represents a differential ordering of the materials, meaning and competences of the practice, as well as differential relationships with the fields of culture and tourism. The examples cited in this book depict an overlapping raft of cultural niches, which together constitute the cultural tourism field. The general cultural tourist will often travel between niches as they seek new sources of EE, combining a visit to an art museum with sampling local gastronomy and taking in a cityscape or rural landscape.

Seen this way, the continual rearrangement of the practice elements outlined by Shove et al. (2012) in cultural tourism creates a series of consumption junctions (Weenink and Spaargaren, 2016), or contexts at which producers and consumers meet to co-create experiences. These provide the focus of the interaction ritual chains identified by Collins (2004). Participation in the ritual develops the competences of the actors, generating increased meaning and necessitating the employment of a greater range of materials. We see this process unfolding, for example, in the 'reinvention of the local for tourism', as Russo and Richards (2016) outline. Pioneering tactical tourists (Wolfram and Burnill-Maier, 2013) or creative tourists (Pappalepore, 2010) explore new areas following the ritual of 'off the beaten track' or 'live like a local' experiences, thus generating internal goods. These new spaces become meeting grounds for consumers and new cultural intermediaries who see opportunities to secure external goods by increasing the articulation of tourism and local culture. This drives a search for new means of consumption (or materials), such as the walking tours, bike tours and tuk-tuks that are now a stock in trade of the new urban tourism. Markers of the local are generated through storytelling and embedded in place using emotion. The EE generated by getting closer to the local stimulates a repetition of the ritual in other places, another art museum visit, local shopping trip, walking tour or street art experience.

All these practice elements and the actors involved in the practice come together in places, or destinations. This illustrates an important element of Collins' (2004) theory of interaction rituals: the need for physical co-presence, which is also developed by Tutenges (2015), who outlines the 'group mind' or a state in which 'people have lost their individuality in favor of a common mind with the same intentions, thoughts, and feelings' (p. 292). This highlights one of the tensions in tourism research, between the traditional focus on the motivation of the individual and the more recent attention for the structures produced by social groups. Collins' (2004) approach helps to unite both perspectives by giving the individual a motive contingent upon their membership of the group. One challenge of this approach is that Collins emphasizes face-to-face interaction. The reality of many contemporary social practices is that they lack physical co-presence, either because they are virtual or because they are practised individually. In both cases, however, we can still argue for a social dimension that effectively creates co-presence. As outlined earlier in the chapter, adherents to a practice are accompanied by previous practitioners, so their rituals are still performed collectively in accordance with internal norms (MacIntyre, 1981). In the online world, we still form part of a community around the practice, often in support of the physical, offline experience (Simons, 2019). More exploration of the solitary and virtual contexts of co-presence are required, but these are also likely to be important in the practices of cultural tourism.

CONCLUSION

The development of a new model of cultural tourism practices helps us to rethink the relationships in this field. We can consider how actors and contexts combine to create different interaction rituals, which are supported by the production of internal and external goods. This holistic vision also combines different levels of analysis, centred on the meso-level of social groups suggested by Collins (2004), which enables us to understand what drives group as well as individual behaviour. The production of EE through ritual interactions provides the motivation for individual consumption of cultural tourism, as well as explaining how this produces social structures and behaviours.

The ritual practice of cultural tourism has many consequences, intended and unintended, for the practitioners, as well as the contexts in which the practice unfolds. Cultural consumption can stimulate learning and develop skills for the individual participant, as well as generating EE for the group. It may also add to the local buzz of the places visited, helping to support the local cultural ecology and providing pipelines to link destinations to global flows of resources. Cultural tourism may therefore be an important source of external goods for cultural actors in a liberalizing climate. But the co-presence that stimulates collective effervescence may also generate negative consequences, such as overcrowding and ignoring local behavioural norms in favour of the internal norms of the practice.

In developing this model, we are trying to rethink cultural tourism in the context of practice theory, but also adding something to existing practice approaches. Building on first generation practice theories that sketched the building blocks of social practices, and the second generation theories that help us analyse different types of practices and their dynamics, we move towards a third generation approach that conceptualizes practices-as-performances in which different actors meet and interact, also considering their links with wider social groups and networks. The application of interaction ritual theory in this new approach also provides a trigger for action, or what 'makes things happen' as Bærenholdt (2017) suggests. In the following chapter, we consider how these emerging rituals have shaped the actors and contexts of contemporary cultural tourism.

REFERENCES

Ajuntament de Barcelona (2017). *Perfil i hàbits dels turistes a la ciutat de Barcelona 2017*. Barcelona: Ajuntament de Barcelona.

Alemida-García, F., Cortés-Macías, R., and Balbuena-Vázquez, A. (2019). Tourismphobia in historic centres: the case of Malaga. *Boletín de la Asociación de Geógrafos Españoles*, *83*(2823), 1–32.

Aoyama, Y. (2009). Artists, tourists, and the state: cultural tourism and the flamenco industry in Andalusia, Spain. *International Journal of Urban and Regional Research*, *33*(1), 80–104.

Artal-Tur, A., Briones-Peñalver, A.J., and Villena-Navarro, M. (2018). Tourism, cultural activities and sustainability in the Spanish Mediterranean regions: a probit approach. *Tourism & Management Studies*, *14*(1), 7–18.

Attard, S. (2018). The evolution of Malta's tourism product over recent years. *Quarterly Review, 2018:4*, 41–55.

Bærenholdt, J.O. (2017). Moving to meet and make: rethinking creativity in making things take place. In J. Hannigan and G. Richards (eds), *The Sage Handbook of New Urban Studies* (pp. 330–42). London: Sage.

Bakas, F.E., Duxbury, N., and Vinagre de Castro, T. (2019). Creative tourism: catalysing artisan entrepreneur networks in rural Portugal. *International Journal of Entrepreneurial Behavior & Research*, *25*(4), 731–52.

Banks, M. (2012). MacIntyre, Bourdieu and the practice of jazz. *Popular Music*, *31*(1), 69–86.

Bargeman, B. and Richards, G. (2020). A new approach to understanding tourism practices. *Annals of Tourism Research*, *84*, 102988.

Bendixen, P. (1997). Cultural tourism – economic success at the expense of culture? *International Journal of Cultural Policy*, *4*(1), 21–46.

Besculides, A., Lee, M.E., and McCormick, P.J. (2002). Residents' perceptions of the cultural benefits of tourism. *Annals of Tourism Research*, *29*(2), 303–19.

Boissevain, J. (1996). 'But we live here!': perspectives on cultural tourism in Malta. In L. Briguglio (ed.), *Sustainable Tourism in Islands and Small States: Case Studies* (pp. 220–40). London: Pinter.

Buda, D.M., d'Hauteserre, A.M., and Johnston, L. (2014). Feeling and tourism studies. *Annals of Tourism Research*, *46*, 102–14.

Burzinski, M., Buschmann, L., and Pröbstle, Y. (2018). *Kulturtourismusstudie 2018: Empirische Einblicke in die Praxis von Kultur- und Tourismusakteuren*. Ludwigsburg: Institut für Kulturmanagement.

Bywater, M. (1993). The market for cultural tourism in Europe. *Travel and Tourism Analyst*, *6*, 30–46.

Capocchi, A., Vallone, C., Pierotti, M., and Amaduzzi, A. (2019). Overtourism: a literature review to assess implications and future perspectives. *Sustainability*, *11*(12), 3303.

Chhabra, D. (2008). Positioning museums on an authenticity continuum. *Annals of Tourism Research*, *35*(2), 427–47.

Cisneros-Martínez, J.D. and Fernández-Morales, A. (2015). Cultural tourism as tourist segment for reducing seasonality in a coastal area: the case study of Andalusia. *Current Issues in Tourism*, *18*(8), 765–84.

Cohen, E. (1979). Rethinking the sociology of tourism. *Annals of Tourism Research*, *6*(1), 18–35.

Cohen, E. (1988). Authenticity and commoditization in tourism. *Annals of Tourism Research*, *15*(3), 371–86.

Collins, R. (2004). *Interaction Ritual Chains*. Princeton, NJ: Princeton University Press.

Conti, E., Forlani, F., and Pencarelli, T. (2020). Visiting a cultural city in the experiential perspective: the case of Urbino. *Rivista fondata da Massimo Montella*, *21*, 391–424.

Cousin, S. (2008). The nation state as an identifying image: traditions and stakes in tourism policy, Touraine, France. *Tourist Studies*, *8*(2), 193–209.

Csapo, J. (2012). The role and importance of cultural tourism in modern tourism industry. In M. Kasimoglu (ed.), *Strategies for Tourism Industry – Micro and Macro Perspectives* (pp. 201–32). London: Intech Open.

D'Auria, A. (2009). Urban cultural tourism: creative approaches for heritage-based sustainable development. *International Journal of Sustainable Development*, *12*(2–4), 275–89.

Davis, P. (2004). Ecomuseums and the democratization of cultural tourism. *Tourism Culture & Communication*, *5*(1), 45–58.

de Geus, S.D., Richards, G., and Toepoel, V. (2016). Conceptualisation and operationalisation of event and festival experiences: creation of an event experience scale. *Scandinavian Journal of Hospitality and Tourism*, *16*(3), 274–96.

Di Lascio, F.M.L., Giannerini, S., Scorcu, A.E., and Candela, G. (2011). Cultural tourism and temporary art exhibitions in Italy: a panel data analysis. *Statistical Methods & Applications*, *20*(4), 519–42.

Diekmann, A. and Smith, M.K. (2015). *Ethnic and Minority Cultures as Tourist Attractions*. Bristol: Channel View.

Dietvorst, A.G.J. (1994). Cultural tourism and time-space behaviour. In P.J. Larkham and G. Ashworth (eds), *Building a New Heritage: Tourism, Culture and Identity in the New Europe* (pp. 69–89). London: Routledge.

du Cros, H. and Jolliffe, L. (2011). Bundling the arts for tourism to complement urban heritage tourist experiences in Asia. *Journal of Heritage Tourism*, *6*(3), 181–95.

Ebejer, J. (2019). Urban heritage and cultural tourism development: a case study of Valletta's role in Malta's tourism. *Journal of Tourism and Cultural Change*, *17*(3), 306–20.

Frey, O. (2009). Creativity of places as a resource for cultural tourism. In G. Maciocco and S. Serreli (eds), *Enhancing the City* (pp. 135-54). Springer: Dordrecht.

García García, L.R. (2020). Identificación del turista cultural flamenco. La influencia del flamenco sobre el mercado turístico en la ciudad de Córdoba. PhD thesis, University of Córdoba.

Giddens, A. (1979). *Central Problems in Social Theory: Action, Structure and Contradiction in Social Analysis.* Berkeley, CA: University of California Press.

Giddens, A. (1984). *The Constitution of Society: Outline of the Theory of Structuration.* Cambridge: Polity Press.

Gkoumas, A. and D'Orazio, F. (2019). Public-space tactical intervention as urban tourist allure. *International Journal of Tourism Cities*, *6*(4), 711–30.

Gratton, C. and Richards, G. (1996). The economic context of cultural tourism. In G. Richards (ed.), *Cultural Tourism in Europe* (pp. 71–87). Wallingford: CABI.

Guccio, C., Lisi, D., Martorana, M., and Mignosa, A. (2017). On the role of cultural participation in tourism destination performance: an assessment using robust conditional efficiency approach. *Journal of Cultural Economics*, *41*(2), 129–54.

Guerreiro, M., Mendes, J., Fortuna, C., and Pinto, P. (2020). The dynamic nature of the city image: do image components evolve over time? *Tourism: An International Interdisciplinary Journal*, *68*(1), 83–99.

Herrero, P.L., Sanz, D.M., González, I., and Sanz, L.J. (1998). Economía de la Cultura en Castilla y León: Turismo Cultural y Museos. *Gestión Turística*, *3*, 77–105.

Jansen-Verbeke, M.C. (1990). *Toerisme in de binnenstad van Brugge: een planologische visie.* Nijmegen: Katholieke Universiteit Nijmegen.

Jenkins, L.D. and Romanos, M. (2014). The art of tourism-driven development: economic and artistic well-being of artists in three Balinese communities. *Journal of Tourism and Cultural Change*, *12*(4), 293–306.

Jovicic, D. (2016). Cultural tourism in the context of relations between mass and alternative tourism. *Current Issues in Tourism*, *19*(6), 605–12.

Kim, H., Kim, Y.G., and Woo, E. (2020). Examining the impacts of touristification on quality of life (QOL): the application of the bottom-up spillover theory. *The Service Industries Journal*, 1–16.

Kneafsey, M. (1994). The cultural tourist: patron saint of Ireland. In U. Kockel (ed.), *Culture, Tourism and Development: The Case of Ireland* (pp. 103–16). Liverpool: Liverpool University Press.

Lage, B.H.G and Milone, P.C. (1995). Cultura, lazer e turismo. *Revista Turismo em Análise*, *6*(2), 7–25.

Lamers, M. and Pashkevich, A. (2018). Short-circuiting cruise tourism practices along the Russian Barents Sea coast? The case of Arkhangelsk. *Current Issues in Tourism*, *21*(4), 440–54.

Law, C.M. (1992). Urban tourism and its contribution to economic regeneration. *Urban Studies*, *29*(3–4), 599–618.

Leiper, N. (1990). Tourist attraction systems. *Annals of Tourism Research, 17*(3), 367–84.

López-Gay, A., Cocola-Gant, A., and Russo, A.P. (2020). Urban tourism and population change: gentrification in the age of mobilities. *Population, Space and Place.* doi: 10.1002/psp.2380.

Lowenthal, D. (1985). *The Past is a Foreign Country.* Cambridge: Cambridge University Press.

Luxemburg and Greater Region (2008). *Luxemburg and Greater Region, Cultural Capital of Europe 2007. Final report.* Luxemburg: Luxemburg 2007.

MacCannell, D. (1976). *The Tourist: A New Theory of the Leisure Class.* New York: Schocken.

MacIntyre, A. (1981). *After Virtue: A Study in Moral Theory.* London: Duckworth.

Malta Tourism Authority (2020). *Tourism in Malta: Facts & Figures 2019.* http://www .mta.com.mt/en/file.aspx?f=34248 (accessed 18 December 2020).

Markwick, M. (1999). Malta's tourism industry since 1985: diversification, cultural tourism and sustainability. *Scottish Geographical Journal, 115*(3), 227–47.

Markwick, M. (2018). Valletta ECoC 2018 and cultural tourism development. *Journal of Tourism and Cultural Change, 16*(3), 286–308.

Martínez-Pérez, Á., García-Villaverde, P.M., and Elche, D. (2016). The mediating effect of ambidextrous knowledge strategy between social capital and innovation of cultural tourism clusters firms. *International Journal of Contemporary Hospitality Management, 28*(7), 1484–507.

Matteucci, X. (2014). Forms of body usage in tourists' experiences of flamenco. *Annals of Tourism Research, 46*, 29–43.

Mayor of London (2017a). Cultural tourism vision for London. https://www.london .gov.uk/what-we-do/arts-and-culture/cultural-places-and-creative-spaces/cultural -tourism-vision-london (accessed 18 December 2020).

Mayor of London (2017b). *Take A Closer Look: A Cultural Tourism Vision for London 2015–2017.* London: Mayor of London.

McNamee, M. (1994). Valuing leisure practices: towards a theoretical framework. *Leisure Studies, 13*(1), 288–309.

Millán Vázquez de la Torre, M.G., Millán Lara, S., and Arjona-Fuentes, J.M. (2019). Flamenco tourism from the viewpoint of its protagonists: a sustainable vision using lean startup methodology. *Sustainability, 11*(21), 6047.

Munsters, W. (1994). *Cultuurtoerisme* (1st edn). Leuven: Garant.

Munsters, W. (2001). *Cultuurtoerisme* (3rd edn). Leuven: Garant.

Munsters, W. (2011). Malta's candidature for the title of European Capital of Culture 2018: the cultural tourism perspective. https://surfsharekit.nl/publiek/zuyd/bfc1e641 -877c-4996-848c-6a9d0ec34990 (accessed 18 December 2020).

Munsters, W. and Melkert, M. (2010). Objective authenticity in cultural tourism: thinking the unthinkable. *Journal of Hospitality & Tourism, 8*(2), 14–29.

Myerscough, J. (1988). *The Economic Impact of the Arts in Britain.* London: Policy Studies Institute.

Nicula, V. and Chindriş, C. (2017). Implications of festival culture in tourism development in the city of Sibiu. *Revista Economică, 69*(6), 120–7.

Noonan, D.S. and Rizzo, I. (2017). Economics of cultural tourism: issues and perspectives. *Journal of Cultural Economics, 41*, 95–107.

Nurse, K. (2001). Festival tourism in the Caribbean: an economic impact assessment. Report prepared for Inter-American Development Bank. Washington, DC: Inter-American Development Bank.

O'Connor, J. (2009). Creative industries: a new direction? *International Journal of Cultural Policy*, *15*(4), 387–402.

Ollero, J.L.S., Capellán, R.U., and Pozo, A.G. (2019). The impact of cultural and urban tourism on housing. *Journal of Tourism and Heritage Research*, *2*(4), 257–72.

Packer, J. and Ballantyne, R. (2016). Conceptualizing the visitor experience: a review of literature and development of a multifaceted model. *Visitor Studies*, *19*(2), 128–43.

Page, S.J. (1993). Urban tourism in New Zealand: the National Museum of New Zealand project. *Tourism Management*, *14*(3), 211–17.

Pappalepore, I. (2010). Tourism and the development of 'creative' urban areas: evidence from four non-central areas in London. PhD thesis, University of Westminster.

Parlett, G., Fletcher, J., and Cooper, C. (1995). The impact of tourism on the old town of Edinburgh. *Tourism Management*, *16*(5), 355–60.

Pasquinelli, C. (2015). Urban tourism(s): is there a case for a paradigm shift? *Cities Research Unit Working Papers no. 14*. L'Aquila, Gran Sasso Science Institute.

Pearce, P.L. (1995). From culture shock and culture arrogance to culture exchange: ideas towards sustainable socio-cultural tourism. *Journal of Sustainable Tourism*, *3*(3), 143–54.

Plaza, B. (2010). Valuing museums as economic engines: willingness to pay or discounting of cash-flows? *Journal of Cultural Heritage*, *11*(2), 155–62.

Prentice, R. (2003). Conceptualising cultural tourism. Paper presented at the 2nd de Haan Tourism Management Conference, University of Nottingham, December.

Pulido-Fernández, J.I., Cárdenas-García, P.J., and Carrillo-Hidalgo, I. (2016). Trip cultural activities and tourism expenditure in emerging urban-cultural destinations. *International Journal of Tourism Research*, *18*(4), 286–96.

Putnam, R.D. (2000). *Bowling Alone: The Collapse and Revival of American Community*. New York: Simon and Schuster.

Re, A. (2018). Cultural routes and heritage systems at the territorial scale: questions of management. In H. Porfyriou and B. Yu (eds), *China and Italy: Routes of Culture, Valorisation and Management* (pp. 35–43). Rome: National Research Council of Italy.

Richards, G. (1995). The politics of national tourism policy in Britain. *Leisure Studies*, *14*, 153–73.

Richards, G. (1996). *Cultural Tourism in Europe*. Wallingford: CABI.

Richards, G. (2001). *Cultural Attractions and European Tourism*. Wallingford: CABI.

Richards, G. (2007). The authenticity of a traditional event – the views of residents and visitors. *Event Management*, *11*, 33–44.

Richards, G. (2010). The traditional quantitative approach. Surveying cultural tourists: lessons from the ATLAS cultural tourism research project. In G. Richards and W. Munsters (eds), *Cultural Tourism Research Methods* (pp. 13–32). Wallingford: CABI.

Richards, G. (2011). Creativity and tourism: the state of the art. *Annals of Tourism Research*, *38*(4), 1225–53.

Richards, G. (2015). Gastronomic experiences: from foodies to foodscapes. *Journal of Gastronomy and Tourism*, *1*, 5–18.

Richards, G. (2016). Placemaking in Barcelona: from 'Paris of the South' to 'Capital of the Mediterranean'. *MNNieuws*, 12 September, 8–9.

Richards, G. (2017a). Emerging models of the Eventful City. *Event Management*, *21*(5), 533–43.

Richards, G. (2017b). The development of creative tourism in Asia. In C. Silver, L. Marques, H. Hanan, and I. Widiastuti (eds), *Imagining Experience: Creative Tourism and the Making of Place* (pp. ix–xiv). New York: Springer Science+Business Media.

Richards, G. (2018). Cultural tourism: a review of recent research and trends. *Journal of Hospitality and Tourism Management, 36,* 12–21.

Richards, G. and Marques, L. (2018). *Creating Synergies between Cultural Policy and Tourism for Permanent and Temporary Citizens.* Barcelona: UCLG/ICUB.

Richards, G. and Rotariu, I. (2015). Developing the Eventful City in Sibiu, Romania. *International Journal of Tourism Cities, 1*(2), 89–102.

Richards, G. and van der Ark, L.A. (2013). Dimensions of cultural consumption among tourists: multiple correspondence analysis. *Tourism Management, 37,* 71–6.

Richards, G. and Wilson, J. (2004). The impact of cultural events on city image: Rotterdam Cultural Capital of Europe 2001. *Urban Studies, 41*(10), 1931–51.

Richards, G. and Wilson, J. (2005). Social capital, cultural festivals and tourism in Catalunya. *Anuario Turismo y Sociedad, 4,* 170–81.

Richards, G., King, B., and Yeung, E. (2020). Experiencing culture in attractions, events and tour settings. *Tourism Management, 79,* 104104.

Riganti, P. and Nijkamp, P. (2008). Congestion in popular tourist areas: a multi-attribute experimental choice analysis of willingness-to-wait in Amsterdam. *Tourism Economics, 14*(1), 25–44.

Romão, J., Kourtit, K., Neuts, B., and Nijkamp, P. (2018). The smart city as a common place for tourists and residents: a structural analysis of the determinants of urban attractiveness. *Cities, 78,* 67–75.

Rotariu, I. and Stela, M.M. (2017). Addressing public economic development programs in terms of gastronomic tourism objectives of the Sibiu–European Region of Gastronomy 2019 program. *Revista Economică, 69*(3), 102–11.

Russo, A.P. (2002). The 'vicious circle' of tourism development in heritage cities. *Annals of Tourism Research, 29*(1), 165–82.

Russo, A.P. and Richards, G. (2016). *Reinventing the Local in Tourism: Producing, Consuming and Negotiating Place.* Bristol: Channel View.

Saayman, M. and Saayman, A. (2006). Does the location of arts festivals matter for the economic impact? *Papers in Regional Science, 85*(4), 569–84.

Sanagustín-Fons, M., Tobar-Pesántez, L.B., and Ravina-Ripoll, R. (2020). Happiness and cultural tourism: the perspective of civil participation. *Sustainability, 12*(8), 3465.

Sánchez, J., Urrestarazu, R., and Garcia, A. (2019). The impact of cultural and urban tourism on housing. *Journal of Tourism and Heritage Research, 2*(4), 257–72.

Sandell, R. (2003). Social inclusion, the museum and the dynamics of sectoral change. *Museum and Society, 1*(1), 45–62.

Schatzki, T.R. (1996). *Social Practices: A Wittgensteinian Approach to Human Activity and the Social.* Cambridge: Cambridge University Press.

Schouten, F. (2007). Cultural tourism: between authenticity and globalization. In G. Richards (ed.), *Cultural Tourism: Global and Local Perspectives* (pp. 25–37). New York: Howarth Press.

Scitovsky, T. (1976). *The Joyless Economy: An Inquiry into Human Satisfaction and Consumer Dissatisfaction.* Oxford: Oxford University Press.

Sequera, J. and Nofre, J. (2018). Shaken, not stirred: new debates on touristification and the limits of gentrification. *City, 22*(5–6), 843–55.

Shove, E., Pantzar, M., and Watson, M. (2012). *The Dynamics of Social Practice: Everyday Life and How It Changes.* London: Sage.

Silberberg, T. (1995). Cultural tourism and business opportunities for museums and heritage sites. *Tourism Management*, *16*(5), 361–5.

Simons, I. (2019). Events and online interaction: the construction of hybrid event communities. *Leisure Studies*, *38*(2), 145–59.

Singh, J.P. and Hart, S.A. (2007). Sex workers and cultural policy: mapping the issues and actors in Thailand. *Review of Policy Research*, *24*(2), 155–73.

Smith, M.K. (2009). *Issues in Cultural Tourism Studies* (2nd edn). London: Routledge.

Steiner, L. and Frey, B.S. (2012). Correcting the imbalance of the World Heritage List: did the UNESCO strategy work? *Journal of International Organizations Studies*, *3*(1), 25–40.

Stone, M.J., Migacz, S., and Wolf, E. (2019). Beyond the journey: the lasting impact of culinary tourism activities. *Current Issues in Tourism*, *22*(2), 147–52.

Stylianou-Lambert, T. (2011). Gazing from home: cultural tourism and art museums. *Annals of Tourism Research*, *38*(2), 403–21.

Sultana, T. and Attard, M. (2016). Measuring the impact of ECoC Valletta 2018 on travel motivations and behaviour of tourists in Malta. Paper presented at the 14th Global Forum on Tourism Statistics, Venice 2016, Session 5: Tourism, Culture and Creative Industries, 24 November.

Suntikul, W. and Jachna, T. (2016). The co-creation/place attachment nexus. *Tourism Management*, *52*, 276–86.

Therkelsen, A., Jensen, O.B., and Lange, I.S.G. (2019). Constructing 'empty' places: discourses and place materiality in the wake of disruption. *Space and Culture*, 1206331219877623.

Thimm, T. (2014). The flamenco factor in destination marketing: interdependencies of creative industries and tourism – the case of Seville. *Journal of Travel & Tourism Marketing*, *31*(5), 576–88.

Tighe, A.J. (1985). Cultural tourism in the USA. *Tourism Management*, *6*(4), 234–51.

Tutenges, S. (2015). Pub crawls at a Bulgarian nightlife resort: a case study using crowd theory. *Tourist Studies*, *15*(3), 283–99.

UNWTO (2018). *Report on Tourism and Culture Synergies*. Madrid: UNWTO.

van der Zee, E., Bertocchi, D., and Vanneste, D. (2020). Distribution of tourists within urban heritage destinations: a hot spot/cold spot analysis of TripAdvisor data as support for destination management, *Current Issues in Tourism*, *23*(2), 175–96.

van Loon, R. and Rouwendal, J. (2017). Travel purpose and expenditure patterns in city tourism: evidence from the Amsterdam Metropolitan Area. *Journal of Cultural Economics*, *41*(2), 109–27.

van Puffelen, F. (1987). The economic importance of the arts in Amsterdam. In W.S. Hendon, H. Hillmann-Chartrand, and H. Horowitz (eds), *Paying for the Arts* (pp. 231–42). Ohio: Association for Cultural Economics.

Vargas, M. (2015). 'Catalonia is not Spain': projecting Catalan identity to tourists in and around Barcelona. *Journal of Tourism History*, *7*(1–2), 36–53.

Viljoen, J. and Henama, U.S. (2017). Growing heritage tourism and social cohesion in South Africa. *African Journal of Hospitality, Tourism and Leisure*, *6*(4), 1–15.

Weenink, D. and Spaargaren, G. (2016). Emotional agency navigates a world of practices. In G. Spaargaren, D. Weenink, and M. Lamers (eds), *Practice Theory and Research: Exploring the Dynamics of Social Life* (pp. 60–84). London: Routledge.

Wolfram, G. and Burnill-Maier, C. (2013). The tactical tourist: growing self-awareness and challenging the strategists – visitor groups in Berlin. In M. Smith and G. Richards (eds), *The Routledge Handbook of Cultural Tourism* (pp. 382–9). London: Routledge.

World Tourism Organization (1985). *The State's Role in Protecting and Promoting Culture as a Factor of Tourism Development and the Proper Use and Exploitation of the National Cultural Heritage of Sites and Monuments for Tourism*. Madrid: WTO.

Zatori, A., Smith, M.K., and Puczkó, L. (2018). Experience-involvement, memorability and authenticity: the service provider's effect on tourist experience. *Tourism Management, 67*, 111–26.

Zukin, S. (2010). *Naked City: The Death and Life of Authentic Urban Places*. Oxford: Oxford University Press.

# 5.	New rituals and the dynamics of cultural tourism practices

INTRODUCTION

The approach outlined in the previous chapters allows us to analyse the components and dynamics of cultural tourism practices. The previous chapters have intimated the decline of more traditional practices and the rise of Cultural Tourism 3.0 and 4.0 approaches based on co-creation and digital technologies. The crumbling meaning-making systems of traditional cultural tourism have seen the guidebook buried by the information cascade of big data and destination management enhanced by curated cultural tourism experiences. These shifts have engaged new audiences and given meaning to cultural spaces for networked publics (Grevtsova and Sibina, 2018).

Charting the dynamics of cultural tourism practices requires a broader approach to research, and the development of destination management and marketing into a broader concept of placemaking. Previous research on cultural tourism has tended to take a relatively static approach: analysing cultural tourists visiting cultural attractions at a specific point in time. The practice approach adopted here highlights the need to consider a broad range of actors who interact dynamically with each other, their interactions moulded by the context of cultural tourism experiences to generate a range of consequences, both intended and unintended. Although we applied Collins' (2004) concept of interaction rituals to explain the motivations of actors in Chapter 4, we have not considered what makes things happen in practices (Bærenholdt, 2017).

The key to understanding how cultural tourism happens lies in places, and the practice bundles, actors and flows of resources these bring together. In the previous chapter, we outlined the approach taken by Shove, Pantzar and Watson (2012) in analysing the dynamic relations between materials, meanings and competences, and how these elements shift as practices develop. Bærenholdt (2017) argues that we need to broaden our view to include the ways in which practice elements and actors 'move to meet' in events that can literally 'take place' and make things happen. For this, more attention should be paid to mobilities of actors, ideas and materials, and how these are organized into specific events and places that can attract cultural tourists, and, in so doing, create relationships that can initiate placemaking processes.

In making these connections, we transform the view of cultural tourism from an experience developed by producers for cultural tourists into a relational view of a dynamic field of cultural tourism practices. Cultural tourism, drawing on the views of Shove, Bærenholdt and Collins, can be conceptualized as a ritual process causing actors to move, meet and co-create experiences. The places where these meetings happen (destinations, in traditional terminology) represent an assemblage of people and things, linked by the connective authenticity constituted by the local. What links the actors in the cultural tourism ritual is their mutual focus on travelling to encounter culture, and this requires an understanding of enthusiasm, morality and performance that generate positive outcomes for those actors. Because these rituals take place in specific contexts, they are also supported and moulded by the structures of the context. Looking to Cohendet, Grandadam and Simon's (2010) structuring of the creative city, for example, we could argue that the urban cultural tourism ritual is shaped by the relationships between the Underground, Middleground and Upperground, and how actors in these areas interact. This also begins to explain why certain places, even though not rich in cultural resources, become hubs for cultural tourism production and consumption. This practice approach throws new light on cultural tourism as a relational process of placemaking. In this chapter, we outline a range of practices, or interaction rituals, which illustrate the developing dynamics of contemporary cultural tourism, beginning with the placemaking process itself.

PLACEMAKING AND CULTURAL TOURISM

Cultural tourism happens in places. As Pavoni (2015, p. 472) notes, the spatial turn in social science and the humanities calls attention to the fact that 'our being-in-the-world is always an inhabiting-the-world, which always entails a praxis of world-making, a coming together of humans and non-humans in the co-production of the common spaces in and through which we live'. The different elements of spatial practice come together in places that are lived, imagined and physically shaped by practice, and which in turn shape the practices that make them.

Increasingly, cities and regions are utilizing many different aspects of place to profile themselves in competitive markets and attract residents, workers, investors and tourists. This generates increasing attention for sense of place, emotional attachment to place and spatial embedding. Perhaps most importantly, there is also a growing recognition that places can be consciously made better through collective effort. The concept of placemaking is not new – it dates back to the work of Jane Jacobs in the 1960s (Friedmann, 2010). But whereas early work on placemaking centred on neighbourhoods and relatively small-scale physical interventions, today placemaking is being used in more strategic and holistic senses, which involve bringing meaning back into whole communities, cities and regions.

Placemaking is also more important in cultural tourism, as the realization dawns that places should not just be made more attractive for tourists, but that attracting tourists can also actively make places. For example, Frey (2009, p. 140) outlines how cultural tourism and creativity are becoming integrated. He sees cultural tourism not as a passive activity, but as a means of creating places:

> The cultural capital and creative resources of places are a resource for attracting cultural tourists. In this context, 'creative milieus' – as specific social groups of cultural tourists – are considered cultural pioneers who by their ways of producing and consuming space in the 'niches' of neighbourhoods re-evaluate 'doubtful' places and have a decisive influence on them.

Cultural tourists can therefore help to forge new creative or trusting spaces and play an active placemaking role. Certain groups of cultural tourists (or creative tourists) can read and understand the languages of creative places, and the complexity of structural, social, economic and cognitive factors that form a specific local identity (Frey, 2009). Because of these creative skills, cultural tourists seek out the local and the defining elements of the atmosphere of places. This enables them not only to see or experience a place, but to live and dwell in the culture itself.

Frey (2009, p. 142) argues that the 'resource of place' has four dimensions: the physical-material constitution of the place, a cultural symbolism which creates an identity, a neighbourhood structured by use and infrastructural features, and the connection of places to city structures. These dimensions largely mirror the spatial model of Lefebvre (1991) in terms of physical space and infrastructural features (concrete space), cultural symbolism (imagined space) and utilization and activation (lived space).

Frey (2009) sees the amalgamation of these different narratives as constituting the genius loci of a place, echoing one of the key placemaking dimensions suggested by Sacco and Blessi (2007). Successful places manage to coordinate these cultural-creative resources to make themselves more attractive as places to live, work, enjoy leisure and invest in, thereby increasing the quality of life. In the network society, the vital function that enables places to achieve this is the ability to link different networks into 'regimes' that can manage local (space of places) and global (space of flows) resources effectively (Richards, 2015a).

In line with general network theory, Frey (2009) argues that successful creative places are those that can generate bridging social capital (to link to the space of flows and to other communities) and bonding social capital (to bring people together locally). The essential quality of such places is fluidity, which enables different people to meet, so that 'there are unexpected situations, spontaneous actions, as well as heterogeneous and varied lifeworlds and that in this way points of view besides usual paths and routines may develop' (Frey, 2009, p. 147). This echoes the basic arguments of Bærenholdt (2017) on placemaking.

This process is difficult to manage: Frey (2009) argues there must be support for creative processes and the open structures that creative people need for their work and leisure. Thus, apart from focussing on place as a creativity-developing resource, we must consider the producers of creativity and their ability to meet and co-create new knowledge and innovations. In this context, the functions of trust, solidarity and context-bound, implicit knowledge in creative milieus are important. The meetings and moments of co-presence established through networks also create opportunities for risk-taking and surprise, which are vital to the creative process and to relational placemaking (Pierce, Martin and Murphy, 2011).

RELATIONAL PLACEMAKING AND CULTURAL TOURISM IN DEN BOSCH

Our work on the role of creative placemaking in developing cultural tourism (Richards and Duif, 2019) has evolved from a long-term research project on the Dutch city of 's-Hertogenbosch (Den Bosch). Our research focussed on celebrations for the 500th anniversary of the death of the painter Hieronymus Bosch, who lived and worked in the city. Den Bosch is a small city (population 150,000) with an attractive historic centre, but it has struggled to compete with similar heritage cities and to attract international cultural tourists. As the birthplace of a famous medieval painter, the city should be a leading art tourism destination. Den Bosch previously ignored this option, because Bosch's paintings are spread around museums in Europe and the USA – a lack of physical resources that undermined the meaning of the painter for the city. In 2006, however, the city decided to develop a programme of events commemorating the 500th anniversary of Bosch's death in 2016, taking on a major challenge to reunite his oeuvre in the city. This was achieved by creating new relationships and changing the resources, meaning and creativity of the city, attracting large numbers of cultural tourists, and generating significant long-term effects. Resources were the first challenge – as the city had no Bosch paintings, it had to convince other museums spread around the world to loan their works for the exhibition. The city established the Bosch Research and Renovation Project, which paid for the analysis and restoration of paintings held by other cities. Participation in the project had a catch: it was linked to loaning the paintings for a major exhibition in Den Bosch. This strategy was so successful that the city managed to gather 17 of the 25 surviving paintings and many of the drawings. The exhibition attracted over 420,000 visitors, taking 10th position in the *Art Newspaper* Old Master exhibition rankings in 2016. This was described as 'achieving the impossible' by the *Guardian* newspaper, and it generated global media coverage of the city and the exhibition. This was also important in strengthening the link between the painter and the city, as well as pushing Bosch centre stage as a pivotal artist of his time with contemporary relevance and resonance.

The cultural tourism impacts of the exhibition were significant, not just in terms of visitor numbers, but also in a qualitative shift in visitor type. The event attracted large numbers of visitors from other parts of the Netherlands and abroad, and there was an increase in dwell time in the city and overnight stays, driving a significant growth in visitor spending. While external meaning was generated by framing Den Bosch as the city of the painter, internal meaning was developed through involving the local population and giving Bosch new relevance for them. Schoolchildren were engaged in many events in the programme. Creative development was supported by a raft of smaller projects, including the Bosch Dinner cooking competition between different neighbourhoods, and the Bosch Parade, a floating artistic display on the river around the city centre. These were successful in attracting visitors and bringing people together to share creative activities and build social cohesion (Richards, 2020).

Richards and Duif's (2019) analysis of placemaking in Den Bosch takes Lefebvre's (1991) spatial triad as its starting point, and maps the practice of placemaking onto Shove's dynamic model of practices (Shove et al., 2012), envisaging a placemaking practice consisting of the interplay of resources (concrete space), meaning (lived space) and creativity (conceived space). This combination encompasses the view of Sacco and Blessi (2007) that the design of creative places should consider the use of endogenous and exogenous resources (or in the terminology developed in the previous chapter, internal and external goods). It also contains the idea that these resources need to be given meaning through creative use and representation, as suggested by Della Lucia and Trunfio (2018). Richards and Duif (2019) argue that placemaking should be a strategic, holistic process, emphasizing integrated programmes rather than single events. They define a programme as: 'a relational device that links stakeholders in the city and beyond to a series of actions that together are designed to produce beneficial effects' (2019, p. 48).

Richards (2020) charts the different types of value generated by the Bosch 500 programme. Networks such as the Bosch Cities network (global) and the

Bosch Grand Tour (regional) helped to lever resources and generate institutional value. The networks relied on clear vision and political will, which is often a challenge for small cities. The new-found iconic status of Bosch for the city (which mirrors Barcelona's exaltation of Catalan architect Antonio Gaudí; Richards, 2004) helped in branding and marketing. It also gave the city's museum a new confidence to stage more exhibitions, and to build links with another local with global status, Vincent van Gogh. The result was long-term growth of cultural tourism, increased event visits and rising business activity, generating instrumental value.

The most important effect of the Bosch 500 programme was increasing institutional value, which derives from 'the processes, techniques and practices that organisations adopt in working to create value for the public' (Richards, 2020). This form of value is often ignored, particularly because it is difficult to measure. In the case of Den Bosch, however, there is ample evidence to show that the city benefitted from the formal and informal links created between the global space of flows and the local space of places (Fisker, Kwiatkowski and Hjalager, 2019; Richards, 2015a), creating what Bathelt, Malmberg and Maskell (2004) term 'local buzz' that could be levered at global level through the 'pipelines' created by the city in terms of networks, branding and communication (see Chapter 3).

It was also important to ensure that the different elements of resources, meaning and creativity were effectively utilized, and that the Uppground, Middleground and Underground elements of the cultural city (Cohendet et al., 2010) all contributed to the programme. Cultural tourism research has traditionally been focussed on Uppground institutions: major museums and cultural institutions that provide a permanent base for tourism experiences and which are normally well funded. But if these Uppground institutions operate in splendid isolation without engaging the Middleground or the Underground, conflicts between stakeholders can rapidly arise. Richards and Duif (2019) recount a specific incident in the development of the Bosch programme when the directors of leading cultural institutions in the city (the Uppground) exerted pressure on the Municipality to change the strategic direction of the programme. Maintaining the city's original aims meant finding allies in the Middleground, the Underground, and among the public, who represented wider interests than the Uppground institutions alone.

FROM CULTURAL TO CREATIVE TOURISM

The growing role of relationality in cultural tourism is also evident in the recent shift towards creative tourism. Kjaer Mansfeldt (2015) places the creative turn as the latest in a series of revolutions in tourism studies, such as the mobilities turn and the performative turn (see Chapter 1). However, as Richards (2011) discusses, there is debate as to whether creative tourism is a radical reaction to the growth of mass cultural tourism or simply an extension of previous modes of cultural tourism. We can see indications of both explanations, for example, in policies that explicitly refer to 'cultural and creative tourism' (Carvalho, Ferreira and Figueira, 2016; Gordin and Matetskaya, 2012) and the development of creative tourism by sun, sea and sand destinations in southern Europe as a source of diversification (Remoaldo and Cadima-Ribeiro, 2019).

Whichever explanation is most adequate, there are some key differences between cultural and creative tourism. Richards and Marques (2012) argue that creative tourism generates more active involvement of the consumer in the creative life of the destination, a stronger link to people and place, and an emphasis on contemporary creation rather than past heritage. Many creative tourism programmes have emerged that offer experiences related to local forms of creativity and opportunities for tourists to actively learn local skills.

Creative tourism was originally defined as developing individuals' creative potential through participation in learning experiences that characterize a destination (Richards and Raymond, 2000). This means direct involvement in local culture and proactive co-creation of it, rather than mere admiration of others' creativity. The interaction with the local environment and local people means the traveller can engage first-hand with a genuine experience of the destination which yields a sense of achievement and unique learning experiences (Hung, Lee and Huang, 2016).

Oliveira (2019) also views 'aesthetic cosmopolitanism' as disposing the contemporary consumer towards new aesthetic and artistic experiences, and places are rapidly developing creative experiences to cater for this demand. Melpignano and Azara (2019) see the production of festivals and live events at non-traditional venues as confirmation of the increasing importance of creative tourism in attracting those tourists who seek entertainment as a form of distinction. Tan, Lim, Tan and Kok (2020) also argue that creativity is essential for the sustainability of intangible heritage. They present a '5As framework', comprising the interaction of 'actor (skills and knowledge; characteristics)', 'affordance (support; opportunity)', 'artifact (general; souvenirs)', 'audience (local; tourist)' and 'apprentice'. All these elements are needed in the production and maintenance of creative resources, underlining the need for different actors and resources to interact in the creative system.

Such arguments focus on the roles of collective creativity and the everyday in producing cultural and creative tourism experiences. Many places have seen a rise in more active involvement and learning, as Tolkach, Chon and Xiao (2016) identify in the Asia Pacific region. These activities are generally placed in everyday, rather than specialized, tourism contexts. Chopra (2015) sees everyday spaces as sites of multiple social and economic transactions, where numerous experiences accumulate in a single location. In such spaces, tourists and residents increasingly interact. Pasquinelli (2015) underlines that the basic benefits sought by residents from everyday places, such as leisure, quality of life, cultural amenities and entertainment, are also those sought by tourists.

Richards (2020) linked the recent development of creative tourism to the convergence between the creative economy and tourism, which is extensively documented by the OECD (2014). This convergence is based on basic synergies between these sectors: tourism benefits from added symbolic value generated by creativity, and the creative economy benefits from greater tourist activity. These synergies are identified by Richards (2020) at different geographic scales and in both urban and rural locations.

In Thailand, creative tourism has been developed at national level by the Designated Areas for Sustainable Tourism Administration (DASTA), which has developed creative experiences centred on 20 villages around the country (Richards, 2020). Local facilitators and community-based organizations supported the development of creative tourism through a range of creative activities, including ceramics, carving, weaving and cooking. Wisansing and Vongvisitsin (2019) argue that this is a bottom-up approach based on the community's own well-being and the involvement of local people in the measurement of project outcomes. Creative content development stimulates local communities to utilize their artistic and storytelling skills to develop engaging and participative experiences. Residents are also stimulated to think about their own culture and assets from the view of the outsider, who values different aspects of local practices. This local programme has generated explicit knowledge through the development of the *Creating Creative Tourism Toolkit* (Richards, Wisansing and Paschinger, 2019).

Other examples of creative tourism development in Asia include *Saung Angklung Udjo* (SAU) in Bandung, Indonesia, where visitors can learn to play the angklung musical instrument (Musthofa, 2020). Also in Bandung, creative neighbourhoods have been developed in informal settlements, such as Dago Pojok kampung. The development of creative tourism there was led by a local artistic group, *Komunitas Taboo*, headed by artist Rahmat Jabaril. They set up a creative learning centre, a murals project, a creative stage, a batik workshop and an annual festival that brought many visitors into the area, including international tourists (Richards, 2017a). This project was curtailed as a placemaking initiative by objections from some residents of this Islamic community to the artistic dimension of the experience (Akbar, 2020).

In the light of the model of ritual practices developed in the previous chapter, one could explain the shift from cultural to creative tourism as a result of actors being able to generate more Emotional Energy from the new practice of creative tourism.

ON PHOTOGRAPHY: A CULTURAL TOURISM RITUAL REINVENTED?

One area where the creative shift is evident is the field of tourist photography. As Picard and Robinson (2016) remark, tourism involves taking photographs, and carrying a camera used to be a marker of the traditional cultural tourist. Today, taking photos with a smartphone has become one of the means of practising creative tourism, as Airbnb Experiences based on creative smartphone photography attest.

In *On Photography*, Susan Sontag encapsulates the role of the camera as actor in cultural tourism practices: 'Most tourists feel compelled to put the camera between themselves and whatever is remarkable that they encounter' (1977, p. 10). The reason for this is that 'To photograph is to appropriate the thing photographed. It means putting oneself into a certain relation to the world that feels like knowledge – and, therefore, like power' (p. 4). In traditional modes of cultural tourism, therefore, 'Taking photographs has set up a chronic voyeuristic relation to the world which levels the meaning of all events' (p. 11). With the advent of the smartphone, the role of the camera changed. It seems that everybody has a camera, wherever they go, so the marker of being the tourist, and the use of the camera, has changed. Taking photographs is now a routine activity, which no longer gives the cultural tourist the same distinction that Sontag suggested in the analogue era. As Chen and Shannon (2020) note, more than a billion photographs are now taken every day.

The camera used to be a tool of appropriation, through which the cultural tourist expressed power over the cultures they travelled to see. The passive tourist gaze (Urry, 1990) emitted through the camera lens was tightly controlled, with 'no photo' signs being a common marker of important cultural property in museums. The cultural tourist could gaze, but not take away the image as a photo (unless they bought a postcard in the gift shop). In the modern museum, the role of photography has changed thanks to the smartphone and social media.

Dunleavy (2006) argues that the rituals of digital photography provide new forms of social interaction compared with film photography, largely because of its instantaneous nature. Making images has become a routine, everyday act, no longer the preserve of the tourist or the press photographer. But the ritual imposes certain internal standards: photos should be of a certain quality and capture a meaningful moment. They create a rapport with the subject and/or the eventual audience when posted on social media. Our photo albums used to stay in the home – now they can travel anywhere.

Today, tourists are often encouraged to take photos (still no flash, please) and to post them. Museums around the globe participate in Museum Selfie

Day, when visitors are encouraged to be creative with their phones and take selfies with their favourite artwork. As Folgoso (2019) observes, this is because there are already countless images of museums and their objects on the Internet. Museums therefore employ the creativity of the selfie-tourist to create a personal connection and distinction relative to other museums and images. Now, as Stylianou-Lambert (2012, p. 1822) states, 'The camera is a tool that encourages and even requires active performances related to self-identity.'

Cultural tourism research has highlighted the objects and framing of tourist photography – what, or more usually who, tourists take photos of, and how they assemble visual stories about their travels. Bærenholdt, Haldrup and Larsen (2008) analyse the relationship between photography and cultural tourism at two sites in Denmark: Hammershus Castle and the Viking Ship Museum in Roskilde. The analysis of tourist photographs showed that they were often taking postcard-like views and performing their own photographic dramas by visiting cultural sites. The argument is that tourists travel to consume representations rather than places, and to see and photograph the representations they have already consumed, for example though the media. However, as Bærenholdt et al. argue, this ignores the interaction of tourists with the physical site (and other tourists) itself. Cultural sites are increasingly designed as 'view-producing machines', which encourage photography and seek to co-create visual narratives of cultural experience with and through visitors (even more now through social media). Through photography, cultural tourists also produce social relations by posing and framing people and places.

Context is also extremely important. As Wels (2002, p. 64) notes in his examination of photography in cultural tourism in Africa, 'Europeans want to see the Africans and the African landscape in the same way as they are taught to see them during our formative years of image-moulding during the colonial period.' The cultural tourism image of Africa and African peoples was forged in the minds of European cultural tourists through photographic representations of the colonial era. Ethnocentric aesthetics related to landscape and African people played an important role in the representations through tourist photographs. Photographs and photo-taking by cultural tourists therefore reflect social relations and power relations, which are strongly influenced by the context in which they find themselves.

Researchers are now using photos posted on social media to trace and analyse cultural tourist activity. For example, Nguyen, Camacho and Jung (2017) analysed geotagged photos from Flickr and Instagram (together with tags, comments and likes) from cultural heritage sites in Vietnam and in Korea. Many researchers have also used the digital footprints of tourists on social media to analyse hotspots (Girardin, Calabrese, Fiore, Ratti and Blat, 2008). More sophisticated analysis can enable collective narratives to be derived from the photo-taking behaviour. Straumann, Cöltekin and Andrienko (2014) compared user-contributed, georeferenced photographs of Zurich for foreign and domestic tourists, arguing that these have meaning for the photographers. Through photos, the tourist photographer gives spaces meaning, engaging in an act of placemaking. They explored the digital movement patterns of visitors to develop a narrative about the city from their movements. Based on the number of photographers, pictures taken and shared, in terms of time and location, they built a picture of how tourist photographers move throughout the city. They found significant overlap in the pictures of domestic and foreign visitors, but there were also some areas not visited by foreigners. These included a traditionally industrial and poorer neighbourhood, which is a trendy quarter, attracting young people. This type of analysis may therefore be useful in identifying the development of new tourist areas in cities (see Chapter 3).

GASTRONOMY AND TOURISM

The consumption of place is not just visual, but involves all the senses, including taste. The links between tourism and gastronomy have long been evident (Hjalager and Richards, 2002), and recently gastronomy has also been positioned as a specific form of culture for tourism consumption. Gastronomy is a particularly attractive option for developing cultural tourism, since food cultures are found everywhere, and there is growing consumer interest in food, wine and gastronomy (Richards, 2015b).

The OECD (2012) argued that food provides a basis for tourism experiences by:

1. Linking culture and tourism.
2. Developing the meal experience.
3. Producing distinctive foods.
4. Developing the critical infrastructure for food production and consumption.
5. Supporting local culture.

All these elements are basically related to cultural tourism, which has long relied on local gastronomic practices (Richards, 2002). Gastronomic experiences are increasingly employed in marketing and branding of tourism destinations, particularly where this can be linked to the landscape, livelihoods and culture of the destination (Leng and Badarulzaman, 2014). In line with the growth of intangible heritage in cultural tourism, there are also more UNESCO designations of gastronomic elements of World Intangible Heritage. Designations related to gastronomy now include: the gastronomic meal of the French, the Mediterranean diet, the Art of Neapolitan 'Pizzaiuolo', Ancient Georgian traditional Qvevri wine-making, Turkish Coffee, Arabic Coffee, Traditional Mexican cuisine, Kimjang, or making and sharing kimchi in the

Republic of Korea, Croatian Gingerbread Making, and Washoku, traditional dietary cultures of the Japanese. Several other countries and regions are now making efforts to have their culinary heritage recognized. There is a campaign in Catalunya to have their gastronomy listed, and in Peru signatures were collected to have Peruvian gastronomy listed as UNESCO Intangible Heritage. This was unsuccessful, so Peru then nominated ceviche (fresh raw fish cured in lime juice, onions, salt and yellow chili peppers) as a candidate in 2019 (so far without success).

Deacon (2011) argues that these food-related nominations to the Intangible Heritage list are part of general promotional campaigns:

> The Mexican nomination seems to be linked to tourism rather than the food trade. The Conservatory of Mexican Gastronomic Culture and the Don Vasco Cultural and Tourism Route project will work with traditionally-trained cooks to set up small enterprises and provide training in business administration, hygiene and marketing in a project to create 'culinary hubs' around the country, promoting local cuisines. (Deacon, 2011)

She predicted that awareness of the links between gastronomy, intangible heritage and cultural tourism would increase in future, in the same way as the World Heritage designation has done for tangible heritage sites. This also seems to be the case. The first UNESCO City of Gastronomy, Popayán in Colombia, was designated in 2005. By 2020 there were 36 UNESCO Creative Cities of Gastronomy, including Bergamo, Burgos, Chengdu, Phuket, Hyderabad and Tucson. Brazil, China, Turkey and Italy all have at least three Cities of Gastronomy. The timeline of designations shows a steep rise from 2015 onwards, with 28 of the 36 designations having taken place between 2015 and 2019.

To be approved as a City of Gastronomy, cities need to meet several criteria set by UNESCO, including having a well-developed gastronomy that is characteristic of the location, a vibrant gastronomy community with numerous traditional restaurants, endogenous ingredients used in traditional cooking and traditional culinary practices, food markets and festivals (Pearson and Pearson, 2017).

Despite assertions that the UNESCO creative city designation generates increased tourism (Pearson and Pearson, 2017), very little empirical evidence is available to back up such claims. As Emmendoerfer, Emmendoerfer and Ashton (2016) argue in the case of Florianopolis in Brazil, the main reasons for cities to bid for the designation relate to the brand value of the UNESCO label, and the opportunity to add meaning to basic local resources. Gastronomy is particularly useful as an intangible, symbolic resource for tourism development, because it provides links to place, intangible culture and the symbolic economy, facilitating the use of a new range of assets. It also allows traditional cultural resources to be updated to contemporary, creative meanings.

Richards (2015b) identifies three 'moments' in this process of increasing integration between gastronomy and tourism: a first generation of gastronomic experiences based on the production of themed experiences for consumers; a second generation of experiences co-created by producers and consumers; and the third generation of gastronomic experiences related to the development of communities around gastronomy and food. This process reflects a shift from gastronomic tourism driven by the preferences of individual foodies to the development of entire foodscapes designed to cater for the needs of a wide range of consumers.

The development of foodscapes parallels what Loda, Bonati and Puttilli (2020) refer to as 'foodification'. In Florence, they note growing integration of food and tourism through the expansion of catering activities; the substitution of existing retail businesses; and the tailoring of food-related activities to tourism demand. These processes seem to be ubiquitous, as Savela (2016, p. 95) notes in Finland: 'food has become central in creative urban economies, foodism and even spatial practices, turning into forms of community participation and "DIY urbanisms"'. Savela notes that Finnish food culture is not urban – so the practices that underpin the development of food culture in Helsinki are essentially imported. Instead of feeding off traditional gastronomic practices, the food culture of Helsinki is based on growing urban diversity and globalized urban lifestyles.

In this third generation of gastronomic experiences, 'the holistic nature of food experiences is highlighted by their ability to connect people around the shared consumption of products that involve all the senses' (Richards, 2015b, p. 5). These include more relational experiences, such as the Balinese home cooking classes described by Bell (2015), where local people provide an interactive foodscape for interested tourists. This third generation experience allows tourism to penetrate the private space of the home, but there are also larger-scale gastronomic tourism contexts emerging. Eataly (a combination of the words 'Eat' and 'Italy') is a large-scale establishment offering a variety of restaurants, food and beverage counters, bakery, retail items and a cooking school. *The New York Times* described it as a 'megastore' that 'combines elements of a bustling European open market, a Whole-Foods-style supermarket, a high-end food court and a New Age learning center'. The first Eataly opened in Torino in 2007 in an old vermouth factory, and the company now has 40 locations worldwide. As Colombino (2018) reports, Eataly sells a 'taste' of, and vicarious travel to, an imaginary Italy where consumers can see, smell, touch, hear and eat the gastroscape of Italy.

Such new gastronomic settings support the cultural tourists' search for new experiences, the acquisition of new skills and new means of distinction

(Richards, 2011). Some countries have used these trends to boost cultural tourism. For example, Italy has 825 food and wine products with a denomination of origin label, which helps to raise their profile with consumers and tourists (Garibaldi, 2020). As with many other forms of branding, the number of such labels has been increasing rapidly in the last 20 years. Italy combines these brands with five UNESCO World Heritage designations related to food, the highest number together with France.

The research on different gastronomic settings reveals a general growth in food-related practices among tourists. But there has been relatively little research on the mobility of these practices from one setting to another, or the different food practices of individual tourists (Santos, Santos, Pereira, Richards and Caiado, 2020). It seems unlikely that many tourists will stick to single food practices during their holiday, and many will combine different types of food, settings and knowledge during their trip.

WALKING CULTURE

Walking tours are an important cultural tourism product, thanks to the growth of walking as a social practice in the 20th century, and its emergence as a prime form of urban consumption in the new Millennium, stimulated by free walking tours and new urban tourism (Giddy and Hoogendoorn, 2018).

Walking has long been associated with rural holidays. As Snape (2004) explains in his analysis of the practice of walking holidays in the UK, the Co-Operative Holidays Association (CHA) was formed with the specific aim of encouraging working-class people to enjoy the countryside through walking. Founded at the end of the 19th century, the CHA espoused countryside recreation as an alternative to the popular seaside holiday, with its frivolous distractions. A typical one-week walking holiday comprised non-optional daily walks of up to 30 kilometres, accompanied by a lecturer.

The slower pace of walking 'encouraged a reflective appreciation of one's surroundings and thus a cultural contextualization of the countryside being traversed' (p. 146), allowing participants to develop an interpretative relationship with the landscape. Snape argues that the CHA was engaged in the 'cultural construction of the countryside as a leisure space' (p. 147), which posed the countryside as the 'other' relative to urban space. The CHA provided simple, affordable accommodation, promoting greater access to the countryside, and welcoming women on equal terms. According to Snape, the legacy of the CHA 'lies not in footpath preservation nor in increased land access, but in its promotion of a cultural context' (p. 155). In this context, a bounded ritual flourished: standards of dress and simplicity in lifestyle were imposed by self-discipline not usually compatible with holiday freedom. The practice revolved around shared values and sense of identity, and the members also met regularly beyond their annual holiday (providing an early example of the temporal and spatial extension of a tourism ritual). The shared meanings included the cultural symbolism of the countryside, particularly in opposition to the city and popular leisure destinations.

Similar practices continue, although they have gained new labels and meanings through time and with shifting contexts. Plate (2006) provides a comprehensive analysis of the practice of urban walks, centring on literary walking tours linked to the author Virginia Woolf. Plate places such tours in a tradition of walking as a cultural, critical and aesthetic practice in which the city is mapped through a reading of the streets and a performance of the text to produce an embodied experience of urban space. The 'present obsession with heritage and cultural memory' links Virginia Woolf and the London district of Bloomsbury:

> Everywhere, writers are remembered by tracing their (or their characters') steps through the spaces described in their books, their names evoked to attach to place, their memory celebrated in rituals that involve complex engagements between local inhabitants and tourists in transit, 'city branding' and the marketing of space as 'cultural capital' in both senses of the term. (p. 102)

Plate argues such acts of placemaking are 'characteristic of a form of contemporary tourism that calls itself "cultural", which has been spreading across Europe since the 1970s' (p. 102). This is quite literally a practice invented by cultural tourism. It is also a very specific form of cultural tourism practice in which 'the pedestrian movement is the necessary corollary of a cultural heritage construed as spectacular environment'. The link between walking and the embodiment of the city in Europe contrasts, for example, with the experience of North American cities of spectacle and fantasy (Hannigan, 1998), built for consumption from the motor car or tour bus (Venturi, Robert, Brown, Izenour and Steven, 1977).

The focus of walking cultural tourism experiences is therefore on the means of consumption as much as the content. The physical act of walking is a means of transporting the modern tourist back in time and recreating the past. Literary tourists are invited to see the city or the countryside through the eyes of the writer, to see what they saw – sometimes with the help of poetic licence, or augmented reality. The literary walking tour recreates the role of the *flâneur* as an urban stroller whose knowledge is indigenous, local, and in harmony with the place. The tourist gains access to cultural meaning, allowing for the anchoring of self in the social past to acquire a sense of identity, continuity and belonging (Plate, 2006). The urban walk is a form of resistance to the rise of the spectacular, commodified city with its emphasis on speed and flow. The walking tour invariably entails slowing down and gazing at the city in new ways and appreciating the daily lives of others. Walking as a practice arguably reduces the distance between the tourist and the local, bringing them to street level and removing the physical barrier of the tour bus window (Morris, 2018).

However, even these attempts at physical equalization may not be sufficient, as Giddy and Hoogendoorn (2018) describe in the case of Johannesburg. They argue that walking tours have been stimulated by the demand for authentic experiences, particularly in poor neighbourhoods of major cities globally. The passage of tourists through poorer areas with relatively vulnerable populations raises potential ethical concerns, such as the strengthening of territorial stigma and the association of inner-city areas with 'slum tourism'.

Walking tours may also be used as a means of linking cultural and creative resources in cities, as du Cros and Jolliffe (2011) show in the case of the Hong Kong Artwalk. The staging of this event at night arguably adds to its appeal, highlighting urban nightlife in the surrounding areas. Du Cros and Jolliffe argue this provides an engaging mix of arts, late-night shopping and heritage. In Hong Kong, art walks are organized both in distinct historic and city centre areas and industrial heritage areas in the urban periphery. The sense of place created by the presence of local artists is important in linking these different cultural assets together and creating a dialogue between people and place.

Art walks aiming to link visitors with the artistic scene are now common, as in the case of artwalksparis.com, an opportunity to 'learn what inspires artists, curators, and enthusiasts', organized by an expat. The Friday Night Art Walk organized in the Dutch city of Rotterdam provides a more professional curation of art galleries, attracting those with an interest in art and architecture, who see the walk as a means of contacting a lot of different creatives in a short period of time. The walks attract a lot of locals, but also many 'tourists': arts professionals from other cities in the Netherlands. Again, the organizer is an expat.

Cultural tourism walks have also been used to reimagine rural space, as Hawkes (2012) describes in rural Britain in the wake of the mad cow disease outbreak in the 1990s. He analyses the development of a walking trail called the 'Coleridge Way Walk' across the Quantock Hills and Exmoor National Park, which aimed to change the image of the area from that of disease and death to a more Romantic idea of literary imaginings of the rural. The Coleridge branding of the 80 kilometre walk removes the link with contemporary diseases and rolls the area back into the Romantic era, with new memories and perceptions being derived from previous (literary) memories. Walking is also connected to health and well-being, a feeling strengthened by images of people happily walking over the landscape, and a relational narrative: Ian was:

> the first person to walk the Coleridge Way back in 2005 and has walked it a further three times in the past year with his faithful companion, Ozy the Labrador. Ian

lives at the beginning of, and *on*, the Coleridge Way and is (probably) the most knowledgeable person on all aspects of the path. (www.coleridgewaywalk.co.uk/coleridge-way-guide/)

Running can also be a relational means of placemaking, as Larsen and Bærenholdt (2019) show in the Etape Bornholm run in Denmark. This event mobilizes actors across the small island, and their engagement makes the event possible. The internal goods generated by the bonding social capital in the local community support the production of external goods and the creation of bridging capital between locals and tourists. For many tourist participants, the ritual of running in the event is more important than the novelty of seeking out new courses. The small island context of Bornholm and the five-day duration of the event provide an intense social setting that links tourists to the local space of places and links the island to the global space of flows.

NEW URBAN TOURISM

The development of new styles of urban (cultural) tourism has stimulated discussion of a ritual of 'new urban tourism' (Füller and Michel, 2014; Pasquinelli, 2015). This can be viewed as a new bundle of practices related to cultural tourism in urban environments. Elements of this urban ritual include infiltrating the everyday culture of the city, growing relational engagement, creative modes of tourism and a cosmopolitan ethos. The practice is supported by a growing array of the means of consumption, including collaborative economy accommodation, bike rentals, tuk tuk tours and guided walking tours (Richards, 2016).

Urban tourism has been growing considerably in recent years, bolstered by the growth of budget airlines and 'collaborative economy' accommodation platforms (Dredge and Gyimóthy, 2017). But the development of new urban tourism styles has been long in the making. New urban tourism was first mentioned by Roche (1992, p. 594) as a 'force in the economic regeneration or micro-modernisation of old industrial cities in western society'. The increasing integration of tourist and everyday practices was also noted by Maitland (2007) in his observation of a new form of tourism that turns residential neighbourhoods into tourist destinations. The new practices of urban tourism see the urban traveller actively engaging in construction of the urban experience.

The search for urbanity has supplemented more traditional cultural tourism practices related to high culture. Pasquinelli (2015) identifies a paradigm shift in urban tourism, marked by increasing relational engagement with the city and local community. The new urban travellers are often pioneering tastemakers for whom travelling represents 'unrenounceable lifestyle consumption'. For this group, the right to travel becomes an extension of the right to the city. Pasquinelli argues that the new urban traveller is actively engaged with construction of the urban experience through experiential learning (creative tourism), which involves learning about the 'urban ordinary' and the link between the city's history and the future. Creativity becomes a tool in the new urban tourists' search for 'infiltration points' into the everyday life of places.

Learning about ordinary urban life is a moral imperative for the urban traveller and implies the establishment of relationships and connections with locals brokering local culture. To meet the locals and find an authentic city experience, urban travellers must go 'off the beaten tourist track' (Füller and Michel, 2014, p. 1306), compromising the idea of a tourist city as a differentiated tourist space (Richards, 2017b). In fact, as Condevaux, Djament-Tran and Gravari-Barbas (2016) note, 'any area will be ordinary until it is discovered by tourists'. After this discovery, however, the everyday must be made accessible for tourist consumption by presenting the ordinary as authentic (Füller and Michel, 2014).

The vast array of elements of everyday culture sought by the new urban tourists suggests that they are not looking for specific elements of the urban environment, but rather a general atmosphere of urbanity or cosmopolitanism (Picard, 2013). Many cities now deliberately position themselves as urbane and cosmopolitan places, emphasizing their openness and ease of infiltration for the new cultural tourist. For example, Lisbon underlines its role as an 'open city', welcoming to tourists, refugees and other temporary citizens (Richards and Marques, 2018).

Tourist in Your Own City

New urban tourism practices have also changed the meaning of tourism itself. As the traditional tourist has gone in search of the local, now locals are also becoming tourists in their own city (Richards, 2017b), a trend strengthened by the Covid-19 pandemic.

The globalization of tourist practices and related means of consumption have created opportunities for people to adopt touristic practices in the places where they live as well. The idea that home can also be a tourist location long predates the development of Airbnb and other means of turning home into an object of consumption (Roche, 1992). The tourist in your own city idea can be traced back to a cartoon story published in the magazine *Ons Amsterdam* (our Amsterdam) in 1997. In *Toerist in eigen stad* (Tourist in your own city), van Driel and Blokker (1997) sketched a bored inner-city dweller who puts on a safari outfit to explore the multicultural suburbs of Amsterdam. Growing segregation of city neighbourhoods meant people sometimes knew less about other parts of their own city than they did about places on the other side of the globe. In fact, just as cultural diversity is under threat in many traditional tourist destinations, large cities and regions are now hotbeds of diversity where residents, workers, tourists, expats, students and lifestyle migrants create a cosmopolitan mix of cultures that people can travel to and through without leaving 'home' (Richards and Marques, 2018). In these circumstances:

> the phenomenon of the tourist in their own city is not really a surprise, but rather a logical outcome of a number of social and cultural processes linked to the development of tourism and society in general in recent decades. Although it may be argued that local residents cannot be 'tourists' in their own city in the formal sense, we are increasingly consuming places, including those we live in, in a touristic way. Such is our desire for tourist-like experiences that we continue to visit tourist places even after they have apparently been 'overrun' by tourists and uninhabitable for locals. (Richards, 2017b, p. 16)

As Lim and Bouchon (2017) observe, people can now get off the beaten track in their own city at the same time as visitors are trying to 'do as the locals do' and immerse themselves in the local environment, leading to 'a serially reproduced infusion of tourism and recreation practices repeated in all the global cities where visiting middle class meets local middle class in joint consumption' (p. 15). Visitors experience the excitement of being part of a new city, whereas residents seek the excitement of discovering secret corners of their own city. Spatial coincidence of local and tourist cultural consumption is now being noted in some studies. In Barcelona, Richards (2014) shows that many key sites, including La Pedrera, Park Güell and the Barri Gotic, were visited by a large number of residents and tourists, and between 2005 and 2015, visits by residents to most major tourist sites grew (Richards, 2016). In the case of Hangzhou, China, Zheng, Ritchie, Benckendorff and Bau (2019) found that over 76 per cent of local residents consumed cultural tourism experiences, and these activities generated more positive attitudes towards tourism development.

Different effects are noted in South Africa, where Hoogendoorn and Hammett (2020, p. 15) find a reverse movement of suburbanites to the inner city of Johannesburg as 'resident tourists':

> The Johannesburg inner city has been off the tourist map for more than 25 years, yet produces a classic example of the dichotomy of the tourist gaze that exemplifies both the ordinary and the extraordinary ... Resident and nonresident tourists therefore may be looking for 'authentic' experience of a vibrant African city, learning about the history, or exploring places they have not seen before in ways which are simultaneously ordinary and extraordinary.

The inner-city residents are positioned as locals in this practice, in which the resident tourist becomes non-local and different to the local 'other'. In the case of South Africa, social rather than spatial distance creates the conditions for resident cultural tourism. Hoogendoorn and Hammett (2020) also note that photography is an important creative practice for resident tourists, who use the opportunity for creative community networking and showing off their photographic and other creative skills.

TIME-SHIFTING

Time is a resource employed to increase the distinctiveness and flexibility of cultural tourism practices: changing time to change the experience of space. For example, Fistola and La Rocca (2018) evaluate the possibilities of designing cultural routes such as the Via Francigena to slow down travel and make it more sustainable. In Poland, Pawlusiński and Kubal (2018) analyse plans to develop a 'slow quarter' in a district of Krakow, using creative tourism strategies. Because creativity involves a learning process that requires immersion in place, creative tourism experiences should arguably be slower than traditional forms of cultural tourism.

There is also scope for places to bend or manipulate time by changing how people experience it, for example by increasing absorption in experiences and creating a sense of 'flow' (Csikszentmihalyi, 2000). These kinds of changes can generate a greater experience of happiness in cultural tourism (Filep, 2009). We can also change notions of standardized time by literally putting the clocks back. During the Oerol Festival on the Dutch island of Terschelling in 2008, the clocks on the island were turned back two hours to Greenwich Mean Time, which had been used on the island at the beginning of the 19th century (Richards and Palmer, 2010).

One of the most widespread models of time-shifting in cultural tourism is the development of *nuit blanche* (white night) programmes and museum nights. The *nuit blanche* concept emerged in Paris in 2002, although the basic idea of having a nocturnal cultural programme in cities dates to the 1990s (Evans, 2020). Night events enable cities to extend their cultural tourism offer into 'creative city tourism' (Evans, 2007), spreading tourism activity, reducing overcrowding, improving the visitor experience and reaching new markets. In Greece, Doxanaki, Dermitzaki, Tzortzi, Florou and Andriopoulou (2020) attribute the phenomenon of staging 'Lates' to growing competition and the search for new markets. The late-night opening of the Industrial Gas Museum of Athens provides a balance of entertainment and learning, addressed to generation Y as a new target audience segment. In their study of Lates at the National Museum of Scotland, Barron and Leask (2017) conclude that these events increase the social and economic sustainability of the museum via audience development by attracting non-traditional museum visitors from generation Y. However, these visitors had limited engagement with the permanent exhibitions, and therefore arguably require more entertainment elements to be added to the traditional learning functions of these exhibitions.

The extension of cultural consumption into the night has spawned other new practices. For example, the company Sound Diplomacy promotes the concept of using music as a development strategy to cities worldwide:

> We are the global experts in delivering economic growth to cities and regions, and the tourism and real estate sectors using strategies focused on music and the night time economy … We defined the 'music cities model', which uses music and culture in a deliberate and intentional way to deliver economic, social and cultural growth in cities and places. (www.sounddiplomacy.com)

Sound Diplomacy has turned a practice that was already evident in many places into a business model, in which tourism, hospitality and the creative industries become parts of a 'music ecosystem' for the city. Much of this music ecosystem inhabits the night, which can be a cause of friction between residents and visitors. In the case of Lisbon (Richards and Marques, 2018), the Municipality has a specific policy related to nightlife as a cultural activity that attracts international and domestic tourists as well as residents. But the city also tries to separate what it defines as nocturnal cultural venues, combining performance and food and drink, from those that offer alcohol only.

The commodification of time in cultural tourism practices is also evident through the growth of timed ticketing for exhibitions, as well as the sale of premium 'jump the queue' tickets at busy cultural attractions. In some cities, such as Amsterdam, there have been attempts to shift the time patterns of cultural tourism consumption by giving visitors real time information about queues at popular attractions (Gemeente Amsterdam, 2019).

In other cases, the cultural differentiation of time can be an unintended consequence of social practices. For example, Simoni (2015) describes the encounters between tourists in Cuba and their hosts, who have different views of the anachronisms forced on the island by the American blockade. The feeling of being a country 'stuck in time' and having to be creative with obsolete technology was a source of pride for the hosts, even though they wanted 'to belong to a fast paced world' from which they felt excluded. For the tourists, on the other hand, obsolete technology was a culturally attractive anachronism rather than a barrier to the global space of flows.

THE EMERGENCE, CIRCULATION AND DISRUPTION OF PRACTICES

As we discussed in Chapter 4, it is important to consider how practices emerge, are maintained or propagated and eventually disappear or change. In this section, we consider how new cultural tourism practices emerge and are copied around the world, and finally how practices are disrupted.

Richards (2014) mentions several cultural tourism models that have been copied around the globe, including the tourist bus, the city museum card, the rental bike and the guided tour. These are examples of the expansion of the means of consumption, which provide new consumption opportunities, as Ritzer (1999) argues. One of the important elements of the means of consumption is theming, which aids instant recognition and familiarity, and therefore overcomes cultural barriers that might otherwise hamper or slow consumer decision-making.

For example, the archetypal city bus tour was first developed in Barcelona, where there are now three routes serving 2 million passengers a year. The *Barcelona Bus Turístic* has been operating since 1987, and was a pioneer of the 'hop on, hop off' system, which has since become a standard for tourist cities worldwide. The bus is one of the mainstays of the mass cultural tourism product in Barcelona, taking in the major attractions in the city centre, as well as linking to specific sites such as Camp Nou (home of FC Barcelona and the Barca Museum) further afield. In fact, the Green Line of the Bus Turístic was specifically developed for the 2004 Forum of Cultures, which developed new cultural attractions at the edge of the city (Richards, 2004). In this way, developing new means of transport adds to the means of consuming the destination, and spreading tourists to new places.

The basic template of open top double-decker buses offering a hop on, hop off service has now been globalized through the activities of commercial companies, such as City Sightseeing, Big Bus and Greyline. City Sightseeing was created in 1999 in Seville, Spain, as an open-top, sightseeing tour bus operator. It now provides tour bus services in more than 100 cities around the world. It uses a franchise system, under which operators must use the City Sightseeing red base colour, logo and a global booking website. Greyline highlights the fact that it has been operating as a bus company for over 100 years, and labels itself as 'the Local Expert'.

Slum tourism has also emerged as a globalized practice, the mobility of which is discussed by Frenzel, Koens, Steinbrink and Rogerson (2015). They show that the slum tourism concept first emerged in slums in Brazil and South Africa in the early 1990s, spreading to other parts of Latin America and Africa and more recently to Asia. The concept was arguably transported by actors moving between these locations, including entrepreneurs, consultants and volunteer tourists. The practice provides economic resources for slum dwellers as well as many intermediaries, but it can also have other consequences. In Johannesburg, Frenzel (2014) argues that the relationality generated by new urban tourism can be a source of value. Although tourists may be attracted to inner-city areas by their very invisibility, their visits help to make these areas visible, also for policy makers. He also sees similar processes in Rio de Janeiro, where tourists have penetrated previously taboo favelas, helping to open them up for better-off expats and locals, creating a buzz around them and facilitating new encounters and opportunities.

New cultural tourism practices have also arisen in opposition to tourism itself, as in the rise of anti-tourism sentiment and alternative tourism guides (Anthony, 2005). In the case of Athens, Ioannides, Leventis and Petridou (2016) describe the ways in which a culture of resistance generated by the economic crisis in 2008–09 helped spark new cultural and creative tourism experiences. Rejecting the neo-liberal transformation of the city and the austerity programme of the EU, Alternative Tours of Athens (ATA) was founded to give visitors a different view of the city (www.atathens.org). As well as providing tours of the creative scene, art, design and gastronomy, they also run tours devoted to activism, urban movements and 'money, culture and identity'. The ATA team also offer themselves as 'fixers' for people wanting to organize educational trips or mount creative projects, such as film making and staging cultural events. The group also runs an urban garden and stages Street Art Parties to showcase urban art.

Cultural tourism as resistance has also been employed as a political tool in Italy, where Addiopizzo Travel brings visitors directly into the fight against the mafia (Forno and Garibaldi, 2016). Local activists-hosts and their Italian or foreign clients take part in shared indirect anti-mafia experiences and preventive activities which eventually lead to co-construction of the touristic destination. Addiopizzo Travel is an anti-racket organization founded in 2004 in Palermo, Sicily, supporting businesses that refuse to pay the pizzo (mafia) for protection, with a mobilization campaign aimed at consumers: 'change your shopping habits to fight the pizzo'. This is an example of a Cultural Tourism 3.0 model, in which new relationships have enabled local people to obtain political and economic leverage in their fight against the mafia by working with tourists.

Anti-corruption tours have sprung up in many other locations around the world in recent years. Corrupt Tour has been offering sightseeing tours in Prague since 2011, featuring corruption scandals from the post-communist era. It highlights the activities of Prague's so-called Godfathers and their luxurious villas. In Mexico, Corruptour, a free bus tour run by volunteers, has been running in Monterrey since 2014, and now also operates in Mexico City. The free tours run every Sunday on an old school bus, and at each stop an audio-guide, featuring two fictional characters, introduces the property and explains its significance. Volunteer guides are also on hand to encourage debate and discussion. In the UK, Kleptocracy Tours was launched in 2016, organizing sightseeing of properties owned by allegedly corrupt foreign businesspeople.

Disrupted Practices

If the emergence of new cultural tourism practices is stimulated by the local and global mobility of actors, concepts, materials and meanings, practices can also be disrupted or ended by interruptions to these flows. More research is needed in this area, because practice research often concentrates on routine and everyday behaviour, and therefore the continuity of practices. This can obscure the fact that practices and rituals change or disappear. Often such change is incremental, sometimes imperceptible, but on other occasions rituals can be abruptly ended or disrupted, as in the case of the Covid-19 pandemic. As Condevaux et al. (2016) observe, the end of tourism practices has not been researched, and the study of 'previously tourist areas' could be fruitful in shedding light on why certain practices are discontinued.

Sometimes cultural tourism practices are deliberately interrupted or stopped by specific groups of actors. This was the case in the ban on tourists climbing Uluru (or Ayer's Rock) in Central Australia. Climbing was banned from 26 October 2019, to coincide with the 34th anniversary of the return of Uluru to its traditional owners, the Anangu. The Anangu had long requested visitors not to climb Uluru because it is a sacred site, and because they felt a cultural responsibility over the high number of deaths and injuries involved in climbing. One unexpected consequence of the ban was a rush of tourists climbing Uluru before the ban took effect.

In cities, established tourist practices have also been altered because of the unintended consequences of mass cultural tourism. In Amsterdam, for example, the famous Begijnhof now limits tourist access to certain areas and visitors are told not to photograph the homes in the alms-house complex. In early 2020, a ban was placed on guided tours taking groups past the famed windows in the city's red-light district. More controversially, an incoming left-wing city government removed the iconic 'I-Amsterdam' sign from Museumplein in 2018. It was estimated that the sign attracted some 6000 selfies a day, but it was considered too 'individualistic'. This is an example of a practice being ended because it violated cultural norms – in this case, appropriate collective modes of behaviour in the symbolic cultural heart of the city.

These examples show that many cultural tourism practices are vulnerable to disruption. The way in which practices are disrupted, changed or transformed depends on their form and context. Practices that are dependent on specific materials and resources, such as visits to museums and monuments, tend to be less mobile or transferable. Some smaller material objects can be physically transferred to a new location, as in the case of the I-Amsterdam sign, currently at Schiphol Airport. But it is much easier to move concepts to new contexts. The basic idea of revealing and combatting corruption through the development of a tour as a framing device, for example, can be transferred to any location where there is enough corruption.

The creation, transfer and disruption of practices are potential sources of innovation in tourism. The examples cited in this book show a continual stream of new cultural tourism concepts and experiences. As Gravari-Barbas and Delaplace (2015) observe, these are not replacing visits to famous tourist spots, but instead augmenting cultural tourism supply. This creates an overlaying of practices – new ones are created faster than old ones are discarded, which may have to do with the attractions of the new for consumers and the need to innovate on the part of producers.

Discontinued tourism practices suddenly became much more visible in 2020 with the Covid-19 pandemic, with many destinations shifting abruptly from too many to too few tourists. The longer-term impact of the Covid-19 pandemic on cultural tourism is not yet evident, but it will be dramatic. Not only are there far fewer tourists, but cultural institutions have been closed as well. Many cultural institutions will find it difficult to survive (UNESCO, 2020), and some have already closed permanently, including the Handbag Museum in Amsterdam and the World of Speed museum in Oregon. There seems to be a particular challenge for the new generation of 'postmodern museums', which are more reliant on private funding and tourist audiences.

The Covid-19 pandemic is already shaping the future of cultural tourism. The pandemic hastened the digital transformation of museums, with an explosion in virtual visits. Between 12 March and 22 May 2020, the Louvre's website received 10.5 million visitors, compared to 14.1 million in all of 2019. By June 2020, there were over 2200 virtual museum tours listed by the Google Arts and Culture website. Other types of cultural events also emerged. The Frick Collection in New York organized digital 'Cocktails with a Curator' events, pairing short lectures on artists such as Bellini, Bronzino and Holbein with drink recommendations. Some museums also extended their virtual collections to the normally hidden artworks held in the depot. In Italy, Agostino, Arnaboldi and Lampis (2020) show that museums increased their online interaction with publics during the first weeks of the pandemic. This changed the relationship between institutions and their visitors, and how people consumed museums and their objects. Visits increased, but they became much shorter and more selective, opening the possibility of more personalized museum experiences in future.

The movement to virtual experiences and the growth of smaller-scale, more intimate, more exclusive experiences are likely to continue. The shift to more intimate settings may carry the danger of exclusion for many. Some places may also find it hard to support cultural provision in the absence of tourism, which often delivers considerable economic support to cultural institutions. UNESCO (2020) predicted that around 13 per cent of museums may never reopen. CNN (2020) reported that cultural events have also been cancelled on a massive scale, causing catastrophic financial losses, which can also affect the entire cultural ecosystem around the event. In 2019, Art Basel in Hong Kong attracted 90,000 visitors from over 70 countries, whereas in 2020 galleries were exhibiting virtually via online viewing rooms on the original dates of the cancelled event. Many other events have been organized online (such as the Edinburgh Festival) or with hybrid online/offline combinations, such as the Classics Week music event in the Netherlands.

Although the pandemic is currently still in full swing, there is already research emerging on the effects of Covid-19 on cultural tourism. For example, Carr (2020) examines the challenges for indigenous tourism in New Zealand, arguing that Covid-19 can act as a new colonizing force in Māori communities. However, there is still an aspiration that the 'new normal' will usher in empowerment of indigenous peoples and give them a chance to reconnect with nature. In China, Chen, Huang and Li (2020) examined the Chinese news coverage of Covid-19 and its effects and found that the response of cultural institutions to the pandemic was an important area of concern. From an Italian perspective, Iguman (2020, p. 165) reviewed the responses of heritage organizations and concluded that 'If visitors won't go to Heritage, Heritage must go to visitors' through digitization. As the *Art Newspaper* (Grant, 2020) asked: 'can digital platforms offer a satisfactory alternative to experiencing art in the real world?' If the answer is yes, then we may see a decline in cultural tourists visiting physical museums in future.

As Richard Sennett (1992, p. xiii) once remarked, a major challenge will be to 'revive the reality of the outside as a dimension of human experience'. It seems that the pandemic may have done something to meet this challenge, with streets becoming temporary living rooms, and cafes and restaurants expanding their open-air operations. In Vilnius, Lithuania, many public spaces were used to support the city's restaurants and cafes. They could make free use of public space for their operations during 2020, and about 400 establishments took up the offer. This has helped many businesses to survive by serving more customers, particularly at night. But this also had consequences in terms of increased noise and litter in the city centre. The challenge is that crowds of people create emotional energy and excitement, and now cities are keen to avoid such gatherings. In future, we might even see public, shared spaces giving way to private, individualized space, reducing the opportunities for tourists and residents to interact. Given the sudden shift we have seen in 2020 from overtourism to undertourism, we might speculate whether we have already seen 'peak cultural tourism'?

An interesting study of the consequences of a previous pandemic suggest not. The effects of the Spanish flu in 1918/19 in the Brazilian city of Rio de Janeiro were examined by do Nascimento (2020), who pictures deserted streets reminiscent of the 2020 lockdown. At the end of the Spanish flu outbreak, however, the city erupted into the ritual joy of Carnival, which in 1919 'dramatized death, by transforming mourning into joy, and the tragic, into joke' (p. 182). More importantly, Carnival also marked the rejuvenation of the city's cultural sector, and the beginning of a new stream of international tourism. There is hope that the current pandemic will also trigger the transformation of traditional models of cultural tourism and the growth of more innovative and creative practices. This example may also suggest that the internal goods of the practice are more important for continuation of the practice than external goods, particularly where these support a history of the practice that can inspire future participants.

CONCLUSIONS

Following the cultural tourism practice model developed in Chapter 4, we can see that many practices develop into rituals of consumption and production, which as Collins (2004) argues, begin to form chains of experiences, with actors moving from one to another in search of emotional energy. In these Interaction Ritual Chains (IRCs), the behaviour of actors is heavily determined by their previous experiences of related practices as well as the history of the practice itself.

The extension of the cultural tourism field is driven by actors seeking both internal and external goods to increase their own well-being and secure their position in the ritual. A growing range of practices provides more opportunities for actors to differentiate themselves by acquiring external goods, and increasing levels of competence developed through repeated participation in particular practices or related bundles of practices enable actors to derive enhanced levels of emotional energy, ensuring continuation of the IRCs.

The IRCs developed in cultural tourism practices enable actors to 'move to meet' in events that literally 'take place' and facilitate action. In cities we see dynamic relationships between the Upperground, Middleground and Underground providing the 'buzz' that enables new cultural tourism practices to develop. These can subsequently be circulated through the global pipelines that connect different locations, particularly through the mobility of actors such as expats, who act as conduits for concepts to be embedded in new contexts.

Some new practices or rituals such as creative tourism or being a tourist in your own city can involve alchemy, or a transformation of one practice into something completely different (Maitland, 2013). In many cases, however, what we witness is a change in the ingredients of the ritual, a subtle shift in the materials, meanings or competences of the practice. Because cultural tourism has moved out of the museum and into the arena of everyday culture, these processes are now more complex than they were in the past. We now have a vast range of resources that can be framed as cultural tourism, and a growing army of actors involved in the framing process.

Understanding these processes requires more attention to be paid to the ways in which practices emerge, are maintained, and are disrupted or ended (Bargeman and Richards, 2020). At present, we seem to be witnessing a steady sedimentation of new practices on top of old ones. Existing practices of mass cultural tourism are augmented by innovative and alternative new practices, expanding the cultural tourism field as a whole. With the disruption of Covid-19 and the reactions to the unintended negative consequences of mass cultural tourism, we may see a thinning out of cultural tourism practices in future. The final chapter now turns to consider the potential future trajectories of cultural tourism and cultural tourism research.

REFERENCES

Agostino, D., Arnaboldi, M., and Lampis, A. (2020). Italian state museums during the COVID-19 crisis: from onsite closure to online openness. *Museum Management and Curatorship*, 1–11.

Akbar, P.N.G. (2020). Place-making in urban informal settlements: a case of Indonesian Kampungs. PhD thesis, Erasmus University Rotterdam.

Anthony, R. (2005). *The Lonely Planet Guide to Experimental Travel*. Melbourne: Lonely Planet.

Bærenholdt, J.O. (2017). Moving to meet and make: rethinking creativity in making things take place. In J. Hannigan and G. Richards (eds), *The Sage Handbook of New Urban Studies* (pp. 330–42). London: Sage.

Bærenholdt, J.O., Haldrup, M., and Larsen, J. (2008). Performing cultural attractions. In J. Sundbo and P. Darmer (eds), *Creating Experiences in the Experience Economy* (pp. 176–202). Cheltenham, UK and Northampton, MA, USA: Edward Elgar Publishing.

Bargeman, B. and Richards, G. (2020). A new approach to understanding tourism practices. *Annals of Tourism Research*, *84*. https://doi.org/10.1016/j.annals.2020 .102988.

Barron, P. and Leask, A. (2017). Visitor engagement at museums: Generation Y and 'Lates' events at the National Museum of Scotland. *Museum Management and Curatorship*, *32*(5), 473–90.

Bathelt, H., Malmberg, A., and Maskell, P. (2004). Clusters and knowledge: local buzz, global pipelines and the process of knowledge creation. *Progress in Human Geography*, *28*(1), 31–56.

Bell, C. (2015). Tourists infiltrating authentic domestic space at Balinese home cooking schools. *Tourist Studies*, *15*(1), 86–100.

Carr, A. (2020). COVID-19, indigenous peoples and tourism: a view from New Zealand. *Tourism Geographies*, 1–12.

Carvalho, R., Ferreira, A.M., and Figueira, L.M. (2016). Cultural and creative tourism in Portugal. *PASOS. Revista de Turismo y Patrimonio Cultural*, *14*(5), 1075–82.

Chen, H., Huang, X., and Li, Z. (2020). A content analysis of Chinese news coverage on COVID-19 and tourism. *Current Issues in Tourism*, 1–8.

Chen, M. and Shannon, M. (2020). *Photography: A 21st Century Practice*. London: Routledge.

Chopra, D. (2015). Place. People. Praxis: collective engagements towards mediated urban futures. In S. Golchehr (ed.), *MEDIATIONS: Art & Design Agency and Participation in Public Space* (pp. 31–44). London: Royal College of Art.

CNN (2020). Cultural events are being cancelled amid the coronavirus. So what? 22 March. https://edition.cnn.com/style/article/cultural-events-impact-coronavirus/index.html (accessed 19 December 2020).

Cohendet, P., Grandadam, D., and Simon, L. (2010). The anatomy of the creative city. *Industry and Innovation*, *17*(1), 91–111.

Collins, R. (2004). *Interaction Ritual Chains*. Princeton, NJ: Princeton University Press.

Colombino, A. (2018). Becoming Eataly: the magic of the mall and the magic of the brand. In U. Ermann and K. Hermanik (eds), *Branding the Nation, the Place, the Product* (pp. 67–90). New York: Routledge.

Condevaux, A., Djament-Tran, G., and Gravari-Barbas, M. (2016). Before and after tourism(s). The trajectories of tourist destinations and the role of actors involved in 'off-the-beaten-track' tourism: a literature review. *Via Tourism Review*, *9*. doi: journals.openedition.org/viatourism/413.

Csikszentmihalyi, M. (2000). Happiness, flow, and economic equality. *American Psychologist*, *55*(10), 1163–4.

Deacon, H. (2011). Food nominations to the Intangible Heritage Convention's Lists. http://www.apc.uct.ac.za/apc/projects/archival_platform/food-nominations-intangible-heritage-conventions-lists (accessed 19 December 2020).

Della Lucia, M. and Trunfio, M. (2018). The role of the private actor in cultural regeneration: hybridizing cultural heritage with creativity in the city. *Cities*, *82*, 35–44.

do Nascimento, A.F. (2020). The tourist topicality of the case of the Spanish flu in the city of Rio de Janeiro (Sep. 1918–Mar. 1919). *Revista Brasileira de Pesquisa em Turismo*, *14*(3), 176–88.

Doxanaki, A., Dermitzaki, K., Tzortzi, K., Florou, M., and Andriopoulou, D. (2020). Experiencing a museum after dark: the practice of 'Lates' in the Industrial Gas Museum of Athens. In A. Kavoura, E. Kefallonitis, and A. Giovanis (eds), *Strategic Innovative Marketing and Tourism* (pp. 745–54). Cham: Springer.

Dredge, D. and Gyimóthy, S. (2017). *Collaborative Economy and Tourism: Perspectives, Politics, Policies and Prospects*. Cham: Springer.

du Cros, H. and Jolliffe, L. (2011). Bundling the arts for tourism to complement urban heritage tourist experiences in Asia. *Journal of Heritage Tourism*, *6*(3), 181–95.

Dunleavy, D. (2006). Photography as ritual. https://ddunleavy.typepad.com/the_big_picture/2006/08/the_wedding_par.html (accessed 19 December 2020).

Emmendoerfer, M.L., Emmendoerfer, L., and Ashton, M.S.G. (2016). Analysis of the Heritage Requalification Process to the recognition of a UNESCO Creative City of Gastronomy. Paper presented at the INFOTA Conference Tourism and Cultural Landscapes: Towards A Sustainable Approach, Budapest, 12–16 June.

Evans, G. (2007). Creative spaces, tourism and the city. In G. Richards and J. Wilson (eds), *Tourism, Creativity and Development* (pp. 57–72). London: Routledge.

Evans, G. (2020). Events, cities and the night-time economy. In S.J. Page and J. Connell (eds), *The Routledge Handbook of Events* (pp. 554–69). London: Routledge.

Filep, S. (2009). Tourists' happiness through the lens of positive psychology. PhD thesis, James Cook University.

Fisker, J.K., Kwiatkowski, G., and Hjalager, A.M. (2019). The translocal fluidity of rural grassroots festivals in the network society. *Social & Cultural Geography*, 1–23. doi: 10.1080/14649365.2019.1573437.

Fistola, R. and La Rocca, R.A. (2018). Slow mobility and cultural tourism. Walking on historical paths. In R. Papa, R. Fistola, and C. Gargiulo (eds), *Smart Planning: Sustainability and Mobility in the Age of Change* (pp. 301–22). Cham: Springer.

Folgoso, F.J.F. (2019). El patrimonio histórico artístico ante el turismo Cultural: una aproximación crítica desde la historiografía del arte. *Anales de historia del arte, 29*, 443–58.

Forno, F. and Garibaldi, R. (2016). Ethical travel: holidaying to fight the Italian mafia. In A.P. Russo and G. Richards (eds), *Reinventing the Local in Tourism: Producing, Consuming and Negotiating Place* (pp. 50–64). Bristol: Channel View.

Frenzel, F. (2014). Slum tourism and urban regeneration: touring inner Johannesburg. *Urban Forum, 25*(4), 431–47.

Frenzel, F., Koens, K., Steinbrink, M., and Rogerson, C.M. (2015). Slum tourism: state of the art. *Tourism Review International, 18*(4), 237–52.

Frey, O. (2009). Creativity of places as a resource for cultural tourism. In G. Maciocco and S. Serreli (eds), *Enhancing the City* (pp. 135–54). Dordrecht: Springer.

Friedmann, J. (2010). Place and place-making in cities: a global perspective. *Planning Theory & Practice, 11*(2), 149–65.

Füller, H. and Michel, B. (2014). 'Stop Being a Tourist!' New dynamics of urban tourism in Berlin – Kreuzberg. *International Journal of Urban and Regional Research, 38* (4), 1304–18.

Garibaldi, R. (2020) *Rapporto sul Turismo Enogastronomico Italiano 2020: Trend e tendenze*, Bergamo: Associazione Italiana Turismo Enogastronomico.

Gemeente Amsterdam (2019). Stad in balans. https://www.amsterdam.nl/bestuur -organisatie/volg-beleid/stad-in-balans/ (accessed 19 December 2020).

Giddy, J.K. and Hoogendoorn, G. (2018). Ethical concerns around inner city walking tours. *Urban Geography, 39*(9), 1293–9.

Girardin, F., Calabrese, F., Fiore, F.D., Ratti, C., and Blat, J. (2008). Digital footprinting: uncovering tourists with user-generated content. *IEEE Pervasive Computing, 7*, 36–43.

Gordin, V. and Matetskaya, M. (2012). Creative tourism in Saint Petersburg: the state of the art. *Journal of Tourism Consumption and Practice, 4*(2), 55–77.

Grant, D. (2020). America's virtual museums take on new significance as Covid-19 lockdown deepens. *The Art Newspaper*, 18 March. https://www.theartnewspaper .com/news/covid-19-pushes-museums-to-embrace-the-virtual-world (accessed 19 December 2020).

Gravari-Barbas, M. and Delaplace, M. (2015). Le tourisme urbain 'hors des sentiers battus'. Coulisses, interstices et nouveaux territoires touristiques urbains. *Téoros. Revue de recherche en tourisme, 34*, 1–2.

Grevtsova, I. and Sibina, J. (2018). *Entre los espacios físicos y virtuales. Turismo cultural en el mundo digital*. Munich: GRIN Verlag.

Hannigan, J. (1998). *Fantasy City: Pleasure and Profit in the Postmodern Metropolis*. New York: Routledge.

Hawkes, L. (2012). Walking the Coleridge Way: using cultural tourism to change perceptions of Somerset after the Foot and Mouth Epidemic of 2001. *Social Alternatives, 31*(3), 21–4.

Hjalager, A.M. and Richards, G. (2002). *Tourism and Gastronomy*. London: Routledge.

Hoogendoorn, G. and Hammett, D. (2020). Resident tourists and the local 'other'. *Tourism Geographies*, 1–19. doi: 10.1080/14616688.2020.1713882.

Hung, W.L., Lee, Y.J., and Huang, P.H. (2016). Creative experiences, memorability and revisit intention in creative tourism. *Current Issues in Tourism*, *19*(8), 763–70.

Iguman, S. (2020). If visitors won't go to Heritage, Heritage must go to visitors. Digitisation of Heritage in time of Corona. In F. Burini (ed.), *Tourism Facing a Pandemic: From Crisis to Recovery* (pp. 165–72). Bergamo: University of Bergamo.

Ioannides, D., Leventis, P., and Petridou, E. (2016). Urban resistance tourism initiatives in stressed cities: the case of Athens. In A.P. Russo and G. Richards (eds), *Reinventing the Local in Tourism: Producing, Consuming and Negotiating Place* (pp. 229–50). Bristol: Channel View.

Kjær Mansfeldt, O. (2015). The inbetweenness of tourist experiences. PhD thesis, Royal Danish Academy of Fine Arts, Copenhagen.

Larsen, J. and Bærenholdt, J.O. (2019). Running together: the social capitals of a tourism running event. *Annals of Tourism Research*, *79*, 102788.

Lefebvre, H. (1991). *The Production of Space*. Oxford: Blackwell.

Leng, K.S. and Badarulzaman, N. (2014). Branding George Town World Heritage Site as city of gastronomy: prospects of creative cities strategy in Penang. *International Journal of Culture, Tourism and Hospitality Research*, *8*(3), 322–32.

Lim, S.E.Y. and Bouchon, F. (2017). Blending in for a life less ordinary? Off the beaten track tourism experiences in the global city. *Geoforum*, *86*, 13–15.

Loda, M., Bonati, S., and Puttilli, M. (2020). History to eat. The foodification of the historic centre of Florence. *Cities*, *103*, 102746.

Maitland, R. (2007). Tourism, the creative class and distinctive areas in cities. In G. Richards and J. Wilson (eds), *Tourism, Creativity and Development* (pp. 73–87). London: Routledge.

Maitland, R. (2013). Backstage behaviour in the global city: tourists and the search for the 'real London'. *Procedia – Social and Behavioral Sciences*, *105*, 12–19.

Melpignano, C. and Azara, I. (2019). Conserving Italian World Heritage Sites through live music events: exploring barriers and opportunities. *Event Management*, *23*(4–5), 641–54.

Morris, B. (2018). The Walking Institute: a reflexive approach to tourism, *International Journal of Tourism Cities*, *4*(3), 316–29.

Musthofa, B.M. (2020). The dynamics of traditional and contemporary Angklung development as a tourist attraction based on social creativity in Saung Angklung Udjo. In *Proceedings of the 3rd International Conference on Vocational Higher Education (ICVHE 2018)* (pp. 347–52). Atlantis Press. https://doi.org/10.2991/assehr.k.200331.165.

Nguyen, T.T., Camacho, D., and Jung, J.E. (2017). Identifying and ranking cultural heritage resources on geotagged social media for smart cultural tourism services. *Personal and Ubiquitous Computing*, *21*(2), 267–79.

OECD (2012). *Food and the Tourism Experience*. Paris: OECD.

OECD (2014). *Tourism and the Creative Economy*. Paris: OECD.

Oliveira, N. (2019). A Lisboa cosmopolita e o fascínio da diversidade. *Cidades. Comunidades e Territórios*, *39*, 115–28.

Pasquinelli, C. (2015). Urban tourism(s): is there a case for a paradigm shift? *Cities Research Unit Working Papers No. 14*. L'Aquila, Gran Sasso Science Institute.

Pavoni, A. (2015). Resistant legacies. *Annals of Leisure Research*, *18*(4), 470–90.

Pawlusiński, R. and Kubal, M. (2018). A new take on an old structure? Creative and slow tourism in Krakow (Poland). *Journal of Tourism and Cultural Change, 16*(3), 265–85.

Pearson, D. and Pearson, T. (2017). Branding food culture: UNESCO creative cities of gastronomy. *Journal of Food Products Marketing, 23*(3), 342–55.

Picard, D. (2013). Cosmopolitanism and hospitality. In M.K. Smith and G. Richards (eds), *The Routledge Handbook of Cultural Tourism* (pp. 165–71). London: Routledge.

Picard, D. and Robinson, M. (eds) (2016). *The Framed World: Tourism, Tourists and Photography*. London: Routledge.

Pierce, J., Martin, D.G., and Murphy, J.T. (2011). Relational place-making: the networked politics of place. *Transactions of the Institute of British Geographers, 36*(1), 54–70.

Plate, L. (2006). Walking in Virginia Woolf's footsteps: performing cultural memory. *European Journal of Cultural Studies, 9*(1), 101–20.

Remoaldo, P. and Cadima-Ribeiro, J. (2019). Creative tourism as a new challenge to the development of destinations: the Portuguese case study. In M. Peris-Ortiz, M. Cabrera-Flores, and A. Serrano-Santoyo (eds), *Cultural and Creative Industries: Innovation, Technology, and Knowledge Management* (pp. 81–99). Cham: Springer.

Richards, G. (2002). Gastronomy: an essential ingredient in tourism production and consumption? In A.M. Hjalager and G. Richards (eds), *Tourism and Gastronomy* (pp. 17–34). London: Routledge.

Richards, G. (2004). *Symbolising Catalunya*. Unpublished report for the Catalan Department of Higher Education. http://www.academia.edu/10649130/Symbolising _Catalunya_culture_tourism_and_place (accessed 19 December 2020).

Richards, G. (2011). Creativity and tourism: the state of the art. *Annals of Tourism Research, 38*(4), 1225–53.

Richards, G. (2014). Tourism and creativity in the city. *Current Issues in Tourism, 17*, 119–44.

Richards, G. (2015a). Events in the network society: the role of pulsar and iterative events. *Event Management, 19*(4), 553–66.

Richards, G. (2015b). Evolving gastronomic experiences: from food to foodies to foodscapes. *Journal of Gastronomy and Tourism, 1*(1), 5–17.

Richards, G. (2016). El turismo y la ciudad: hacia nuevos modelos? *Revista CIDOB d'Afers Internacionals, 113*, 71–87.

Richards, G. (2017a). The development of creative tourism in Asia. In C. Silver, L. Marques, H. Hanan, and I. Widiastuti (eds), *Imagining Experience: Creative Tourism and the Making of Place* (pp. ix–xiv). New York: Springer Science+Business Media.

Richards, G. (2017b). Tourists in their own city – considering the growth of a phenomenon. *Tourism Today, 16*, 8–16.

Richards, G. (2020). The value of event networks and platforms: evidence from a multi-annual cultural programme. *Event Management.* https://doi.org/10.3727/ 152599520X15894679115501.

Richards, G. and Duif, L. (2019). *Small Cities with Big Dreams: Creative Placemaking and Branding Strategies*. New York: Routledge.

Richards, G. and Marques, L. (2012). Exploring creative tourism: editor's introduction. *Journal of Tourism Consumption and Practice, 4*(2), 1–11.

Richards, G. and Marques, L. (2018). *Creating Synergies between Cultural Policy and Tourism for Permanent and Temporary Citizens*. Barcelona: UCLG/ICUB.

Richards, G. and Palmer, R. (2010). *Eventful Cities: Cultural Management and Urban Revitalisation*. London: Routledge.

Richards, G. and Raymond, C. (2000). Creative Tourism. *ATLAS News*, *23*(8), 16–20.

Richards, G., Wisansing, J. and Paschinger, E. (2019). *Creating Creative Tourism Toolkit* (2nd edn). Bangkok: DASTA.

Ritzer, G. (1999). *Enchanting a Disenchanted World: Continuity and Change in the Cathedrals of Consumption*. Thousand Oaks, CA: Pine Forge Press.

Roche, M. (1992). Mega-events and micro-modernization: on the sociology of the new urban tourism. *British Journal of Sociology*, *43*(4), 563–600.

Sacco, P.L. and Blessi, G.T. (2007). European culture capitals and local development strategies: comparing the Genoa 2004 and Lille 2004 cases. *Homo oeconomicus*, *24*(1), 111–41.

Santos, J.A., Santos, M., Pereira, L., Richards, G., and Caiado, L. (2020). Local food and changes in tourist eating habits in a sun-and-sea destination: a segmentation approach. *International Journal of Contemporary Hospitality Management*, *32*(11), 3501–21.

Savela, M. (2016). Guerilla Eats and Bicycle Espresso. The changing contemporary food culture of urban Helsinki. *The Journal of Public Space*, *1*(1), 95–112.

Sennett, R. (1992). *The Conscience of the Eye: The Design and Social Life of Cities*. New York: W.W. Norton & Company.

Shove, E., Pantzar, M., and Watson, M. (2012). *The Dynamics of Social Practice: Everyday Life and How It Changes*. London: Sage.

Simoni, V. (2015). Feeling stuck but eager to accelerate: tourism and 'Cuban Time'. In F. Martínez and P. Runnel (eds), *Hopeless Youth!* (pp. 104–6). Tartu: Estonian National Museum.

Snape, R. (2004). The Co-operative Holidays Association and the cultural formation of countryside leisure practice. *Leisure Studies*, *23*(2), 143–58.

Sontag, S. (1977). *On Photography*. New York: Farrar, Straus and Giroux.

Straumann, R.K., Cöltekin, A., and Andrienko, G. (2014). Towards (re) constructing narratives from georeferenced photographs through visual analytics. *The Cartographic Journal*, *51*(2), 152–65.

Stylianou-Lambert, T. (2012). Tourists with cameras: reproducing or producing? *Annals of Tourism Research*, *39*(4), 1817–38.

Tan, S.K., Lim, H.H., Tan, S.H., and Kok, Y.S. (2020). A cultural creativity framework for the sustainability of intangible cultural heritage. *Journal of Hospitality & Tourism Research*, *44*(3), 439–71.

Tolkach, D., Chon, K.K., and Xiao, H. (2016). Asia Pacific tourism trends: is the future ours to see? *Asia Pacific Journal of Tourism Research*, *21*(10), 1071–84.

UNESCO (2020). COVID-19: UNESCO and ICOM concerned about the situation faced by the world's museums. https://en.unesco.org/news/covid-19-unesco-and-icom-concerned-about-situation-faced-worlds-museums (accessed 19 December 2020).

Urry, J. (1990). *The Tourist Gaze*. London: Sage.

van Driel, G. and Blokker, B. (1997). Toerist in Eigen Stad. *Ons Amsterdam*, *49*(5), 124–5.

Venturi, R., Robert, I.V., Brown, D.S., Izenour, S., and Steven, R.V.D.S.B. (1977). *Learning from Las Vegas: The Forgotten Symbolism of Architectural Form*. Cambridge, MA: MIT Press.

Wels, H. (2002). A critical reflection on cultural tourism in Africa: the power of European imagery. In J. Akama and P. Sterry (eds), *Cultural Tourism in Africa: Strategies for the New Millennium* (pp. 55–67). Arnhem: ATLAS.

Wisansing, J.J. and Vongvisitsin, T.B. (2019). Local impacts of creative tourism initiatives. In N. Duxbury and G. Richards (eds), *A Research Agenda for Creative Tourism* (pp. 122–36). Cheltenham, UK and Northampton, MA, USA: Edward Elgar Publishing.

Zheng, D., Ritchie, B.W., Benckendorff, P.J., and Bao, J. (2019). The role of cognitive appraisal, emotion and commitment in affecting resident support toward tourism performing arts development. *Journal of Sustainable Tourism, 27*(11), 1725–44.

6. Emerging research agendas in cultural tourism

INTRODUCTION

Cultural tourism has evolved from the simple combination of culture and tourism it was considered when the field first emerged in the 1980s. The basic elements of the cultural tourism practice, materials, meanings and competences are becoming more complexly interrelated as our view of culture broadens and the range of actors involved in cultural tourism experiences expands.

The expansion of cultural tourism in recent years reflects de Haan's (1997) observation that cultural tourism is driven by the expansion of global tourism consumption and production. This has also stimulated growing diversity, as the range of cultural phenomena considered worthy of tourist attention has grown to include 'high', 'popular' and 'everyday' culture and creativity. The practice approach outlined in this book underlines the mutual dependency of the elements of the cultural tourism practice. Cultural tourism has evolved through increased demand, accessibility of and interest in culture, enabled by the actions of cultural intermediaries, governments, technology providers and a range of other actors. Shifts in the resource base of cultural tourism have in turn been linked to changing meanings – from the preserve of the elite to an everyday mass pursuit. Linking the growing raft of cultural resources with these new meanings has also stimulated creativity in developing new practices, formats, models and contexts for cultural tourism.

Cultural tourism has grown to embrace many new practices, with different contexts and constellations of actors. This expansion has, as the UNWTO (2018) suggests, also stimulated increasing collaboration between tourism and cultural actors. Many different stakeholders are involved in the governance of cultural tourism, and new forms of partnership and networking are required to develop and manage it. Different actors have also emerged on the consumption side: tourists, expats, refugees, third culture kids and other mobile groups mix at cultural sites and events. In reviewing the changing geographies of urban tourism, Richards (2016a) analyses how expats act as 'switchers' in Barcelona, being responsible for a large proportion of Airbnb hosting (Arias Sans and Quaglieri Domínguez, 2016), bike rentals, art tours and other cultural experiences (Richards, 2020). Pappalepore and Smith (2016) also examine how tourism experiences are co-created by residents as 'hosts', workers and other leisure visitors. Thanks to the blurring boundaries between tourism and every-day life, social interactions between these different groups are becoming more important in the cultural tourism experience, and encounters are increasingly facilitated by peer-to-peer tourism platforms.

This chapter considers the research agendas emerging from the evolution of cultural tourism. We relate this research agenda to practices, and particularly to the elements that comprise them and support the rituals of cultural tourism, namely, materials, meanings and competences (Shove, Pantzar and Watson, 2012).

THE MATERIALS AND RESOURCES OF CULTURAL TOURISM PRACTICES

Shove et al. (2012) see materials as a basic building block of all practices. As Richards and Duif (2019) argue, however, cultural systems also contain many non-material, intangible elements, and so it is probably better to talk about a wider concept of 'resources'. All cultural tourism practices make use of a range of resources, including tangible elements such as museums and monuments and intangible elements such as traditions and pastimes. In most cases, these resources are made available for tourism through the activities of a series of different actors, including those involved in the tourism, cultural and creative sectors, both in the public and private sectors.

The growing range of resources involved in cultural tourism creates a need for research in many areas, including the appearance of new forms of culture (new museums, monuments, events), new means of consumption (particularly new media and technologies) and changes in the power relations attached to these resources. We focus on a key contemporary resource issue: the use of new technologies.

New Technologies and Media in Cultural Tourism

The application of new technologies to cultural tourism was signalled by Marianna Sigala (2006) in her analysis of the use of multi-media information systems in cultural heritage, noting that early studies 'merely focused on tech-nical issues' (p. 168). Sigala argued that new technologies would stimulate 'experience-centric innovation', enabling online museum experiences to be more spiritual, engaging, moving and social, driven by three features of new technologies, namely, interactivity, connectivity and convergence.

All these aspects have been stimulated by the development of applications in tourism, heritage and culture. The ability to use an app on our smartphone to access information, book tickets or record our experiences has changed the cultural tourism experience. Boiano, Bowen and Gaia (2012) report on the development of the Malta Culture Guide, a mobile app for a destination. They predicted a growth in such apps, and a subsequent extension of virtual communities built around cultural tourism experience. In fact, apps have developed quickly to give users new experiences of cultural sites through Augmented Reality (AR) and Virtual Reality (VR), as Bollini, De Palma, Nota and Pietra (2014) note. Many studies have emerged of the development of AR and VR applications and their use in (cultural) tourism (Barrado-Timón and Hidalgo-Giralt, 2019; Garau, 2017; Han and Jung, 2018). Jung, tom Dieck, Lee and Chung (2016) argue that these technologies blur the boundaries between the real and the virtual world, increasing the potential for immersion in tourism experiences.

Although the basic technology for AR has been around for some time (for example, Fritz, Susperregui and Linaza, 2005), recently the availability of more mobile and cheaper technology has enabled their widespread use. The advent of smartphones made AR applications available to visitors at cultural sites, who could view information overlays on their mobile devices. Tscheu and Buhalis (2016) reviewed the value creation process of AR apps in cultural heritage, emphasizing that value creation should be a process that involves all stakeholders. This is not an easy process, particularly when there is limited understanding of new technologies. Stiller and Beex (2017) review apps developed for archaeological heritage in the Netherlands, finding that many apps were not downloaded or installed very often. They relate this to the lack of planning among local authorities, and their lack of understanding of the role of apps. There is often no clear idea why, or for whom, the app is being made: the goal was to have an app because 'everyone else has an app'. The funders had no idea about the target users, the use they would make of the app, what content it should have, or how this should be kept relevant. The result of this haphazard provision of technology is predictable: the maximum number of downloads never exceeds 1000 installations. Even for popular museums and exhibitions in the Netherlands, the downloads did not exceed 7 per cent of visitors. Given the vast amounts of money being spent on app development, it seems important to assess the effectiveness of these tools, and to advise funders on how best to invest in them.

It is also important to analyse the ways in which they are taken up by visitors, and how they affect the visitor experience. VR, for example, because it uses a headset that encompasses the field of vision, often accompanied by sound via headphones, provides a more immersive experience, arguably more engaging for the visitor (Bec, Moyle, Timms, Schaffer, Skavronskaya and Little, 2019). Jung et al. (2016), argue that AR and VR are both promising tools to enhance the visitor experience at cultural tourism sites because they give additional digital content to tourists without disrupting the physical environment. Han, Weber, Bastiaansen, Mitas and Lub (2019) emphasize that AR and VR have two very different approaches to enhancing 'reality'. AR provides an overlay of digital content into the user's vision through mobile devices such as smartphones, tablet computers or, more recently, smart glasses. VR, on the other hand, aims to immerse the user into an alternative completely computer-generated world. Using standalone devices such as the Oculus Rift or HTC Vive, or mobile phone-based alternatives such as Google Daydream and Samsung Gear VR, VR headsets completely cover the user's vision. VR technology therefore permits immersion in cultural tourism experiences, as well as 'a sense of presence'. 'The result is that, rather than experiencing the environment where s/he truly is, the user experiences immersion in a virtual world with which s/he interacts, and from which s/he obtains sensory responses' (Barrado-Timón and Hidalgo-Giralt, 2019, p. 2).

New technologies also affect visitor outcomes in terms of memorability and engagement. Barrado-Timón and Hidalgo-Giralt (2019) identify a number of themes in the relationship between AR and cultural tourism, including 'Nomadic Museography', or the integration of functions into a single device that enables new relationships between museums and their users, social inclusion of disadvantaged groups and entrepreneurship and innovation. They found that most studies report benefits of VR and AR technology in promoting new ways of accessing knowledge, which increases engagement with heritage sites. Engagement is also central to the 'gamification' of cultural tourism. Mortara, Catalano, Bellotti, Fiucci, Houry-Panchetti and Petridis (2014) found that turning user interactions with urban heritage into a game accessed via a mobile device generated greater user involvement, reinforcement of knowledge and helped to disseminate missing or partially preserved heritage. This was also a strategy adopted by the Hieronymus Bosch 500 programme in Den Bosch (Richards and Duif, 2019), where a competition was organized for developers to produce a game around the life and works of the medieval painter. The European Union project SmartCulTour (Smart Cultural Tourism as a Driver of Sustainable Development of European Regions) aims to use 'serious games' as a means of increasing the sustainability of cultural tourism. Stakeholders including those involved in the tourism and cultural industries, policy makers and resident groups will be able to play out different scenarios for the development of cultural tourism and experience how this will affect the actors involved.

Some authors have also pointed to unintended negative effects of new technologies, although there is little research in this area. Han et al. (2019) argue that there are negative implications of technologically enhanced heritage, such as the trivialization of heritage, the creation of virtual tourist bubbles separated from the real world and potential barriers for some user groups in accessing these technologies. Bec et al. (2019, p. 118) underline the need to balance contested heritage with accurate information or known facts. AR and VR also have the potential to change concepts of authenticity. Shehade and Stylianou-Lambert (2020) argue that modern technology, and especially VR/ AR, may facilitate existential authenticity by enabling visitors to play with the materials provided to them and to produce their own interpretations of reality.

New technologies may also cause spatial uncoupling, with VR rendering culture and heritage effectively 'placeless', producing what Garau and Ilardi (2014) called 'neo-places', or places created in digital media environments. This may not be intrinsically negative, but rather a compromise between what they describe as 'old places' (traditional cultural spaces) and what Augé (1995) termed 'non-places'. Neo-places can arguably provide a balance between personalization (consumerism) and enduring social connections (or citizenship), enabling individual memories to connect to broader historical narratives, facilitating the rediscovery of 'old places' as heritage which can be used, protected and projected.

Geographical changes in cultural tourism flows are also having an influence on the application of new technologies. For example, China is now one of the major areas for cultural tourism development, driven by large tourist numbers and promotion by the state. It is also an area of rapid technological development in cultural tourism, as many cities and attractions have adopted a smart tourism approach involving the use of big data and new data capture methods.

There are likely to be generational differences in the uptake and use of digital technologies. The attitudes of 'digital natives' are likely to be very different. Studies by the World Youth Student and Educational Travel Confederation (2018) and ATLAS (Richards, 2015) indicate that Generation Y and Generation Z have similar consumption patterns in terms of cultural tourism or visits to cultural events, but Generation Z makes much more use of different social media platforms and information channels.

With the growth of new technology, cultural tourism is increasingly combining physical travel to sights with vicarious travel to websites and social media platforms. Ilja Simons' research illustrates how offline and online experiences are intertwined in cultural events (Simons, 2020), and there is significant scope to expand this work to cover other contexts and actors. In the case of street art, Campos and Sequeira (2020) argue that physical tourism activities are becoming increasingly hybrid, with co-creation of experiences being facilitated by new technologies. Hybrid experiences also provide interesting examples of consumption junctions in practices (Bargeman and Richards, 2020). Consumption junctions are (physical or virtual) settings or specific contexts in practices where actors from the demand and supply side come together or interact (for example, cultural attractions, cultural events, social media posts). Spaargaren (2006) argues that consumption junctions are the most promising places to analyse the matches or mismatches in the interactions between demand and supply. This principle is also actively being followed by experience suppliers, as the development of street art experiences by Culture Trip shows (see Chapter 2).

The change in cultural tourism resources implied by new technologies also alters the meanings of practices as well as the competences required from cultural tourists.

MEANINGS OF CULTURAL TOURISM PRACTICES

The changing resources and competences in cultural tourism practices also alter the meanings of the practice. One recent example is the development of mass cultural tourism (see Chapter 4), which has challenged the meaning of cultural tourism as an inherently 'good' form of tourism (Richards, 2001). Changing meanings are also evident in the competitive struggles between different cultural destinations. When Spanish cities began to challenge the supremacy of Italian cities as cultural destinations around the turn of the Millennium, this reflected years of cultural investment after the restoration of democracy. In reclaiming their cultural symbols and giving them new meaning, cities such as Barcelona also experienced the unintended consequence of attracting droves of cultural tourists (Richards, 2007).

The advance of technology is changing the meaning of authenticity and the role of both human and non-human actors in the production of cultural experiences. Shehade and Stylianou-Lambert (2020) ask whether new technologies have turned cultural tourism from a quest for the original (as opposed to the replica) into a quest for pure entertainment without any desire for authenticity. They speculate whether VR, AR and other technologies will offer a mere substitute of the original or a new form of entertainment. In the end, they conclude that neither scenario will dominate. However, recent years have seen the construction of many replicated cultural attractions, including replicas of urban centres and cultural theme parks.

Discussions about the level of involvement and depth of experience desired by cultural tourists still rage, almost 20 years after the pioneering research conducted by McKercher and du Cros (2002). Are there new cohorts of cultural tourists emerging (such as Generation Z), or have the preferences of all cultural tourists changed? Brida, Dalle Nogare and Scuderi (2016) argued that a complete immersion in the cultural experience is not necessary, as many museum visitors prefer a 'light consumption' experience, which is more site-specific. In contrast, Chang, Backman and Huang (2014) proposed the need for a more holistic and engaging form of tourism that involved tourists in longer-lasting forms of cultural experiences by stretching the cultural experience beyond specific site visits.

Shifting meanings are also evident in the recent rise of gastronomic tourism (see Chapter 5). As Jönsson (2020) notes, countries are trying to claim a position as gastronomic nations at the same time as the gastronomic landscape is becoming post-nationalist. New Nordic Cuisine, originally launched as part of a collaboration between the Nordic countries, can be seen as one such post-nationalist project to revalorize food. In 2008, the Swedish Ministry of Rural Affairs launched the vision *Sweden – the New Culinary Nation,* competing with France to be the number one culinary country. Jönsson (2020) argues that not having a gastronomic culture became a springboard to innovation in Sweden. At a more local level, Mashkov and Shoval (2020) examined the changing meaning of the Mahane Yehuda Market in Jerusalem. Their analysis of newspaper articles from the mid-1990s to 2010 shows substantial change in the discourse around the market. Traditional food-buying functions were displaced by tourist uses, linked to phrases describing the buzz and the presence of foodies. The market essentially became a gastroscape integrated into the tourist product of the city, which changed the meaning of the space as well as the roles of the stallholders.

The question of who has the legitimacy to establish the meanings of cultural tourism rituals is important. We have seen a steady shift in power between producers and consumers, with consumers increasingly taking on production roles as prosumers or co-creators. The curatorial turn has ushered in a raft of content producers and selectors, primed to help the cultural tourist navigate both the cultural Upperground and the Underground. Legitimacy is now established by the perceived value and emotional appeal of the narrative rather than the authority of an institution, as the growth of street art indicates (see Chapter 3). The flattening hierarchy of meaning means the cultural tourist will draw from a wider variety of information sources in deciding where to go, and will therefore require greater competence in interpreting these data.

THE COMPETENCES OF CULTURAL TOURISM

Navigating the new cultural landscape requires competences from all the actors involved. For the tourist, there is the challenge of 'reading' the new texts of cultural tourism, and interpreting the value provided by experience curators. Which places will be cool to visit in the future? As Ilaria Pappalepore (2010) suggested, the need to seek out 'cool' places to be will become even more crucial as the hierarchies of places change with increasing speed. Being caught posting pictures of last year's 'coolest neighbourhood' might engender scorn, just as a trip to Benidorm might once have done for the traditional cultural tourist. Avoiding transgressing the norms of the new urban tourism ritual therefore requires skills in coolhunting.

Coolhunting is not just important for the consumer, but also for the producers who need to predict where the cultural tourists will descend next. For the curator concerned to identify the future value of places, the ability to distinguish the paid-for bleating of the influencer from the genuine local buzz of the next 'place to be' is essential. Producers also need to be able to turn their cool concepts into a trend, in a process Gloor (2010) terms 'coolfarming'. Coolfarmers, who seek to grow a market for their cool idea, are also coolhunters, looking for the next big thing. Cool ideas, according to Gloor, need to be new and fresh, to make people part of a community, be fun, and provide meaning. These ideas are now starting to be integrated into cultural tourism development. Novy (2016) discusses how Berlin became Europe's 'Capital of Cool', and Maitland (2017) analyses how suburbs of big cities have become cool places to visit. Perceived coolness has also been shown to influence consumers of creative tourism experiences in Taiwan (Chen and Chou, 2019). Even whole nations have engaged in coolhunting programmes, as the development of the 'cool Britannia' brand for the UK and Cool Japan attest (Funck, 2018). Places increasingly need to capitalize on their position as cool destinations, because other locations are jostling to become the next capital of cool. Apparently, Málaga is the new Barcelona and Leipzig is the new Berlin (Rogers, 2014). The problem for wannabe cities is that they live in the shadow of the original. Barcelona only became a world-leading city when it stopped wanting to be Paris of the South, and instead positioned itself as the Capital of the Mediterranean (Richards, 2016b).

As places compete to be cool, they need to develop storytelling skills. Storytelling has become an important competence for places seeking to attract cultural tourists, and for coolfarmers looking to develop new trends. Engaging stories link tourists to places, and to the people who live there. In New Zealand, Howison, Higgins-Desbiolles and Sun (2017) show that storytelling, which is an important cultural competence for Māori people, also serves to generate connections with tourists. It can attract attention to specific aspects of culture, deliver information, trigger an emotional response from the tourists and contribute to a memorable experience. In the case of Chinese tourists, however, this is a challenge because of language barriers.

Tourists also need cultural competence, and the specific competences are often linked to the context of their travel. Lin, Fan, Tsaur and Tsai (2020) identify four core competences related to culture for Asian tourists engaging in urban cultural tourism: cultural openness, cultural understanding, cultural consciousness, and cultural participation. Acquiring the right skills can enable tourists to 'blend in' (Lim and Bouchon, 2017) or even to engage as temporary citizens in the places they stay in (Richards and Marques, 2018).

Pera (2017) analysed online reviews of a tourism experience, arguing that these can be considered stories, not just comments on experience satisfaction. She found that stories in online reviews generated value by reinforcing participatory and citizenship behaviours, instructing community members on the moral dimension of the practice. This is particularly important in creative tourism and third generation experience communities, where storytelling becomes a collective creative process that enables social interactions by generating an emotional shared experience that confirms the community's identity.

The development of cultural tourism also increases the competences of producers and consumers in co-creating meaningful rituals. For example, Simons (2020) analyses the ritual of the Redhead Days event in the Netherlands, 'the world's largest gathering of redheads'. This was created by an artist who placed an advert for redheads for a photoshoot. He expected 15, but 150 turned up. This kick-started a major annual event, which was held for years in the city of Breda. Simons argues that photographic practices are still central in the performance of identity. Group rituals such as a mass photo shoot and a red hair parade tend to sweep the individual up into the crowd, or 'a giant orange wave'. Such rituals were created from scratch for the event, but 15 editions later, these rituals are obligatory elements of the event. The feeling of belonging and emotional energy created by the interaction ritual attracts visitors from all over the world, generating considerable tourism spending and media coverage. The event has been so successful that it moved from Breda to the larger city of Tilburg in 2020, which also has more resources and greater competence in staging events.

The ability of governments to shift cultural events, as in the case of the Redhead Days, throws light on the power issues surrounding cultural tourism resources. Governments are often responsible for important cultural tourism resources, such as museums and monuments, and can exert influence on tourism through regulation and marketing and development measures. Increasingly, however, governments must deal with a wide range of stakeholders, with whom they can also collaborate to achieve policy goals. The study of different types of governance arrangements or 'regimes' that promote, support and develop cultural tourism is therefore increasingly important. As governments retreat from the direct provision and management of cultural tourism experiences, these are often taken up by public-private partnerships and other governance mechanisms. The complexity and tensions involved in such arrangements is analysed in the Chinese city of Nanjing by Su and Cai (2019), who argue that the cultural sector tends to promote its own interests, but is less engaged with the domestic tourism market, thus failing to support the city's marketing objectives. In many areas we are seeing the construction of cross-border governance bodies, which helps to deal with the mismatch between administrative areas and tourism regions. In the Guangdong-Hong Kong-Macao Greater Bay Area many studies have been made of the development of cross-border governance and its impact on tourism (Kirillova,

Park, Zhu, Dioko and Zeng, 2020; Wong, Chen and Zhang, 2019). These developments raise questions about how these bodies function, the effect that they have on tourism flows, destination development or marketing. Regimes operate in terms of agreed agendas, but what influence does the composition of the regime have on the aims and implementation of the agenda? Do such arrangements lead to the privatization or commercialization of culture, particularly under neo-liberal governance regimes? It is also important to consider the institutional value that can be generated by increasing governance competences, which can often be a more crucial success factor than instrumental or intrinsic value creation (Richards, 2020). For example, Richards and Palmer (2010) have argued that Barcelona has developed a considerable international reputation partly because it is skilled in telling its story as a successful city.

From the analysis of cultural tourism practices provided in this book, it becomes clear that the resources, meanings and competences linked to each practice have a dynamic relationship to one another, and the model provided by Shove et al. (2012) gives a useful starting point in studying them. But as we argue here, it is useful to go even further and to see the ecosystem of materials, meanings and competences as part of a wider ritual of cultural tourism, as discussed in Chapter 4. Such approaches provide a more holistic view of the cultural tourism field and the attendant actors and structures, although generating the information necessary for such an approach also requires new cultural tourism research practices.

NEW RESEARCH METHODS AND APPROACHES

Our view of cultural tourism as a nexus of social practices that include interaction rituals undertaken in contexts offering cultural resources has implications for the ways in which we research the phenomenon. As we have seen in previous chapters, much research on cultural tourism centres on the profile of cultural tourists, their motivations and behaviours. The links between the actors, particularly consumers and producers, and the context of consumption are less often examined. Actor-centred research often focusses on snapshots of cultural tourism behaviour, isolating the visitor from the temporal as well as the spatial context. There is scope for research that attempts to address these gaps in the analysis of cultural tourism practices.

The approach of Collins (2004) to interaction ritual chains can be useful in analysing the dynamics of social practices – the factors that cause people to adopt cultural tourism practices in the first place, those that tend to maintain the practice, and the reasons why people stop engaging with them (Bargeman and Richards, 2020). In terms of the antecedents of consumers, there is much research on the effects of socialization on cultural tourism consumption. Bourdieu (1984) emphasizes the role of habitus and acquired cultural capital in influencing levels and forms of cultural consumption. This is clear in cultural tourism, where many participants are highly educated and have visited museums and other cultural institutions as children (Falk, 1995; Kracman, 1996). More attention could be paid to the mechanisms that tend to sustain such practices into adulthood.

It is also important to analyse how actors become entrained into supplying cultural tourism experiences. The ATLAS research has consistently shown that people with a link to the cultural sector, either through education or employment, have high levels of cultural tourism consumption (Richards, 2007). This underlines the important role of co-creation in cultural tourism, which still requires extensive research. In the network society, information about cultural tourism has shifted from the authorized pages of the guidebook towards peer-to-peer systems, changing the power relations of tourism production and consumption. Social media is now important in stimulating cultural attendance, for example through electronic word of mouth (eWOM) (Márquez-González and Caro Herrero, 2017). Much current research examines the influence of social media on motivations and behaviour, but there is also a need for research on the role of social media in generating social pressure and Fear Of Missing Out (FOMO). Cultural institutions are increasingly adopting social media as a means of marketing, but how effective is it, particularly in influencing new audiences and tourists from different origins? What are the effects of the shift towards intangible heritage and 'new' forms of culture? One could hypothesize that new media should help to generate more interest for popular culture and intangible culture, but is this assumption valid?

The rise of the collaborative economy has made relationality a key research theme (Dredge and Gyimóthy, 2017). There are many actors involved in linking tourists to places, including technology platforms, Airbnb hosts, experience curators and tour guides. Technological advances provide new avenues for tourists to penetrate the urban fabric. Richards (2014) analyses the rise of creative relational spaces in the city, such as new tourist spaces in Barcelona visited by mobile 'post-bohemians'. Frequently temporary citizens who are not integrated into the formal labour market or recorded as official residents, they congregate in neighbourhoods that are readily permeable, with a cosmopolitan atmosphere and the infrastructure to support 'living like a local'. These spaces often bring together the different actors in the Upperground, Underground and Middleground, and provide support for building and embedding local and global networks. As Marques and Gondim Matos (2020) argue, such systems are supported by important elements of network relationality, including temporary belongingness, a priori empathy and technology to bridge to face-to-face interactions. In this more complex contemporary cultural tourism ecosystem, we need to recognize fluidity, mobility, creativity and relationality in cultural tourism research practice, which also calls for new research approaches.

These can include netnography, as employed by Simons (2020), using the vast data of the Internet as an ethnographic source. The use of diary methods, including video diaries (Rakić, 2010), can help to gather rich data on images and impressions, linked to locations, spaces and contexts. Linkages between cultural experiences and specific time-space contexts can be made through experiential sampling methods, which can use mobile phones to elicit real time experiential data from visitors (Moss, Whalley and Elsmore, 2019), including words, photographs, videos and voice recordings. Stienmetz, Kim, Xiang and Fesenmaier (2020) also suggest blueprinting and journey mapping to facilitate the analysis of tourism experiences. These rich data can also be triangulated in several ways as Marques and Gondim Matos (2020) suggest, including data triangulation, multi-methods triangulation and investigator triangulation.

By analysing the behaviour of cultural tourists in time and space, we can understand more about how the different cultural elements of a destination fit together into a holistic experience. Richards, King and Yeung (2020) suggest visitors often undertake a 'destination journey', which includes several different cultural sights and other experiences. Simply profiling cultural tourists based on single site or event visits may produce an incomplete picture. This morning's cultural tourist, stimulated by rainy weather to visit a museum, may be a beach tourist when the afternoon sun appears – the same person, different tourist practices. Vergopoulos (2016) makes a similar point in terms of the development of a tourist career, in which skills and knowledge are developed relative to new contexts and places.

To examine destination journeys and tourist careers, we might usefully return to time-space mapping, a body of work that was pioneered by geographers in the 1990s. These techniques were also applied to the analysis of cultural tourism behaviour (Dietvorst, 1994). Mapping studies of cultural tourism persist, as Rossetto's (2012) cartographic study of embodied tourism practices in Berlin attests. Edwards, Dickson, Griffin and Hayllar (2010) used global positioning system (GPS) devices for tracking cultural tourists in Sydney, and now such analyses are much easier thanks to the use of big data collected from mobile phones (for example, Raun, Ahas and Tiru, 2016; van der Zee, Bertocchi and Vanneste, 2020). To date, however, as Thimm and Seepold (2016) note, tourist-tracking research has focussed mainly on movement patterns and has done little to enlighten us about motivations or the relationships that underpin behaviour.

Such studies also tend to be limited to a brief time period, and they have not unlocked the potential of identifying the 'DNA' of trip patterns – the sequence of visits and behaviours that could illuminate the relationships of tourists to destinations and the role of routine in destination choice (Bargeman and van der Poel, 2006). The importance of routine, an element often over-emphasized in practice studies, has yet to be fully recognized in tourist studies. Why do some people return to the same destination time after time? Are there particular patterns or combinations of cultural experiences that reveal the DNA of the cultural tourist? Tracking studies using mobile technology and experiential sampling may reveal much about how cultural tourists move through the destination, how different environments and sights make them feel during their destination journey, and which sights and locations generate most Emotional Energy.

Collaborative Approaches to Research

Collaborative, networked approaches to research can arguably provide more holistic understanding of the nexus of practices. The use of networks, such as ATLAS or UNESCO's UNITWIN programme, which promote international cooperation and networking between universities, can be a useful strategy to develop new research possibilities. The ATLAS Cultural Tourism Research Group has been a pioneer of open source research projects, in which teams of researchers develop common research strategies and instruments and share data to create transnational and transcultural views of cultural tourism (Richards, 2010). Through networking, research programmes can be sustained over longer time periods and greater geographical extents than individual researchers or universities can manage on their own. The open source approach allows researchers to contribute to the development of the research instruments and to adapt these for their own local needs. Working across cultural and linguistic boundaries is challenging, but it also stimulates greater understanding of the diversity of cultures and cultural tourism, enabling researchers to reflect on their own positionality. The ATLAS Cultural Tourism Research Programme has now been running for 30 years, and in that time has generated tens of thousands of visitor interviews and a wide range of case studies in different countries.

Extending the open source principles developed by ATLAS could provide avenues for crowdsourcing of research, which draws on a large pool of people to gather data, implying reduced cost and increased reach. Crowdsourcing can also be developed into 'citizen science', where citizens – or non-expert members of the public – provide inputs and valuable contributions to research projects. This also helps to promote dialogue between researchers and citizens (Lichten, Ioppolo, D'Angelo, Simmons and Jones, 2018). There are now many platforms and tools that can support citizen science, such as Zooniverse and Scifabric. These platforms support data collection, data processing, problem solving and idea generation, but they are currently little used in the field of tourism. The involvement of citizens in the research process could potentially be used to address a wide range of research questions, such as the effects of crowding on the experience of culture, the relationships between hosts and guests and the perceived authenticity of different cultural phenomena.

Collaborative research also poses significant challenges. Removed from a single institutional context, the sustainability of such research programmes is less certain. Academic institutions are often too caught up in competitive research activities to collaborate effectively. Researchers also need to carefully consider Intellectual Property and data ownership issues, which have cropped up in the ATLAS Cultural Tourism Project, for example. Further challenges in collaborative projects include the tendency to use English as a common language and western theoretical frameworks, with a relative lack of attention for other contexts/views. This book has underlined the importance of context in understanding cultural tourism, and without the context and insights provided by language our comprehension of culture is much poorer. Although technologies such as Google Translate offer tempting possibilities for translation, they are no substitute for understanding.

EMERGING RESEARCH QUESTIONS FOR A PRACTICE APPROACH

The rise of new forms of cultural tourism such as new urban tourism, street art and creative tourism has highlighted the emergence of new practices combining different materials (for example, technology platforms, means of transport), meanings (encountering the everyday) and competences (reading the city). Analysing these complex practice bundles, or the 'nexus of practices' (Hui, Schatzki and Shove, 2017), suggests a number of key research questions.

1. *The emergence of new practices.* It is important to address how different cultural tourism practices emerge, how are they maintained and eventually are transformed or wither away. This can be extremely challenging, as it implies both a longitudinal and a large-scale approach to capture the behaviour and interaction of different groups over time.
2. *Shifting between practices.* The concept of Interaction Ritual Chains suggests individual actors may build a travel career by shifting between different practices. It would be illuminating to analyse how cultural tourism activities change over the life course of an individual (their cultural tourism travel career), or how rituals change when actors move into a new geographical, social or cultural context.
3. *The construction of cultural tourism journeys.* At a finer scale, we can analyse the construction of cultural experience journeys within individual trips or destinations. How do travellers move between iconic cultural sites and the mundane sites of everyday life? To what extent do people engage in omnivorous consumption, mixing different types of culture during

a trip? This is a practice which is encouraged by many destination marketeers, who are keen to offer visitors a broad palette of high and popular cultural experiences, enabling them to appreciate different facets of place, and engaging with a wide range of stakeholders. However, there are also more specialized cultural consumers, who only visit destinations to experience one specific type of culture and develop their own consumption skills.

4. *The role of routine.* Given the commonplace nature of cultural tourism, it is a routine form of behaviour for some people. Frequent participation in city breaks, for example, might lead to people developing a certain pattern of cultural tourism behaviour. Seeking out a bohemian neighbourhood, visiting the local market or sampling local gastronomy can be as routine for some cosmopolitan consumers as the practice of visiting the iconic cultural sights in a city. Such routines can also be a means of developing the consumption skills required to adapt to new environments, and Lin et al. (2020) argue that they can be developed in different ways by a wide range of different tourists.

5. *Connection between practices.* As tourists move between different cultural practices, they also help to change the connections between them. Studying the changing connections in the nexus of practices also allows us to focus on dynamics – for example, in the way that systems of practice, rather than individual practices, provide the locus for change. In making connections we should consider the relationality of places as actors, as Jacobs (2012) suggests. She highlights the way in which practices, concepts and ideas circulate between places, carried by policy makers and 'policy entrepreneurs' who tour different locations. These actors often meet to exchange ideas at 'field configuring events' (Lange, Power and Suwala, 2014), which helps to create a buzz around concepts. Podestà and Richards (2018) examine the way in which knowledge spillovers are created through a literary festival in Mantua, Italy. They emphasize the role of a small organizing group in linking networks of actors and different practices together, and the effects that these linkages have in local and regional knowledge production. At a global level, Colombo and Richards (2017) trace the practices developed by the Sónar festival to create value through a series of events in different cities that all refer back to the 'hub' event that originated in Barcelona.

6. *Suffusing and threading through.* The routine combination of different cultural elements may relate to two other themes that Hui et al. (2017) identify in practice research: suffusing and threading through. Suffusing refers to the 'atmosphere' created by certain practices. For example, the practice of going to a museum is suffused with a very different atmosphere than attending a music festival or arriving in a city as a pilgrim. If indi-

vidual practices are suffused with their own atmosphere, this could mean that each place can offer a range of different atmospheres depending on the nexus of practices it accommodates or enables. In this sense, we can also conceive of cultural tourists threading their way through the nexus of practices in the destination, linking different practices as they move. The strength of these links, or the thickness of the threads, will depend on the relationships between practices. Some practices, such as the consumption of food and wine, will be closely related, since they link elements that form part of the same cultural system, as well as attracting people who have overlapping knowledge and skills linked to these practices. Other practices may be linked through omnivorous consumption, marking a search for novelty and variety.

If we start to analyse the nexus of practices linked to cultural tourism, and consider how these emerge, are maintained and then cease to be practised, we can open up interesting new perspectives. We can understand how cultural tourists as actors are affected by the contexts or structures they encounter using the tools of first generation practice theory, derived from Giddens and Bourdieu. This can also be linked to an understanding of the dynamics of cultural tourism practices, developed from the insights of second generation practice theory, including the interplay of practice elements described by Shove et al. (2012) and the consumption junctions outlined by Spaargaren, Weenink and Lamers (2016). By adding the insights of Collins (2004) on interaction rituals and MacIntyre's (1981) analysis of the internal and external goods required to support practices, we can arguably better understand what 'makes things happen' in practices (Bærenholdt, 2017). Collins' concept of emotional energy also provides a means of studying the role of emotions in cultural tourism, which is a growing area of research (Hosany, Martin and Woodside, 2020).

Using this combination of insights, the third generation of practice theory might better explain why people adhere to practices such as cultural tourism. A practice theory 3.0 approach might also generate new insights on how actors take up positions in the field of cultural tourism practices to generate internal goods, and how these positions help them to link local cultural practices with the global space of flows to generate external goods (Jarman, 2020).

CHALLENGES OF A PRACTICE APPROACH

It must be recognized that there are numerous criticisms of practice theory, which provides the main basis of our approach. Bargeman and Richards (2020) note that rather than being a coherent theory, practice approaches tend to amalgamate a range of different accounts of social systems. Schmidt (2018) notes several other problems with practice theory, including:

1. The broad range of the practice concept, in which a practice can be 'anything people do'.
2. The lack of a research tradition and body of knowledge, which makes it important to understand the different practice theories and their application.
3. The conceptual foundation of practice theory lacks empirical support.
4. Attempts to create a 'general conception of social life' through practice theory are not feasible.
5. The idea that actors act according to social rules that they themselves are unable to access introduces a circularity of argumentation.

The lack of a clearly defined concept of practices is problematic, because it is difficult to identify and compare practices in different contexts or between groups of actors. We can often recognize similar practice elements, but do these have the same meanings in different contexts? How do practitioners themselves determine what is considered part of a particular practice? Schmidt's (2018) conclusion is that practice theory 'comprises a mixed bag of attempts to devise ontological (or a priori) constructs to "fill the gap" in the philosophy of social science left by now-discredited notions such as culture, tradition, structure, etc. that pretend to explain everything but, in the end, explain nothing'.

Practice theory seen as an all-encompassing explanation of the social is certainly problematic. However, as Bargeman and Richards (2020) argue, a practice approach can help to overcome the actor-structure divide, and when combined with Collins' (2004) approach to interaction rituals, it also provides us with plausible explanations for cultural tourism behaviour. It engages with the practice turn and embodiment in tourism as well as the affective turn, and it gives us tools to deal with routine and linkage of practices. Arguably, what is important in a practice approach to cultural tourism is not so much understanding society as a whole, but the use of practices as a device for understanding social actors and contexts.

Some also argue that practice theory is suitable for studying the detailed actions of everyday life (for example, cooking, driving or visiting cultural attractions), but less suited to larger topics, such as issues of power. However, practice research has also tackled large phenomena, such as world trade and global energy markets (Hui et al., 2017). In the practice approach proposed by Bargeman and Richards (2020), the meso scale of the social group is the main focus, but it also attempts to link the micro scale (of individual motivations driven by emotional energy, for example) with the macro scale (the consequences of group action for society, or global markets). Building on the second wave of practice theory (Shove et al., 2012) encourages us to look for connections and consider the effect of practices at different scales. As Bargeman and Richards (2020, p. 9) note: 'A particular strength of the proposed model is that by seeing the tourist as a person situated at the intersection of an array of practices, and therefore social networks, we can pay more attention to how different tourism practices emerge, are maintained and eventually are transformed or wither away.'

We should also be aware that Collins' (2004) approach has weaknesses, including overreliance on emotional energy as a driving force for participation, and a lack of attention for the context of interaction rituals. Collins is far more concerned about the interactions between participants in a practice than about the different contexts in which these interactions take place. Yet the development of cultural tourism illustrates the important role that changing context has had on the practice of cultural tourism, shifting the focus from the confines of the museum to integration with everyday life, for example.

RETHINKING CULTURAL TOURISM AS A FIELD OF RITUAL PRACTICE

In Chapter 3, we examined cultural tourism as a field. The features of a field are summarized by Warde (2004) in terms of Bourdieu's field theory, which concentrates on the positions and competitive orientations of actors (principally producers). In the decades since Bourdieu outlined these principles, more attention has been focussed on the role of a wider range of actors, including consumers, in the shaping of the field.

In cultural tourism, we can identify all the ingredients of a field. The stakes attached to cultural tourism rituals generate a set of positions, as we see in the role of cultural intermediaries in street art experiences, for example (see Chapter 3). These actors define their authenticity in relation to their position in the field (being close to the artists, for example) and as Collins (2004) suggests, they gain power by taking a more central position in the ritual. This enables them to gather yet more resources to deploy in the cultural tourism practice.

Although cultural tourism is usually a communal practice, it can also be practised alone, or virtually. Individuals can link themselves to collective practices using the thread of history and following the moral guidance of the practice. The power of this phenomenon is underlined by the tendency of tourists to flock together, even when they individually seek to get off the beaten track. The unwritten rules of the practice (such as avoiding other tourists), insider tips (Welk, 2004) and social media all serve to converge cultural tourism behaviour. In this sense, the 'threading through' of individuals leads to collective cultural tourism practices at specific times and places.

Future cultural tourism research could pay more attention to how communities emerge around cultural tourism practices and help to expand the field. With growing attention for the co-creation of experiences (Rihova, Buhalis, Moital and Gouthro, 2015), there is also increased interest in the notion of experience communities (Boswijk, Thijssen and Peelen, 2007), which unite producers and consumers with a stake in a particular experience.

From a producer perspective, Cohendet, Grandadam, Simon and Capdevila (2014) identify the evolution of communities around cultural fields in particular locations at specific moments in time, such as Impressionism in Paris, jazz in New Orleans or new circus arts in Montréal. These movements emerged from informal groupings, which did not constitute pre-existing or formal cultural clusters, but which evolved to have global influence. They are also integrated into important contemporary cultural tourism destinations. These developments are arguably driven by 'epistemic communities', or groups of knowledge-driven agents linked by a common goal, cognitive framework and shared understandings of their work. Cohendet et al. (2014) link the success of such developments to linkages between the informal, creative Underground and the institutionalized Upperground, provided by a rich Middleground comprising places, spaces, events and projects. Drawing on the example of Cubism in Paris, they show how this movement progressed from the artists' studios in the Underground to the museum exhibition halls of the Upperground through a series of phases. This included the formation of a close-knit community of artists centred around Picasso, their linkage with a dense network of buyers and dealers in the Middleground of the city, and their promotion through a series of events and exhibitions. It took 30 years for Cubism to be embraced as a legitimate and marketable artform by the Upperground.

The importance of ritual practices in these processes is made clear by Cohendet et al. (2014), who argue that the production of a manifesto, the construction of a codebook, the development of new practices and the elaboration of a specific discourse are central to the formation of such communities. In other words, the community must produce what MacIntyre (1981) terms 'internal goods' through the development of rituals that can then also attract resources, or 'external goods' (see Chapter 4). The production of internal goods is led by actors in the Underground who strategically engage local resources to legitimize their ideas and gather support. The Middleground helps to make the work of the Underground legible for a wider audience, which then provides the legitimation for the Upperground to frame specific works as 'culture' or 'art'.

With globalization, such developments are no longer confined to individual locations. The validation of the local culture emerging from the space of places in the Underground of a specific location serves to feed a local buzz (Bathelt, Malmberg and Maskell, 2004), which can eventually be promoted by a series of intermediaries to reach global audiences, and travel the pipe-lines linking centres of cultural production to generate a global buzz (Bathelt and Schuldt, 2010). This spatial shift means that many cultural phenomena prosper by utilizing tourism and other mobilities to expand the field and attract a wider audience (Richards and Marques, 2018). Globalization also provides an impulse for the expansion of the field through 'creative jostling' between established and new actors in the field. This jostling for position brings new spaces and events into the field, as we have seen with the growth of street art and suburban cultural tourism. This local creative jostling therefore has real spatial effects, beyond shaping the field itself. What starts as a local ritual practice can quickly expand to other locations, feeding them with external goods and creating competitive tensions between places. These developments open many fertile paths for research. Which mobile actors and intermediaries are important in discovering, curating and disseminating local buzz? How are connections between actors and places formed, what are the processes of knowledge exchange, and how do these benefit the different levels of crea-tivity in each location (Underground, Middleground, Upperground)? How do the connections between the actors in the local place of spaces help to secure a position in the global space of flows?

As Cohendet et al. (2014) suggest, we also need to consider how specific communities of practice emerge in particular locations. Having knowledge, passion and internal goods is not enough, because a failure to generate external resources to support the practice means it will eventually be discontinued. We can also speculate that epistemic communities have a finite life cycle. How long can the practice be sustained in one place? Does the community dissolve when the mission set out in the manifesto is achieved? What happens to these communities in the digital, post-Covid era when virtual platforms are already challenging what Collins (2004) views as the requirement for face-to-face interaction? Cohendet et al. (2014) also argue that the local buzz needs the physical interactions, frictions and clashes that primarily occur offline. Online communities usually represent a single domain of knowledge, which does not stimulate interactions between diverse communities or create new knowledge.

Our rethinking of cultural tourism through ritual practices leads us to a fundamental change in how we view the field. In the past, we thought about cultural tourism as the consumption of culture in discrete locations with a well-established hierarchy of meanings. Recent developments have challenged this relatively static view of the field. We are now more con-cerned with the development of cultural tourism as a dynamic field where many actors, consumers, producers and institutions move to meet, producing emotional energy related to local and global culture. This creative jostling changes the mix of resources, meanings and competences in the cultural ecosystem, marking cool places and generating buzz. Understanding these dynamics requires a more holistic consideration of how this energy is channelled in places to generate internal and external goods that not only sustain, but ultimately change the practice. Then we will have more appreciation of the changes we have observed: from cultural tourism based on tangible high culture, museums and monuments to intangible popular and everyday culture; from the camera as marker of the cultural tourist to the democratization of the smartphone and selfie, from the museum curator to the experience curator; and the interaction of offline and online settings for cultural tourism. A ritual practice approach supports this appreciation by resolving the actor-structure divide, paying more attention to the context of cultural tourism practices and revealing how Emotional Energy drives people to move to meet in cultural tourism.

REFERENCES

Arias Sans, A. and Quaglieri Domínguez, A. (2016). Placing network hospitality in urban destinations: the case of Airbnb in Barcelona. In A.P. Russo and G. Richards (eds), *Reinventing the Local in Tourism: Producing, Consuming and Negotiating Place* (pp. 209–28). Bristol: Channel View.

Augé, M. (1995). *Non-places: Introduction to an Anthropology of Supermodernity.* London: Verso.

Bærenholdt, J.O. (2017). Moving to meet and make: rethinking creativity in making things take place. In J. Hannigan and G. Richards (eds), *The Sage Handbook of New Urban Studies* (pp. 330–42). London: Sage.

Bargeman, B. and Richards, G. (2020). A new approach to understanding tourism practices. *Annals of Tourism Research, 84,* 102988.

Bargeman, B. and van der Poel, H. (2006). The role of routines in the vacation decision-making process of Dutch vacationers. *Tourism Management, 27*(4), 707–20.

Barrado-Timón, D.A. and Hidalgo-Giralt, C. (2019). The historic city, its transmission and perception via augmented reality and virtual reality and the use of the past as a resource for the present: A new era for urban cultural heritage and tourism? *Sustainability, 11* (10), 2835.

Bathelt, H. and Schuldt, N. (2010). International trade fairs and global buzz, Part I: ecology of global buzz. *European Planning Studies, 18*(12), 1957–74.

Bathelt, H., Malmberg, A., and Maskell, P. (2004). Clusters and knowledge: local buzz, global pipelines and the process of knowledge creation. *Progress in Human Geography, 28*(1), 31–56.

Bec, A., Moyle, B., Timms, K., Schaffer, V., Skavronskaya, L., and Little, C. (2019). Management of immersive heritage tourism experiences: a conceptual model. *Tourism Management, 72,* 117–20.

Boiano, S., Bowen, J.P., and Gaia, G. (2012). Usability, design and content issues of mobile apps for cultural heritage promotion: the Malta culture guide experience. doi: 10.14236/ewic/EVA2012.12.

Bollini, L., De Palma, R., Nota, R., and Pietra, R. (2014). User experience and usability for mobile geo-referenced apps. A case study applied to cultural heritage field. In S. Misra, O. Gervasi, B. Murgante, E. Stankova, V. Korkhov, C. Torre, D. Taniar, and

B.O. Apduhan (eds), *International Conference on Computational Science and Its Applications* (pp. 652–62). Cham: Springer.

Boswijk, A., Thijssen, T., and Peelen, E. (2007). *The Experience Economy: A New Perspective*. Amsterdam: Pearson Education.

Bourdieu, P. (1984). *Distinction: A Social Critique of the Judgement of Taste*. London: Routledge.

Brida, J.G., Dalle Nogare, C., and Scuderi, R. (2016). Frequency of museum attendance: motivation matters. *Journal of Cultural Economics*, *40*(3), 261–83.

Campos, R. and Sequeira, A. (2020). Urban art touristification: the case of Lisbon. *Tourist Studies*, *20*(2), 182–202.

Chang, L.L., Backman, K.F., and Huang, Y.C. (2014). Creative tourism: a preliminary examination of creative tourists' motivation, experience, perceived value and revisit intention. *International Journal of Culture, Tourism and Hospitality Research*, *8*(4), 401–19.

Chen, C.F. and Chou, S.H. (2019). Antecedents and consequences of perceived coolness for Generation Y in the context of creative tourism – a case study of the Pier 2 Art Center in Taiwan. *Tourism Management*, *72*, 121–9.

Cohendet, P., Grandadam, D., Simon, L., and Capdevila, I. (2014). Epistemic communities, localization and the dynamics of knowledge creation. *Journal of Economic Geography*, *14*(5), 929–54.

Collins, C. (2004). *Interaction Ritual Chains*. Princeton, NJ: Princeton University Press.

Colombo, A. and Richards, G. (2017). Eventful cities as global innovation catalysts: the Sónar Festival network. *Event Management*, *21*(5), 621–34.

de Haan, J. (1997). *Het Gedeelde Erfgoed*. Den Haag: Sociaal en Cultureel Planbureau.

Dietvorst, A.G.J. (1994). Cultural tourism and time–space behavior. In G.J. Ashworth and PJ. Larkham (eds), *Building a New Heritage: Tourism, Culture, and Identity in the New Europe* (pp. 69–89). London: Routledge.

Dredge, D. and Gyimóthy, S. (2017). *Collaborative Economy and Tourism: Perspectives, Politics, Policies and Prospects*. Cham: Springer.

Edwards, D., Dickson, T., Griffin, T., and Hayllar, B. (2010). Tracking the urban visitor: methods for examining tourists' spatial behavior and visual representation. In G. Richards and W. Munsters (eds), *Cultural Tourism Research Methods* (pp. 104–15). Wallingford: CABI.

Falk, J.H. (1995). Factors influencing African American leisure time utilization of museums. *Journal of Leisure Research*, *27*(1), 41–60.

Fritz, F., Susperregui, A., and Linaza, M.T. (2005). Enhancing cultural tourism experiences with augmented reality technologies. Paper presented at the 6th International Symposium on Virtual Reality, Archaeology and Cultural Heritage (VAST), Geneva.

Funck, C. (2018). 'Cool Japan' – a hot research topic: tourism geography in Japan. *Tourism Geographies*, *20*(1), 187–9.

Garau, C. (2017). Emerging technologies and cultural tourism: opportunities for a cultural urban tourism research agenda. In N. Bellini and C. Pasquinelli (eds), *Tourism in the City* (pp. 67–80). Cham: Springer.

Garau, C. and Ilardi, E. (2014). The 'Non-Places' meet the 'Places': virtual tours on smartphones for the enhancement of cultural heritage. *Journal of Urban Technology*, *21*(1), 79–91.

Gloor, P. (2010). *Coolfarming: Turn Your Great Idea into the Next Big Thing*. New York: AMACOM.

Han, D.I.D. and Jung, T. (2018). Identifying tourist requirements for mobile AR tourism applications in urban heritage tourism. In T. Jung and M.C. tom Dieck (eds), *Augmented Reality and Virtual Reality* (pp. 3–20). Cham: Springer.

Han, D.I.D., Weber, J., Bastiaansen, M., Mitas, O., and Lub, X. (2019). Virtual and augmented reality technologies to enhance the visitor experience in cultural tourism. In T. Jung, M. tom Dieck, and M. Claudia (eds), *Augmented Reality and Virtual Reality* (pp. 113–28). Cham: Springer.

Hosany, S., Martin, D., and Woodside, A.G. (2020). Emotions in tourism: Theoretical designs, measurements, analytics, and interpretations. *Journal of Travel Research*, 0047287520937079.

Howison, S., Higgins-Desbiolles, F., and Sun, Z. (2017). Storytelling in tourism: Chinese visitors and Māori hosts in New Zealand. *Anatolia*, *28*(3), 327–37.

Hui, A., Schatzki, T., and Shove, E. (2017). *The Nexus of Practices: Connections, Constellations, Practitioners*. London: Taylor & Francis.

Jacobs, J.M. (2012). Urban geographies I: still thinking cities relationally. *Progress in Human Geography*, *36*(3), 412–22.

Jarman, D. (2020). Festival to festival: networked relationships between fringe festivals. *Event Management*. doi.org/10.3727/152599520X15894679115510.

Jönsson, H. (2020). A food nation without culinary heritage? Gastronationalism in Sweden. *Journal of Gastronomy and Tourism*, *4*(4), 223–37.

Jung, T., tom Dieck, M.C., Lee, H., and Chung, N. (2016). Effects of virtual reality and augmented reality on visitor experiences in museums. In A. Inversini and R. Schegg (eds), *Information and Communication Technologies in Tourism* (pp. 621–35). New York: Springer International.

Kirillova, K., Park, J., Zhu, M., Dioko, L.D., and Zeng, G. (2020). Developing the competitive destination brand for the Greater Bay Area. *Journal of Destination Marketing & Management*, *17*, 100439.

Kracman, K. (1996). The effect of school-based arts instruction on attendance at museums and the performing arts. *Poetics*, *24*(2–4), 203–18.

Lange, B., Power, D., and Suwala, L. (2014). Geographies of field-configuring events. *Zeitschrift für Wirtschaftsgeographie*, *58*(1), 187–201.

Lichten, C., Ioppolo, R., D'Angelo, C., Simmons, R.K., and Jones, M.M. (2018). *Citizen Science: Crowdsourcing for Research*. Cambridge: THIS. Institute.

Lim, S.E.Y. and Bouchon, F. (2017). Blending in for a life less ordinary? Off the beaten track tourism experiences in the global city. *Geoforum*, *86*, 13–15.

Lin, J.H., Fan, D.X., Tsaur, S.H., and Tsai, Y.R. (2020). Tourists' cultural competence: a cosmopolitan perspective among Asian tourists. *Tourism Management*, *83*, 104207.

MacIntyre, A. (1981). *After Virtue: A Study in Moral Theory*. London: Duckworth.

Maitland, R. (2017). Cool suburbs: a strategy for sustainable tourism? In S.L. Slocum and C. Kline (eds), *Linking Urban and Rural Tourism: Strategies in Sustainability* (pp. 67–81). Wallingford: CABI.

Marques, L. and Gondim Matos, B. (2020). Network relationality in the tourism experience: staging sociality in homestays. *Current Issues in Tourism*, *23*(9), 1153–65.

Márquez-González, C. and Caro Herrero, J.L. (2017). World Heritage Cities of Spain: eWOM as an element of tourism development. *PASOS: Revista de Turismo y Patrimonio Cultural*, *15*(2), 437–57.

Mashkov, R. and Shoval, N. (2020). Merchants' response towards urban tourism development in food markets. *International Journal of Tourism Cities*. doi:10.1108/IJTC-05-2020-0115.

McKercher, B. and du Cros, H. (2002). *Cultural Tourism: The Partnership between Tourism and Cultural Heritage Management*. Binghamton, NY: Haworth Press.

Mortara, M., Catalano, C.E., Bellotti, F., Fiucci, G., Houry-Panchetti, M., and Petridis, P. (2014). Learning cultural heritage by serious games. *Journal of Cultural Heritage*, *15*(3), 318–25.

Moss, J., Whalley, P.A., and Elsmore, I. (2019). Phenomenological psychology & descriptive experience sampling: a new approach to exploring music festival experience. *Journal of Policy Research in Tourism, Leisure and Events*, *12*, 382–400.

Novy, J. (2016). The selling (out) of Berlin and the de- and re-politicization of urban tourism in Europe's 'Capital of Cool'. In C. Colomb and J. Novy (eds), *Protest and Resistance in the Tourist City* (pp. 52–72). London: Routledge.

Pappalepore, I. (2010). Tourism and the development of 'creative' urban areas: evidence from four non-central areas in London. PhD thesis, University of Westminster.

Pappalepore, I. and Smith, A. (2016). The co-creation of urban tourism experiences. In A.P. Russo and G. Richards (eds), *Reinventing the Local in Tourism: Producing, Consuming and Negotiating Place* (pp. 87–100). Bristol: Channel View.

Pera, R. (2017). Empowering the new traveller: storytelling as a co-creative behaviour in tourism. *Current Issues in Tourism*, *20*(4), 331–8.

Podestà, M. and Richards, G. (2018). Creating knowledge spillovers through knowledge-based festivals: the case of Mantua, Italy. *Journal of Policy Research in Tourism, Leisure and Events*, *10*(1), 1–16.

Rakić, T. (2010). Tales from the field: video and its potential for creating cultural tourism knowledge. In G. Richards and W. Munsters (eds), *Cultural Tourism Research Methods* (pp. 129–40). Wallingford: CABI.

Raun, J., Ahas, R., and Tiru, M. (2016). Measuring tourism destinations using mobile tracking data. *Tourism Management*, *57*, 202–12.

Richards, G. (2001). *Cultural Attractions and European Tourism*. Wallingford: CABI.

Richards, G. (2007). *Cultural Tourism: Global and Local Perspectives*. New York: Haworth Press.

Richards, G. (2010). The traditional quantitative approach. Surveying cultural tourists: lessons from the ATLAS cultural tourism research project. In G. Richards and W. Munsters (eds), *Cultural Tourism Research Methods* (pp. 13–32). Wallingford: CABI.

Richards, G. (2014). Tourism and creativity in the city. *Current Issues in Tourism*, *17*, 119–44.

Richards, G. (2015). *ATLAS Cultural Tourism Report 2008–2013*. Arnhem: ATLAS.

Richards, G. (2016a). El turismo y la ciudad: 'hacia nuevos modelos? *Revista CIDOB d'Afers Internacionals*, *113*, 71–87.

Richards, G. (2016b). Placemaking in Barcelona: from 'Paris of the South' to 'Capital of the Mediterranean'. *MNNieuws*, 12 September, 8–9.

Richards, G. (2020). Urban tourism as a special type of cultural tourism. In J. Van der Borg (ed.), *Research Agenda for Urban Tourism*. Cheltenham, UK and Northampton, MA, USA: Edward Elgar Publishing.

Richards, G. and Duif, L. (2019). *Small Cities with Big Dreams: Creative Placemaking and Branding Strategies*. New York: Routledge.

Richards, G. and Marques, L. (2018). *Creating Synergies between Cultural Policy and Tourism for Permanent and Temporary Citizens*. Barcelona: UCLG/ICUB.

Richards, G. and Palmer, R. (2010). *Eventful Cities: Cultural Management and Urban Revitalisation*. London: Routledge.

Richards, G., King, B., and Yeung, E. (2020). Experiencing culture in attractions, events and tour settings. *Tourism Management, 79*, 104104.

Rihova, I., Buhalis, D., Moital, M., and Gouthro, M.B. (2015). Conceptualising customer-to-customer value co-creation in tourism. *International Journal of Tourism Research, 17*(4), 356–63.

Rogers, T. (2014). The life and death of a 'cool' city. Which metropolis will Berlin's tourist hordes descend on next? *The New Republic*, 12 September. https://newrepublic.com/article/119394/life-death-cool-city (accessed 19 December 2020).

Rossetto, T. (2012). Embodying the map: tourism practices in Berlin. *Tourist Studies, 12*(1), 28–51.

Schmidt, K. (2018). Practice theory: a critique. In V. Wulf, V. Pipek, M. Rohde, and G. Stevens (eds), *Socio-informatics: A Practice-based Perspective on the Design and Use of IT Artifacts* (pp. 105–37). Oxford: Oxford University Press.

Shehade, M. and Stylianou-Lambert, T. (2020). Revisiting authenticity in the age of the digital transformation of cultural tourism. In V. Katsoni and T. Spyriadis (eds), *Cultural and Tourism Innovation in the Digital Era* (pp. 3–16). Cham: Springer.

Shove, E., Pantzar, M., and Watson, M. (2012). *The Dynamics of Social Practice: Everyday Life and How It Changes*. London: Sage.

Sigala, M. (2006). New media and technologies: trends and management issues for cultural tourism. In D. Leslie and M. Sigala (eds), *International Cultural Tourism: Management, Implications and Cases* (pp. 167–80). London: Routledge.

Simons, I. (2020). Changing identities through collective performance at events: the case of the Redhead Days. *Leisure Studies*, doi: 10.1080/02614367.2020.1768281.

Spaargaren, G. (2006). The ecological modernization of social practices at the consumption junction. Discussion paper for the ISA-RC-24 conference 'Sustainable Consumption and Society', Madison, Wisconsin, 2–3 June.

Spaargaren, G., Weenink, D., and Lamers, M. (2016). Introduction: using practice theory to research social life. In G. Spaargaren, D. Weenink, and M. Lamers (eds), *Practice Theory and Research: Exploring the Dynamics of Social Life* (pp. 3–27). New York: Routledge.

Stienmetz, J., Kim, J.J., Xiang, Z., and Fesenmaier, D.R. (2020). Managing the structure of tourism experiences: foundations for tourism design. *Journal of Destination Marketing & Management*, 100408.

Stiller, D. and Beex, W.F. (2017). Apps under the surface. Problems with cultural heritage apps. *Studies in Digital Heritage, 1*(2), 326–43.

Su, R. and Cai, H.H. (2019). From cultural governance to cultural tourism: towards an interpretation perspective. *Tourism Culture & Communication, 19*(4), 291–302.

Thimm, T. and Seepold, R. (2016). Past, present and future of tourist tracking. *Journal of Tourism Futures, 2*(1), 43–55.

Tscheu, F. and Buhalis, D. (2016). Augmented reality at cultural heritage sites. In A. Inversini and R. Schegg (eds), *Information and Communication Technologies in Tourism 2016* (pp. 607–19). Cham: Springer.

UNWTO (2018). *Report on Tourism and Culture Synergies*. Madrid: UNWTO.

Van der Zee, E., Bertocchi, D., and Vanneste, D. (2020). Distribution of tourists within urban heritage destinations: a hot spot/cold spot analysis of TripAdvisor data as support for destination management. *Current Issues in Tourism, 23*(2), 175–96.

Vergopoulos, H. (2016). L'effraction ou le sentiment hétérotopique en situation touristique. Une étude de deux cas limites de sortie du tourisme. *Via Tourism Review, 9.*

Warde, A. (2004). Practice and field: revising Bourdieusian concepts. Centre for Research on Innovation & Competition, University of Manchester, Working Paper 65.

Welk, P. (2004). The beaten track: anti-tourism as an element of backpacker identity construction. In G. Richards and J. Wilson (eds), *The Global Nomad: Backpacker Travel in Theory and Practice* (pp. 77–91). Bristol: Channel View.

Wong, C., Chen, Y., and Zhang, M. (2019). Research on Competitiveness Evaluation Index System of Cultural Tourism Enterprises in the Guangdong-Hong Kong-Macao Greater Bay Area. *Journal of Service Science and Management, 12*(5), 573–88.

World Youth Student and Educational Travel Confederation (2018). *New Horizons IV: A Global Study of the Youth and Student Traveller*. Amsterdam: WYSETC.

Index

academic turns 10
accidental cultural tourist 24, 64, 114
Achievement and Autonomy Seekers 24
Actor Network Theory (ANT) 7, 42
actor-structure divide 2, 19, 90, 177, 181
actors in cultural tourism practices
        19–42
agency 7, 10, 20, 23
Agostino, D. 151
Aitchison, C. 27–8
Alarcón, P. 67
Alba, C.A.J. 35
Alemida-García, F. 106
Allcock, J.B. 33
alternative movements and squatter
        movements 60
Amaduzzi, A. 105
Andrienko, G. 136–7
Andriopoulou, D. 146
anti-corruption tours 149–51
anti-tourism sentiment - cultural tourism
        as resistance 149
Aoyama, Y. 100
Arjona-Fuentes, J.M. 99
Arnaboldi, M. 151
Artal-Tur, A. 102
Ashton, M.S.G. 138
Ashworth, G. 4
ATLAS 25–7, 31, 96, 114, 115–16, 165,
        171, 173–4
atmosphere see buzz and atmosphere
Augé, M. 5, 39, 165
Augmented Reality (AR) and Virtual
        Reality (VR) 163–6
authenticity 142, 144, 166, 178
        actors 28, 36–7, 39
        changing contexts 60, 69–70
        connective 128
        consequences of practices 94,
                97–100, 108
        existential 165
        hybrid 98

local as category of 10, 12
        staged 100
        threats to 13
authorized heritage discourse (AHD) 38
Azara, I. 133

Babb, F.E. 28
Backman, K.F. 166
Bærenholdt, J.O. 119, 127–8, 130, 136,
        143
Bakas, F.E. 96–7
Balbuena-Vázquez, A. 106
Ballantyne, R. 21, 49, 94
Bao, J. 145
Bargeman, B. 12, 89–90, 176–8
Barrado-Timón, D.A. 164
Barrera- Fernández, D. 65
Barron, P. 146
Bastiaansen, M. 164
Bathelt, H. 52, 70, 75, 132
Bayno, P.M. 28–9
Bec, A. 165
Beex, W.F. 163
Bell, C. 139
Bellotti, F. 164
Benckendorff, P. 21, 145
Bendixen, P. 101, 114
Berryman, J. 73
Bertacchini, E.E. 71
Bertocchi, D. 105
Besculides, A. 104
Bessière, J. 52
'Bilbao effect' 77
Binkhorst, E. 31
Blessi, G.T. 129, 131
Blokker, B. 144
blueprinting and journey mapping 172
Boiano, S. 163
Boissevain, J. 105
Bollini, L. 163
Bonati, S. 139

187